Constructive Thinking

THE KEY TO
EMOTIONAL INTELLIGENCE

Seymour Epstein

PRAEGER

Westport, Connecticut
London

Library of Congress Cataloging-in-Publication Data

Epstein, Seymour.
    Constructive thinking : the key to emotional intelligence /
Seymour Epstein.
      p. cm.
    Rev. ed. of: You're smarter than you think. 1993.
    Includes bibliographical references and index.
    ISBN 0–275–95884–1 (alk. paper).—ISBN 0–275–95885–X (pbk. :
alk. paper)
    1. Success—Psychological aspects.   2. Emotions and cognition.
I. Epstein, Seymour.   You're smarter than you think. II. Title.
BF637.S8E68   1998
158.1—DC21   97–49277

British Library Cataloguing in Publication Data is available.

Library of Congress Catalog Card Number: 97–49277
ISBN: 0–275–95884–1
    0–275–95885–X (pbk.)

First published in 1998

Praeger Publishers, 88 Post Road West, Westport, CT 06881
An imprint of Greenwood Publishing Group, Inc.

Printed in the United States of America

The paper used in this book complies with the
Permanent Paper Standard issued by the National
Information Standards Organization (Z39.48–1984).

10 9 8 7 6 5 4 3 2

Constructive Thinking

To my wife, Alice, who is my best critic and with whom I can talk about anything; to my daughters, Lisa and Martha, who have been a continuous source of encouragement; and to my students and clients, from whom I have learned as much as I hope they have learned from me.

Contents

PART I

A Tale of Two Minds

Preface

For several years I have taught a college course called "Coping with Stress." I originally decided to offer the course because I wanted to apply a new theory of personality I had developed that I thought could make a practical contribution to improving people's lives. It took some adjusting to finally get the course to operate as I wished, but when it did, it began to produce impressive results. Students told me that it gave them an entirely new outlook on how to deal with stress and cope with their emotions. They said that they used to think there was nothing they could do about having distressing emotions but learn to live with them and control their expression. They learned in the course that they could gain active mastery of their emotions. They noted not only that gaining such control made them feel better but that acquaintances and their parents commented on how much they had changed for the better. I was particularly impressed when students began to photocopy their class notes and give copies to their friends and parents. It was then that I decided to put the material into a book to make it more widely available.

Most people believe their emotions are automatic reactions to events. Events happen and trigger emotions, and that is all there is to it. They are aware, of course, that they can control how they express their emotions but they believe they cannot prevent the emotions from happening in the first place. For example, they think that if someone treats them unfairly, it automatically makes them angry. They can decide whether or not to express the anger and, if so, how, but not whether they will initially feel anger. Few realize that their emotions are determined by how they interpret events, not by the events themselves. As will be repeatedly emphasized in this book, this insight provides a powerful tool for controlling emotions and, relatedly, for becoming the kind of person you want to be. Understanding, however, is only part of the picture. Equally important is implementing the knowledge by practice. You may well understand how a piano works and even a great deal about how you should play it, but that will not make a piano player out of you. To learn to play the piano you have to practice playing it. Likewise, to put the knowledge that interpretations influence emotions to good use, you have to practice improving your interpretations. You have practiced your present ways of automatically interpreting events over most of your lifetime, and you will need a lot of practice in interpreting events differently before the new interpretations become automatic.

One of the major aims of this book is to provide you with techniques for gaining control of your emotions. A second aim is to provide you with a theory for understanding why the techniques in this book work. Theories are important because when you understand how things work, you are able to apply your knowledge more flexibly than when you blindly follow rules. Moreover, understanding the principles behind the rules allows you to apply them in new situations for which there may as yet be no specific rules.

It is widely believed by laypeople and professionals alike that emotions are primary, and thoughts are secondary. We all recognize that when we feel angry, we have aggressive thoughts, and when we feel sad, we have pessimistic thoughts, so it is clear that our feelings shape our thoughts. But the opposite is also true: our thoughts shape our feelings. The difference between the thoughts that precede emotions and the ones that follow them is that the latter are conscious, and the former are automatic and preconscious. As we are normally aware of the conscious but not the preconscious thoughts, it gives us the false impression that emotions come first and thoughts later. As I have already said, how you interpret events determines the feelings you have. Yet, what are your interpretations, if not thoughts? They happen to be automatic thoughts of which you normally are unaware, but nevertheless they are thoughts. If someone steps on your toe and you think it was a deliberate act of provocation, you feel angry, but if you think that it was an accident resulting from the person's muscular dystrophy, you will very likely feel sympathy. Same act, different automatic thought, and therefore different emotion. You may argue that one of the interpretations is correct and the other is not, and therefore only one is appropriate. This, of course, is true for some situations, but many situations in everyday life are ambiguous and therefore can be interpreted with equal accuracy in different ways. It is equally accurate to interpret a glass as half empty or half full. The important point is that how you typically interpret ambiguous events can make a very great difference in your overall adjustment, happiness, and effectiveness.

To a considerable extent this book makes available for use in everyday life the techniques of cognitive therapy, one of the most effective therapies available. If it did that and nothing more, that in itself would justify its existence. However, the book does considerably more. For one, it provides a variety of techniques that go beyond cognitive therapy. For another, even more important, it provides a theory of personality that is based on a new view of the unconscious that can help you understand how you and others operate in a way that no other theory can. Accordingly, the book can be read in different ways, depending on how much you wish to concentrate on its "how-to" feature. Although there is much to be gained from learning the specific techniques that are presented and conducting the practices that are recommended, you can also gain important information by simply reading the book straight through with an emphasis on understanding the principles that are discussed, as if it were not a "how-to" book. Although there is no denying this is a how-to book it differs from most how-to books in that it is grounded in theory and research and can therefore best be regarded as a "thinking person's how-to book," as contradictory as such a designation may seem.

An earlier version of this book was published with Archie Brodsky under the title, *You're Smarter Than You Think: How to Develop Your Practical Intelligence for Success in Living.* The idea behind the title was that we all have an "experiential mind" that has a wisdom of its own that differs from that of our conscious, rational mind. By tuning into and training the experiential mind, we can improve our practical and emotional intelligence. Having decided to update the book by including recent research, extensively rewriting several chapters, and writing two new ones relating the views in this book to similar views expressed in Dan Goleman's popular book, *Emotional Intelligence*, it seemed that a change in title reflecting this new emphasis was in order.

Emotional intelligence is an interesting concept because it draws attention to the limitations of IQ and the value of other kinds of abilities and attributes for success in living, including emotional adjustment. However, there are serious problems with the concept that require further consideration. I thought it important to indicate what is good about the idea and where it needs correction and, most important, to note that it is not emotions that are intelligent or not, but the automatic, preconscious thinking that underlies emotions. It just adds insult to injury to label someone who has periods of depression or anxiety attacks as emotionally unintelligent. It is quite another matter, however, to attempt to understand the maladaptive, automatic thinking that underlies such emotional reactions. This new way of thinking not only is useful for understanding what has been included under emotional intelligence but also provides a realistic source of hope, as it has direct implications for improving emotional intelligence. Given these considerations, it seemed fitting to change the title to *Constructive Thinking: The Key to Emotional Intelligence.*

The first version of this book was written in collaboration with Archie

Brodsky, who helped to rewrite in a more popular style, as requested by the publisher, the preliminary draft that I had written. However, Brodsky did far more than this. As a professional writer whose expertise includes mental and physical well-being, Brodsky made many important observations of his own. I am greatly indebted to him for his invaluable contributions to the first version of the book and have retained almost all of them in the present version. Thus, Brodsky deserves credit for much of what is good in this book as well as in the previous version, but, of course, he cannot be held responsible for whatever is less good as a result of the changes I made.

Acknowledgments

Many people have contributed to this book. The most important is my wife, Alice, who encouraged me to write this book when I was reluctant to divert time from my research and professional writing and who read and constructively commented on every draft.

Others who have read all or part of the book and provided helpful comments are Melanie Bellenoit, John Brockman, Joshua Epstein, Lisa Beth Epstein, Martha Lynn Epstein, Richard Flaste, Gerhard Gschwandtner, Tom Ginocchio, Daniel Goleman, George and Ann Levinger, Katinka Matson, Stacie Melcher, Lynn Robinson, Robert Sederman, Carol Shadoian, Ervin Staub, and Bibi Wein.

The initial book I wrote, while very well received by students in my classes on coping with stress, was too academic for widespread popular appeal. Gail Winston, my editor, convinced me to get a writer who would rewrite it in a more popular style. The result was that I enlisted the help of Archie Brodsky, an accomplished author in his own right. Archie did more than improve the writing style and organization of the first edition of this book. As an authority on health psychology, he added important information and insights of his own.

Gerhard Gschwandtner, editor-in-chief of *Personal Selling Power*, deserves special mention. Gerhard contacted me after reading an article in the *New York Times* on my research and expressed his enthusiasm about the application of my ideas to the business world. He also encouraged me to conduct a study on the practical intelligence of superachievers, and even supplied me with a sample for doing so. The results, published in *Personal Selling Power*, elicited a great deal of interest in the business community, which provided a further incentive for me to have the book written in a form that would reach a wide audience. Gerhard also read the first draft of the entire book and provided me with helpful comments on how to improve it.

Not only were my students and clients a source of stimulation and important feedback, but their reaction to the first version of the book was so positive, including their making photocopies for friends and parents, that it also encouraged me to rewrite the book in popular form. Moreover, without their eager cooperation in testing my views and procedures, I could not have honed the ideas that are presented in the book.

For the second edition of this book, I am particularly indebted to John T. Harney, Dr. James T. Sabin, and John Donohue. I met Harney when he was a book-sales representative who made the rounds at the University of Massachusetts enquiring of professors about writing books that would be of interest to his company. When I told him that the first edition of my book on constructive thinking was out of print, he asked to see it, and was sufficiently impressed with it to find a new publisher, Greenwood Publishing Group, Inc. Dr. James T. Sabin, Director of Academic Research and Development for Greenwood, has been a pleasure to work with. He has been cooperative throughout and always available for discussion of whatever issues arose. John Donohue, production editor for the book, did an outstanding job of editing, and significantly improved the clarity of the final version. I thank them all for smoothing the process of the extensive rewriting that I undertook to bring the book up to date with my latest thinking and research.

Finally, I wish to acknowledge the invaluable support I have received over many years from two grants from the National Institute of Mental Health. One supplied me with sustained support over more than 40 years for conducting research on my theory of two minds. The other provided me with release time from other duties so that I could more fully devote myself to conducting research and developing my theory.

Chapter 1

Emotional Intelligence Revisited

The idea of emotional intelligence has evoked a great deal of interest recently, mainly due to the influence of Dan Goleman's best-selling book, *Emotional Intelligence*. Goleman makes a compelling case for emotional intelligence being important for success in living and very likely more important than intellectual intelligence. People appreciate the message in Goleman's book because they have long resented the excessive importance that has been attributed to IQ. Everyone knows of people with average IQs who are highly successful and of others with very high IQs—stars of their high school classes—who never made it in the real world. This raises the question of what the first group has that the other is missing. Goleman's answer is that it has emotional intelligence.

There is no question but that emotional intelligence is very important. However, as valuable as Goleman's contribution is to an appreciation of the importance of emotional intelligence, it also has several important limitations, among which are a failure to define emotional intelligence, the inclusion of so many different abilities under emotional intelligence as to obscure its meaning, a failure to recognize the importance of those aspects of practical intelligence that are not part of emotional intelligence, and, perhaps most important, a failure to appreciate the influence of preconscious, automatic thoughts on emotion. This latter issue is particularly important for understanding emotional intelligence and what can be done to improve it. From the position that Goleman takes, there is nothing adults can do to improve their experience of emotions, as they are beyond the "neurological window of opportunity" that is available to children. The best adults can hope to do is to control the expression of their inappropriate or "unintelligent" emotions. Ironically, Goleman's analysis would rescue us from the false belief that success in life is determined by our IQs but then present us with an equally restricting false belief, namely that once we are beyond childhood, our success in life is determined by our immutable emotions.

In this and the next chapter, I explore the concept of emotional intelligence, consider what it is and is not, and contrast it with intellectual intelligence, about which a great deal more is known. Most important, I discuss the view that automatic, preconscious thoughts precede and determine emotions and therefore make it possible for people to learn to control the emotions they experience by controlling the underlying preconscious thoughts, a theme that is emphasized throughout this book.

A TALE OF TWO TALES

As a first step toward understanding the difference between emotional and intellectual intelligence, consider the following two perspectives on the meaning of life. As you read each passage, try to answer the following questions: How intellectually intelligent is the protagonist? How emotionally intelligent is he? On what basis did you distinguish between emotional and intellectual intelligence?

The first passage is from *My Confession* by Leo Tolstoi, the great Russian novelist, who describes his thoughts during a period of depression.

When I thought of the fame which my works had gained me, I used to say to myself, "Well, what if I should be more famous than Gogol, Pushkin, Shakespeare, Moliere . . . well, what then?" . . . Such questions demand an answer, and an immediate one; without one, it is impossible to live, but answer there was none. . . . If I wished for something, I knew beforehand that, were I to satisfy the wish, nothing would come of it, I should still be dissatisfied. . . . I knew not what I wanted. . . .

Such was the condition I had come to, at the time when all the circumstances of my life were pre-eminently happy ones, and when I had not yet reached my fiftieth year. I had a good, a loving, and a well-beloved wife, good children, a fine estate, which, without much trouble on my part, continually increased my income; I was more than ever respected by my friends and acquaintances; I was praised by strangers, and could lay claim to having made my name famous. . . .

I could not attribute reasonable motive to any single act, much less to my whole life. I was only astonished that this had not occurred to me before from premises which had so long been known. Illness and death would come . . . , if not today, then tomorrow, to those whom I loved, to myself, and nothing would remain but stench and worms. All my acts, whatever I did, would sooner or later be forgotten, and I myself be nowhere. Why, then, busy one's self with anything? How could men see this, and live? It is possible to live only as long as life intoxicates us; as soon as we are sober again we see that it is all a delusion, and a stupid one.

Now consider the following tale:

A Buddhist monk, being hotly pursued by a vicious tiger, fell off a cliff. By good fortune he landed on a ledge. He could see the tiger waiting hungrily above him, but even if the tiger departed, he knew that the slope was too steep for him to climb. Since there was no escape from above and a sheer drop below, he realized his fate was sealed. No sooner did he have this thought, than the ledge that was supporting him began to develop cracks in it, and it was apparent that it would shortly fall away and hurtle him to his death. As he looked about, he spied a strawberry plant growing out of a crevice in the rock. He plucked a berry from it, ate it very slowly to savor its taste, and thought, "How delicious!"

Having read the two passages, who would you say has the greater intellectual intelligence, Tolstoi or the monk? As one of the greatest literary geniuses of all time, Tolstoi almost certainly had an IQ far above average. Even if you did not know the passage came from Tolstoi, the quality of the writing would indicate that this is someone of superior intellectual ability. As for the Buddhist monk, there is no reason to believe he had above average intelligence. Presumably, then, you rated Tolstoi as the more intellectually intelligent of the two. How about their emotional intelligence? Very likely, you rated the Buddhist monk as the more emotionally intelligent. More important, on what basis did you make the judgment? Was it simply that the monk was happier? I suspect not, for if the sadness of Tolstoi were reasonable in terms of an instigating situation, you would not consider his emotional reaction indicative of poor emotional intelligence. You would not say, for example, that someone is emotionally unintelligent if she were sad following the loss of a loved one. What makes Tolstoi's emotional reaction "unintelligent" is that it is inappropriate for the circumstances of his life, which, by his own appraisal, should make him happy.

Given the awareness of the limited time we all have to live on earth, it is equally logical to conclude that life is futile, and there is no point therefore in living, as to conclude that one might as well make the best of what time one has. Although the two conclusions are equally logical, one is more constructive in the sense that it leads to a more satisfactory way of leading one's life. Does this mean that one should always think positively? Not necessarily, for thinking positively in some circumstances, such as in the face of danger, can lead to disaster. Thinking constructively is not the same as thinking positively. I have much more to say about constructive thinking later in this book. For now, I only wish to emphasize that specific kinds of thoughts precede and determine emotions, that these thoughts occur automatically, that they vary in constructiveness, and that constructive thinking underlies emotional intelligence. If you automatically think constructively, you will exhibit emotional intelligence, and if you don't, you won't.

An interesting question is why Tolstoi had such deeply pessimistic thoughts to begin with. He was consciously aware that his thinking was the source of his misery, but he was powerless to change it. We have all had similar experiences in which we wish to think in different ways from the thinking that automatically arises in our minds but are unable to do so. We may reason with ourselves that it is better for our own peace of mind and even for our health to forgive old insults rather than dwell on them. Yet, when any reminder occurs, the distressing thoughts return, and sometimes they even return without reminders. Why can't we control our own minds? The answer, as I show later, is that we literally operate by two minds, a rational, conscious mind, which is relatively unemotional and which we can normally control, and an automatic, "experiential" mind, which is intimately associated with emotions and past experiences and which operates at the preconscious level, at the fringe of consciousness, and which we cannot as easily control, partly because we are often unaware of its operation. However, if we understood how the experiential mind operates and made a point of attending to its operation, it would put us in an advantageous position for increasing our control of it. How that mind works, you will learn, is by operating in terms of certain principles that differ from those of the rational mind and that involve learning directly from lived experience. Most of the time such learning is adaptive, but not always, for what was learned from previous experience, particularly in early childhood, may not be appropriate for current situations.

Applying the preceding reasoning to Tolstoi's depression, one suspects that he learned to have certain desires in childhood as a result of the frustration of some deep, unfulfilled need, such as, perhaps, the craving for unconditional love, that cannot be satisfied by any later worldly success. This can explain why, once he fulfilled his conscious ambitions, rather than feeling elated, he experienced disillusionment and a loss of direction. He discovered that what he thought would bring him happiness is an illusion. He is thus left without direction as to how to proceed to seek happiness, and he therefore feels helpless and hopeless. The problem is that the desires and beliefs in his experiential mind do not correspond to those in his rational mind, and therefore his rational efforts are of no avail, no matter what his intellectual intelligence.

Note what we have learned about emotional intelligence so far: that at least one aspect of emotional intelligence is the appropriateness of a person's emotions to eliciting situations; that emotions are produced by the interpretation of events (how you think about the world and yourself determines how you feel about the world and yourself); that the thoughts that underlie emotions are preconscious and automatic and therefore not easy to control; and that emotional intelligence is based on the constructiveness of the underlying thoughts. If your automatic thoughts are constructive and appropriate, so, too, will be your emotions. Note that the emphasis here is on the thoughts that underlie emotions. Contrast this with Goleman's position in which he assumes that emotions come before thoughts, presumably through direct physiological channels. From his viewpoint, the thoughts that Tolstoi expresses are the result, not the cause, of his depressive feelings. The solution is not to change his thinking but to take the right pill or to receive electric shock. Who is right? Actually, in this case both of us can be right, because we are dealing here with a mood, not an emotion.

What is the difference between moods and emotions? A helpful way to view the difference is to consider that moods are to emotions as the tides are to the waves. That is, emotions are relatively short-lived reactions that may be superimposed on moods. Moods are more long-lasting and usually increase and decrease gradually. They often occur for no identifiable reason. People may report that they simply woke up in a good or bad mood. Emotions, on the other hand, are always reactions to specific situations. Of particular interest for present purposes, moods can occur for either physiological or psychological reasons. As support for this, depression can be successfully treated with either drugs, electric shock, or psychotherapy, with some people responding better to one, and others to another. Emotions, on the other hand, are almost always produced by the interpretation of events, which means that emotions are almost always produced by thoughts. If you want to change the way you emotionally react, you have to change your thinking. This, of course, has enormous implications for improving emotional intelligence.

As I have already noted, according to Goleman's position, changing emotions through changing thoughts should be possible only during childhood, when there is a presumed "neurological window of opportunity." If you are an adult, you can derive some comfort from blaming your inappropriate emotions on your stupid amygdala, an almond-shaped structure in the temporal lobe of the brain that infuses experience with emotions, learns in a rudimentary manner, and has a rapid alternative pathway to behavior that bypasses your cerebral cortex, the thinking organ of your central nervous system. On the other hand, if you adopt the position recommended in this book, you will recognize that automatic, preconscious thoughts precede emotions and that by training these thoughts, you can "re-form" your emotions, thereby improving your emotional intelligence. Recognizing that thoughts produce emotions will put you in good company. Buddha learned 2,500 years ago, by carefully observing the operation of his mind during meditation, that thought precedes emotions. Five hundred years later the Greek philosopher Epictetus, through logical analysis, came to the conclusion that we react not to events as they objectively occur but to our interpretation (thoughts) of them. More recently, cognitive therapists such as Aaron Beck and Albert Ellis have used this insight to develop the most successful form of psychological treatment known for treating many emotional disorders. I am suggesting in this book that you don't have to be emotionally disturbed to use their techniques. This book will teach them to you, but it also goes beyond those techniques and provides a theory for understanding why they work and the limitations they have that sometimes require supplementation by other procedures, also described in this book.

TWO MINDS AND TWO KINDS OF INTELLIGENCE

If we are to discuss different kinds of intelligence, it would be helpful to have a definition of what we mean by intelligence. A reasonable working definition is that intelligence refers to the cognitive ability to solve problems. By cognitive I mean some form of knowing, broadly conceived, including perception as well as more complex reasoning processes. This view is consistent with the definition in *Webster's Third New International Unabridged Dictionary*, according to which cognition is "the act of knowing in the broadest sense. Distinguished from affection [feelings] and conation [motivation]." Synonyms are listed as "knowledge" and "perception." It is noteworthy that cognition, in this definition, is not restricted to knowledge of which people are consciously aware but, rather, includes conscious and unconscious knowing. Animals have cognition, as do human infants, and there are psychologists who exclusively study the cognitions of preverbal children and nonhuman animals.

My definition of intelligence is in some ways broad and in other ways specific. It is broad in the sense that it includes all problem solving that is accomplished through some form of cognition, which includes conscious, deliberate reasoning as well as information processing that occurs automatically, not necessarily in a person's awareness. Thus, different kinds of intelligence require the ability to solve abstract, mathematical problems in and out of the classroom, the ability to solve practical problems in everyday living, the ability to solve problems that require creativity, the ability to solve problems that require the application of information in known ways, and the ability to solve problems by intuitive procedures. It is specific in that it is restricted to the use of cognition to solve problems and differs, accordingly, from other equally important, noncognitive adaptive reactions and behavior, including emotions, motivation, physiological reactions, and instincts.

From the perspective of the previous definition, it can only add to confusion to regard emotions as having intelligence, as emotions are not a way of thinking but a consequence of preconscious, automatic thinking. Yet, as the term emotional intelligence has caught the popular imagination and is no doubt here to stay, I shall continue to use it, but with the implicit understanding that it is not the emotions themselves that are intelligent or unintelligent but the constructiveness of the automatic, preconscious thinking that underlies the emotions.

In this book I present a theory of the mind that provides a new perspective on understanding emotional intelligence and how it can be trained. A basic assumption in the theory is that human beings operate by two minds, an *experiential mind*, which learns directly from experience, is preconscious, operates automatically, and is intimately associated with emotions and a *rational mind*, which operates according to logical inference, is conscious, deliberative, and relatively emotion-free. All behavior is determined by the combined influence of the two minds, with the degree to which each contributes varying from almost no influence to almost complete dominance, depending on the situation and the person. As the experiential and rational minds provide different ways of solving problems, each has its own form of intelligence. The intelligence of the rational mind is what IQ tests measure, and its essence is the ability to solve abstract problems. The intelligence of the experiential mind includes practical intelligence, social intelligence, and emotional intelligence. To say that each mind has its own form of intelligence is simply to note, according to my definition, that both are cognitive systems (ways of knowing) and that both are used to solve problems.

Note that my definition says nothing about whether the cognition used in solving problems has to be deliberate or conscious to qualify as intelligent, so automatic or intuitive problem solving is considered to be a form of intelligence. Consider, as an example, a person who, when he does not get an expected raise, automatically thinks in a way that works him up into a rage, which leads him to tell off his boss, who fires him. This person might even blame his self-defeating behavior on his "stupid emotions." He would likely add that he lost control of himself because of his rage. However, according to my definition it was not his emotions that were stupid but the automatic thoughts that were the immediate source of the inappropriate rage. The sequence of automatic thoughts responsible for the rage could have consisted of thoughts about how unfair the boss was, how our protagonist does not have to take that kind of treatment from anyone, how someone ought to tell the boss off, and how he is just the kind of person to do so. Given such thoughts, one can work oneself up into getting pretty angry.

As the experiential mind is intimately associated with emotions, I could have called it the emotional mind. However, because it adapts to the world by learning directly from experience, and because it is the cause, and emotions are the result, I prefer to call it the "experiential mind." Moreover, the operation of the experiential mind is not restricted to learning from events that are highly emotional but also includes learning from more mundane situations. The experiential mind is essentially the same mind by which nonhuman animals adapt to their environments. The other mind is strictly a human mind, adapting to the world with the powerful tools of language and logical inference, and I therefore refer to it as the "rational mind."

Which Comes First, Emotions or Thoughts?

I would not be surprised if you doubted my assertion that thought precedes emotions. Most people, including Dan Goleman and a substantial number of other psychologists, believe it is the other way around. Not only is this a very important theoretical issue, but it has important practical implications with respect to controlling emotions. It is, of course, self-evident that people can control the expression of their emotions, so that is not at issue. What is at issue is whether or not people can control experiencing a particular emotion. It is one thing to have an inappropriate emotion and then inhibit its expression, and it is another thing not to have the emotion in the first place. The former amounts to damage control, whereas the latter avoids the damage to begin with. If emotions occur automatically because of hard-wired neurological connections, as Goleman maintains, then there is no possibility of consciously controlling their occurrence.

According to Goleman's view, if someone insults you, you automatically experience anger. You may control how you express your anger or, for that matter, whether or not you express it at all, but you cannot control your initial experience of anger. The reason this is so, Goleman states, citing the neuroscientist Joseph LeDoux, is that there is an alternative, rapid path from the thalamus to the amygdala that bypasses the cerebral cortex, the thinking organ of your central nervous system. However, he fails to consider that this path has little to do with how emotions are normally experienced in everyday life, for only under the most rare circumstances are emotions produced in the absence of interpretation by the cerebral cortex. How people interpret situations normally determines the emotions that they experience, and their interpretations are usually based on an understanding of language, which is well beyond the capacity of the amygdala. Think of some recent emotional experiences of your own. The likelihood is great that they were produced by something that someone said or by your verbal interpretation of what they did.

It is noteworthy that every example of emotionally maladaptive behavior that Goleman cites as a case of a runaway emotion resulting from the short path to the amygdala that bypasses the cerebral cortex is instigated by the interpretation of a situation that involves an understanding of language. Yet, without the neural pathway being routed through the cerebral cortex, which alone understands language, on what basis can the amygdala react? Conceivably, it could react to the tone or loudness of a person's voice or the expression on a person's face. Let us explore this issue by considering the Robles case that Goleman cites as an example of a runaway amygdala reaction that presumably bypassed the cerebral cortex. Robles brutally stabbed two young women to death when robbing their apartment. He reported that he tied the two women up without intending to harm them. However, when one of them said she would remember his face and help the police track him down, he flew into a rage and stabbed both of them over and over with a kitchen knife.

It seems almost certain that the rage was instigated by an understanding of what the woman said and was not simply an automatic response to the tone of her voice or the look on her face. We can never know exactly what went through Robles' mind when he heard her words, but, to make my point, imagine that the thoughts that flashed through his mind were something like the following: "How dare she threaten me when I have her completely in my power and can do anything I want with her. Besides, she's right: she can help them catch me, so I would be better off to get rid of her. I'll show her!" Such thoughts could instigate a state of anger, which the amygdala could then amplify into what Goleman refers to as an "emotional hijacking." I therefore believe that if Robles completely lost control, as he claims, it occurred after, not before, he understood what the woman said, which would mean that the thoughts preceded, rather than followed, the emotion.

Had Robles had other thoughts, such as, "She is talking nonsense because she is scared. In no way is she going to be able to track me down. The poor thing is so terrified she doesn't know what she is saying," not only would he not have flown into a rage, but he might have reassured her that he would not hurt her. Although one cannot know for sure whether the rage reaction occurred before or after Robles understood the woman's words, at the very least it is possible that it occurred after, which means that even in such extreme cases, thoughts may precede and instigate emotions. People do go into a rage over what is said to them, and they do this although the amygdala does not understand a word of English. All that can be legitimately concluded from the neurological evidence Goleman cites is that it is possible for emotional reactions in humans to occur independently from interpretation by the cerebral cortex. What is omitted from this statement is that such circumstances are very unusual, and, with rare exception, emotions are instigated by people's thoughts.

If thought precedes emotions, why do so many people believe it is the other way around? The reason is that the thoughts that precede emotions usually occur automatically and preconsciously, so people are not normally aware of them, whereas the ones that follow emotions are conspicuous in our consciousness. If someone makes us angry, we are consciously aware of thinking about how badly the person behaved and of what we would like to do to even the score. Because we are aware of these thoughts but not of the ones that preceded and instigated the emotion, we have the illusion that emotion precedes thought. Putting it all together, it can be said that preconscious, automatic thoughts, including interpretations of situations, normally precede and induce emotions, which are then followed by conscious thoughts about how to deal with the situation, including whether to express the emotion and, if so, in what manner.

In this chapter I tried to give you an intuitive feeling for the difference between intellectual and emotional intelligence and for the preconscious thoughts that underlie the latter. In the next, I discuss intellectual and emotional intelligence in greater detail and consider what each is and is not and what would have to be accomplished in the measurement of emotional intelligence to establish it as a scientifically viable concept comparable to intellectual intelligence.

Chapter 2

What Is Emotional Intelligence, and How Can It Be Measured?

The first question about emotional intelligence is whether or not it is a meaningful concept in the first place. If it is, the next question is how to measure it. In order to answer both of these questions, it will be helpful to begin with a consideration of what intellectual intelligence is and how it has been successfully measured.

The approach to measuring intellectual intelligence has produced one of the most important instruments with demonstrated predictive power in the history of psychology. This is not to deny that it has often been misused and misinterpreted. It is to suggest that the measurement of intellectual intelligence is a valuable tool for predicting some kinds of human behavior if used and interpreted properly. Moreover, there are important lessons to be learned from the measurement of intellectual intelligence that can be applied to the measurement of other abilities, including emotional intelligence.

Our story about the measurement of intellectual intelligence begins with a French psychologist by the name of Alfred Binet. In 1905, Binet published the first intelligence test, which took American psychologists by storm and became the model for other similar tests, such as the carefully standardized American version, the Stanford-Binet Intelligence test, which is still in widespread use. Binet developed his test at the request of the Paris school authorities, who desired a practical, objective instrument for detecting mentally deficient children who were not expected to profit from attending regular classes. He began with two assumptions: intelligence is a mental ability, and it increases with age through the childhood years. He then determined what kinds of items children of different ages could and could not solve and obtained scores that indicated the age level at which a child performed. A child who performed at the level of a four-year-old was assigned a mental age of 4 and one who performed at the level of a six-year-old was assigned a mental age of 6. The test turned out to fulfill its purpose extremely well and became widely used in this country and elsewhere as an objective measure of mental ability.

In 1914, an American psychologist by the name of Stern proposed that an "intelligence quotient" (IQ) be obtained by dividing mental age by chronological age and multiplying by 100 to get rid of decimals. The IQ had an advantage over mental age in that it was relatively stable over the years, and it allowed children of different ages to be directly compared. For example, a four-year-old child who performed at the level of the average five-year-old and therefore had an IQ of 125 (5/4 × 100) could be expected to have about the same IQ at age 8 and could be judged to be as bright for her age as an eight-year-old who performed at the level of the average ten-year-old. An unfortunate consequence of the surprising degree of stability of the IQ under most circumstances is that people began to interpret it as signifying that IQ was determined by heredity and could not be appreciably changed. It was also assumed not only that IQ was an excellent predictor of school performance but that it was also a good predictor of success in other endeavors. As a result, many people were informed that their capacity for future success was limited, and there was not much they could do about it. Today we know that although there is a considerable hereditary component to IQ, there is also a considerable environmental component, that IQ is less stable than originally believed, that under special circumstances considerable increases or decreases in IQ can occur, that IQ is not nearly as good a predictor of success in the workplace as it is a predictor of success in school, and that other abilities and attributes, such as creativity, motivation, emotional adjustment, and practical intelligence, can be equally as important as or more important than IQ, depending on the particular activity in question. For example, you have to have a very high IQ to be an outstanding physicist or mathematician, but with an average IQ and other superior abilities you can become a successful entrepreneur, movie star, parent, or even president of the United States.

IQ scores for most intelligence tests today are no longer calculated by dividing mental age by chronological age. Rather, the mean, or average score, is set at 100, and the other scores are set at levels that a prescribed percentage of people is expected to obtain. The distribution of scores is made to follow the bell-shaped normal curve, with most scores falling close to the mean and relatively few falling at the extremes. Thus, the IQ no longer means what it used to in terms of mental age. It simply provides a number that indicates where a person stands compared to others of the same age, such as in the upper or lower 20% of the population.

By examining the kinds of items that are included in intelligence tests, we can get a good idea of what the tests are actually measuring. Following is a sample of items representing different mental age levels in the Stanford-Binet test. At the two-year level, a child is expected to place different forms, like triangles and squares, into corresponding holes. At the three-year level, he or she is expected to identify different body parts of a paper doll, such as hair and mouth. At the four-year level, objects, like a toy dog and a toy shoe, are covered, and the child is expected to report what they are from memory. At the seven-year level, a child is expected to indicate in what way two things, such as a ship and an automobile, are alike. At the nine-year level, a child is expected to repeat five numbers backward, define words, and explain proverbs. It is apparent that these items represent a wide range of mental activities, including memory, spatial relations, and abstract reasoning. Together, they provide a broad measure of a child's overall mental ability.

One of the greatest controversies in the history of psychology has been over whether intelligence consists of one general mental ability, referred to as "g", or of several independent mental abilities. Tests like the Stanford-Binet intelligence test are based on the assumption that intelligence is a highly general mental ability. As support for this assumption, the adherents of the general-factor theory note that performance on all the different kinds of items in the test is correlated, meaning that children who do well on one kind of item, such as memory, also tend to do well on other kinds of items, such as abstract reasoning and verbal fluency. In later studies, this issue has been investigated more thoroughly by constructing relatively pure tests of different mental abilities. The most extensive study of this kind was conducted by Thurstone. Through using sophisticated statistical procedures, he found the following seven different kinds of mental ability, which he referred to as the primary mental abilities:

1. Verbal comprehension: the ability to understand and define words
2. Word fluency: the ability to think rapidly of words, as in making an extemporaneous speech or quickly finding the words for a crossword puzzle
3. Number facility: the ability to do numerical problems
4. Spatial ability: the ability to visualize objects and draw them from memory
5. Memory: the ability to memorize and recall information
6. Perception: the ability to notice details and detect similarities and differences
7. Reasoning: the ability to find general rules

Did Thurstone's findings indicate that the advocates of separate mental abilities had won the day? The answer is yes and no, for he also found that the seven primary traits were correlated with each other. That is, as in the case of the Stanford-Binet items, children who did better than others on one kind of ability tended to do better than others on the other abilities. However, the correlations among the primary traits were only modest in strength. Thus, both sides in the argument were right. There is a broad factor of general intelligence, or "g", and there are also separate factors, indicating that to some extent intelligence is general, and to some extent it is specific. It follows that to get a comprehensive picture of a person's intellectual intelligence, it is necessary to know the person's specific strengths and weaknesses in addition to the person's overall score. As an example of how such information could be used, one could say of a particular person that although, in general, he is highly intelligent, he is not uniformly so. He is particularly strong in reasoning and numerical ability, fairly good in verbal comprehension, word fluency, and memory, but only average in spatial and perceptual ability. Another person might be generally good or poor in all of the primary mental abilities.

Although intelligence tests were developed to measure the kinds of mental abilities that are important for success in school, this does not mean that is all they can predict. To some extent, they can also predict success in a wide range of activities in real life, but they do so less well than they predict school success. They are particularly useful for screening purposes. For example, by using tests such as the Army General Classification Test (AGCT) to select candidates for specialized training, the armed services are able to reduce the number of failures and thereby considerably reduce expense. Many errors concerning individuals will be made in such circumstances: some people who are rejected would have made it, and others who are accepted turn out to be failures. However, on average, the test considerably improves the selection process. The same is true for predicting performance in many jobs in industry.

It is important to recognize that intelligence tests merely identify one kind of ability that is important in certain kinds of activities. Other abilities and attributes that are equally or more important in many situations are practical intelligence, or common sense, social ability, emotional adjustment, personality factors, and creativity. Robert Sternberg, a Yale psychologist, who has done a great deal of research on practical intelligence, has demonstrated that the prediction of success in various jobs can be improved by adding measures of other kinds of abilities to measures of intellectual intelligence. In a study he and his associates conducted on the performance of business managers, they found that measures of intellectual intelligence, practical intelligence, and social ability contributed about equally to how well the managers were able to solve realistic business problems. Most important, used together, the three different kinds of ability supplemented each other and produced fairly good overall prediction.

How does IQ relate to solving everyday, real-life problems? A common mistaken belief is that people with high IQs are generally lacking in common sense. The truth of the matter is that people with high IQs have neither more nor less common sense, on average, than others. There are high-IQ people with a lot of common sense and others with very little. We have the illusion that high-IQ people have less common sense than others because we expect more of them. Research has demonstrated that the two kinds of ability are unrelated. Although IQ is related to job performance for some activities, it is unrelated to performance in many others, where common sense is more important. Several studies have found that the ability to solve real-life problems is often unrelated to intellectual intelligence. For example, in one study, it was found that the ability of workers at a milk-processing plant to figure out effective strategies for efficiently filling orders was related neither to their IQs nor to their arithmetic grades in school. In another study, the ability of housewives to choose the best values in grocery stores was unrelated to their IQs. In a study of racetrack handicappers, it was found that their ability to figure out odds, which involved developing mental shortcut methods, was based on experience and was unrelated to intellectual intelligence. Robert Sternberg and his associates have also found that people differed in their ability to pick up useful information while working on a job and that this ability, which was important for advancement, was unrelated to their intellectual intelligence. Other evidence indicating the independence between practical and intellectual intelligence is that they have a different course of development over time. Intellectual intelligence, on average, increases up to young adulthood and then steadily declines. This simply means that people become less bright and mentally sharp as they age. Practical intelligence, on the other hand, keeps increasing until the later years. Thus, people make up in experience for what they lose in mental alertness.

How well do people with very high IQs fare in life? We all know high-IQ people who are unsuccessful in the workaday world and in leading their lives. However, all this tells us is that a high IQ does not guarantee success. The people with high IQs who are failures may be exceptions to the rule rather than representative of it. The best answer to the question of whether or not a very high IQ is related to success in life is provided by a long-term study of mentally gifted children conducted by Lewis Terman. He repeatedly examined a group of children who had IQs over 140, which places them in the upper 1% of the population. After his death, other researchers continued the project, with the latest follow-up being conducted when the participants were over fifty years old. As a result, we now have important information on how very bright children fare in later life. As a group, they did considerably better than average, but there were exceptions. As adults they tended to be healthier, better adjusted, and more successful in their work than others. As for notable accomplishments, a high proportion is listed in *Who's Who* and in *American Men of Science*. Many others have received some other form of professional recognition or have obtained patents for inventions. Most, however, were simply somewhat more successful than average, not outstanding in any way. A few fell by the wayside, dropping out of school at an early age or unable to hold a job. This latter group was found to be poorly adjusted emotionally or socially or to be lacking in the motivation to succeed. This study informs us that a high IQ can be very helpful along the road to success in everyday life, but other factors, including social ability, emotional adjustment, practical intelligence, and motivation, are also important, and although there is a tendency for the very bright to be more creative and successful than others, a high IQ does not guarantee either.

Relatively little research has been conducted on abilities and attributes other than intellectual intelligence and practical intelligence as predictors of performance. Thus, although it is reasonable to suspect that emotional adjustment, social ability, creativity, and personality factors may be as important or even more so than intellectual intelligence for effective performance in many activities, there is not a solid background of evidence on which to base such a conclusion. A good part of the difficulty in collecting such evidence is that there are not yet good measures of most of these other abilities and attributes. It is beyond the scope of this chapter to consider the problems in measuring all of these. Instead, I concentrate on emotional intelligence because it has evoked so much interest and has been presented in such a confusing manner.

Let us take stock of what we have learned about what intellectual intelligence, as measured by intelligence tests, is and is not. It is a composite of mental abilities that are positively related to each other, including reasoning ability, memory, numerical ability, spatial ability, and several others. Both the overall score and the pattern of scores are important, as the latter identifies particular areas of strength and weakness. All of the components of intellectual intelligence are cognitive abilities, as all involve ways of knowing. Intellectual intelligence differs from practical intelligence, which is also a form of intelligence because it is a way of solving problems through the use of cognition, albeit a different kind of cognition than is employed in intellectual intelligence. Examples of important abilities that are something other than forms of intelligence according to my definition are empathy, physical ability, and musical ability. The jury is still out as to whether or not there is a scientifically meaningful concept of emotional intelligence. Nevertheless, as I noted before, I will continue to use the word emotional intelligence because I believe it is here to stay, and, in discussing the views of others who use the term, it is awkward not to do the same.

Before proceeding further, it is helpful to consider some basic principles of psychological testing to provide a background for understanding what would be necessary to effectively measure emotional intelligence.

BASIC PRINCIPLES OF PSYCHOLOGICAL MEASUREMENT

As a result of many decades of working on the development of intelligence tests, aptitude tests, personality tests, and tests of vocational interests, standard procedures have been established for constructing psychological measuring instruments. There are two main requirements of a test: that it be reliable and valid. Two kinds of reliability that have to be demonstrated are internal-consistency reliability and test-retest reliability. Internal-consistency reliability is demonstrated by the use of statistical procedures that show that the different items in a test all measure something in common. However, statistical procedures alone are not sufficient for determining which items belong in a test. The items must also belong together for conceptual reasons, or otherwise items that represent other constructs that happen to be highly correlated with the ability of interest would be included. Test-retest reliability is demonstrated by showing that a test produces the same results on repeated occasions. Validity is established by demonstrating that a test measures what it is supposed to measure, not something else. This is accomplished by showing that the test correlates with appropriate criteria. Intelligence tests do very well with respect to both kinds of reliability and have been demonstrated to be highly valid for predicting school performance. In addition to intelligence tests, reliable and valid tests have been constructed for measuring vocational aptitude and interests, personality attributes, and practical knowledge with respect to certain kinds of jobs. At this point, satisfactory tests of creativity, emotional intelligence, and social ability have not been established, although psychologists are working on it.

THE MEASUREMENT OF EMOTIONAL INTELLIGENCE

If we wish to apply the hard-won knowledge that has been gained from the successful development of other tests to the conceptualization and measurement of emotional intelligence, then the following principles will have to be applied to it, as well. In order for the kind of multifaceted concept of emotional intelligence proposed by Dan Goleman to be scientifically legitimated, it has to be demonstrated that the presumed components of emotional intelligence, such as the ability to discern emotions in others, to feel empathy, to delay gratification, to control one's own emotions, to exhibit social competence, and to be emotionally well adjusted and not suffer from depression, anxiety attacks, and uncontrolled hostility are, in fact, positively correlated with each other and are best conceived of as a single overall ability with semi-independent components. It also has to be demonstrated that reliable and valid measures of the components and of the overall construct can be constructed. Nothing like this has yet been attempted, and, until it is accomplished, all we have is unsupported speculation about the existence of an undefined concept referred to as emotional intelligence. Moreover, on a conceptual basis it is difficult to see, for example, how one can defend the inclusion of social competence as a component of emotional intelligence. Social competence and emotional adjustment are two distinct concepts, and, although related, there is no more basis for including one as a subcategory of the other than the reverse.

Although Goleman's views are highly appealing to people because of his emphasis on the importance of abilities other than intellectual intelligence, they are not very useful for identifying a viable construct of emotional intelligence. What Goleman has accomplished that is very useful is to draw attention to the limitations of intellectual intelligence for success in living and to emphasize the importance of several other abilities and attributes that are equally important, if not more so, including emotional adjustment, social competence, and, at least implicitly, a personality variable, ego strength, which includes the ability to delay gratification, to tolerate frustration, and to regulate impulses. It is unfortunate that he has chosen to include them all under the rubric of an undefined concept that he calls emotional intelligence. A further limitation in Goleman's views is that he ignores the concept of practical intelligence, which refers to solving problems in the real world of everyday experience and which is different from both intellectual and emotional intelligence and equally important for success in living.

An example of a more scientifically defensible approach to emotional intelligence is provided by Peter Salovey and John D. Mayer, who were the ones who introduced the concept of emotional intelligence in the first place. Their conceptualization of emotional intelligence is reasonably much more closely focused on emotions than the far-flung network of concepts included by Goleman. They define emotional intelligence as consisting of four basic skills: the ability to accurately perceive, appraise, and express emotions; the ability to access and/or generate feelings that facilitate thinking; the ability to understand emotions and to utilize emotional knowledge; and the ability to regulate emotions to promote emotional and intellectual growth. According to their definition, people who are more emotionally intelligent than others are better able than others to identify their own and other people's emotions. They can tell when someone is sad, frightened, angry, or jealous and can detect such emotions from subtle cues that elude those who are less emotionally intelligent. They also are in better touch with their own emotions than others. When someone accuses them of speaking in an angry voice, they do not pound their fist on the table and shout that they are not angry. Rather, they know what they feel and can detect subtle shades of feelings in themselves, such as slight irritation or tension, of which others are oblivious. In addition, emotionally intelligent people, according to Salovey and Mayer, accurately express emotions, so others are not confused about the feelings they are projecting. When they are angry, they convey anger, not sadness or some other emotion, and if they wish to pretend to be sad or frightened, they can do so in a compelling manner. Emotionally intelligent people can use their emotions as an aid in their thinking, such as by being able to re-create an emotion in themselves in order to understand what someone else is feeling, having emotions that direct their thinking to issues of significance, and generating emotions that provide a context for thinking in certain ways, such as producing feelings of sadness and happiness to obtain different perspectives on certain issues. Emotionally intelligent people can also understand and analyze emotions, such as distinguishing between shame and guilt and jealousy and envy. They can also control their emotions in a way that promotes intellectual and emotional growth, such as by delaying acting on emotional impulses and taking into account the influence of emotions on their rational thinking.

Currently, Salovey and Mayer are attempting to construct objective tests of the different components of emotional intelligence. It remains to be seen how well they will succeed according to the recognized criteria for evaluating tests. This will require that they develop reliable and valid measures of each of the components and demonstrate that the components are all correlated with each other to a sufficient degree to justify considering them as different aspects of a single, more general concept. Their approach provides an interesting contrast with the one advocated by cognitive-experiential self-theory (CEST), as they emphasize intelligent thinking about emotions, whereas CEST emphasizes the intelligence of the automatic thinking that underlies emotions, which determines the appropriateness of the emotions people actually have. Thus, in their test of emotional knowledge, they ask people to determine the best emotional response in a variety of situations. According to CEST, although such information in the rational system is important, what is even more important is the appropriateness of the emotions people actually have. It is one thing to be knowledgeable about how to emotionally respond, and it is another thing to be able to respond that way. As we know all too well from our own personal experience, emotions do not necessarily respond to our conscious understanding and wishes.

John Gottman, a psychologist at the University of Washington, has studied the emotional development of children in two long-term studies. He found that "emotionally intelligent" children are healthier, happier, and better adjusted, do better in school, and cope better with stress than children who are less emotionally intelligent, which has led him to conclude that emotional intelligence is a better predictor of how children will do in life than anything else. Gottman defines emotional intelligence as consisting of the following components: knowing your own emotions, which includes the ability to control impulses, delay gratification, and cope with frustration; having the ability to recognize emotions in others, which is necessary for empathy; handling relationships with others well; and motivating oneself in an optimistic, self-confident way. It is apparent that, like Goleman, Gottman includes a wide variety of different reactions under emotional intelligence and therefore is subject to the same criticism of treating many different reactions as components of a single concept in the absence of supporting evidence. Certainly, Gottman and Goleman and many others before them have provided impressive evidence that emotional adjustment is extremely important for leading a happy and successful life, including being able to apply one's intellectual abilities in an efficient and constructive manner. But because some attributes are important does not mean they should be considered forms of intelligence. Not only is nothing gained, but something is lost by substituting "emotional intelligence" for the more usual term "emotional adjustment." What is most reasonably viewed as an unfortunate symptom, such as having anxiety attacks or being depressed, is treated as if it is a form of low ability.

One cannot help but wonder why it has recently become fashionable to label a wide variety of abilities and attributes as different kinds of intelligence. This trend began with a book called *Frames of Mind: The Theory of Multiple Intelligences* by Howard Gardner, a professor of education at Harvard University. In this book, Gardner proposed that there is a wide variety of forms of intelligence, including linguistic ability, logical-mathematical ability, spatial ability, musical ability (singing and playing an instrument), bodily-kinesthetic ability (dancing and athletic competence), interpersonal ability (social competence), and intrapersonal ability (self-knowledge). It will be recognized that some of these correspond to Thurstone's primary mental abilities. Others, such as musical ability, bodily-kinesthetic ability, and interpersonal ability, are completely nonintellectual. In effect, Gardner has equated the word "intelligence" with the word "ability," making the word "intelligence" devoid of any special meaning and therefore superfluous. Why has this approach been widely, albeit, to be sure, not universally, accepted? Why is it necessary to call any ability, such as having a fine voice or being a good football player, a form of intelligence rather than just accepting it as a worthwhile activity in its own right?

The answer, I believe, is that it reduces the importance of intellectual intelligence, an outcome that is pleasing to many people. There are at least two reasons people are antagonistic toward intellectual intelligence. One is that there is widespread antipathy in this country to people with high IQs. From grade school on, people with high IQs tend to be viewed negatively, particularly if they are studious. In studies of high school students, teachers in training, and experienced teachers, participants were asked to indicate how attractive they considered the following attributes: brilliant, studious, and athletic. All groups considered the most attractive person to be someone who is athletic, brilliant, and nonstudious and the least attractive person to be someone who is brilliant, studious, and nonathletic. Brilliant individuals are apparently tolerated if they do not capitalize on their brilliance by studying. They can't help it if they were born brilliant, but it is certainly in their power to refrain from studying and making others feel bad by outperforming them. An interesting question to ponder is why people do not resent good athletes who work hard at developing their talent but do resent bright people who do the same.

The second reason that people resent intellectual intelligence is that they have been subjected to the misuse and misinterpretation of the results from intelligence tests. The result is that they are eager to accept any views that deflate the importance of intellect. The danger is that intellectual intelligence, which was originally overvalued, will now be undervalued. The solution, of course, is to accept intelligence testing for what it can legitimately contribute and neither overestimate nor underestimate its importance. It can only add to confusion if, in order to reduce the importance of intellectual intelligence, all other abilities are described as forms of intelligence. Intelligence, as I previously noted, rightly belongs in the realm of cognition. Thinking well is an indication of intelligence. Kicking a football far is not. By the same token, it makes no more sense to consider being emotionally well adjusted as an indication of emotional intelligence than to consider being physically healthy as an indication of health intelligence. As desirable as both may be, that does not make them forms of intelligence.

Because of both warranted and unwarranted antagonism toward the concept of intellectual intelligence and its measurement, people, including many educators, have gone overboard in their acceptance of unsupported views about the nature of other attributes and abilities that are labeled as forms of intelligence, including emotional intelligence. For example, several school programs on training emotional intelligence cited by Goleman include exercises on identifying emotional expressions in photographs of people's faces. This procedure is based on research in which it was found that there is a positive correlation between social adjustment and the ability to identify emotions in photographs of faces. The educators apparently assume that if they train children to recognize the emotions conveyed by people's expressions, they will improve their social ability. This assumption may well be false because a correlation does not establish causality. Rather than the causal relation proceeding in the direction of the ability to identify emotions producing social responsibility, it may be the other way around, or a third factor may be responsible for both. There is no research support for the view that training people to recognize emotions increases their social ability. Moreover, even if there were, it may be a very inefficient way of improving social competence. I suspect direct training in respecting the needs of others is much more effective. After all, someone who is good at reading others' feelings could just as well use this ability for destructive as for constructive ends.

As another example of how people go overboard in the interpretation of research on emotional intelligence, Goleman emphasizes the importance of the ability to delay gratification, which he considers an aspect of emotional intelligence, with respect to later adjustment and success in life. In support of this view he cites a study by Walter Mischel and his associates, who observed that four-year-old children who were able to delay gratification by accepting two marshmallows later rather than one right away, when followed up when they were graduating from high school, were found to be more socially competent and better able to manage stress than those who took the one marshmallow right away. Moreover, the two-marshmallow group performed better in school and obtained higher Scholastic Aptitude Test (SAT) scores than those who exhibited poorer impulse control at age 4. It is a gross oversimplification to assume that the better all-around performance at age 18 can be attributed to the ability to delay gratification at age 4, as many other factors are likely involved. For example, the parents who trained the children to delay gratification at age 4 very likely trained them to acquire other desirable attributes, such as high self-esteem and social competence, and it may be these other attributes that are mainly responsible for the later success of the children. Moreover, the parents who were present when the children were 4 were in most cases present later, and it could be that their prolonged influence, not simply how they trained their children up to age 4, accounts for the long-term differences between the two groups of children.

Summing up what might reasonably be included under emotional intelligence, we have the following promising candidates: the ability to recognize one's own and other people's emotions, the ability to accurately display the emotions one wishes to display, the ability to control and otherwise manage one's emotions, and the ability to have appropriate emotions, which may be the most important of all. Some people are fortunate in that they can freely express and act on their emotions, as they know that their emotions are almost always appropriate. Others have to be on guard against expressing their emotions, which means that they have to pay a high price in order to behave appropriately.

Even if it is demonstrated that it is feasible to construct a test of emotional intelligence, as useful as such a test might be, it would not be able to provide an answer to what determines emotional intelligence. For this, it is necessary to have a theory, such as cognitive-experiential self-theory, that describes how the emotional mind operates. In addition to accounting for emotional intelligence, cognitive-experiential self-theory can elucidate another important kind of intelligence, namely practical intelligence, which is no less important for success in everyday life than intellectual and emotional intelligence.

In summary, I am suggesting that there are basically two forms of intelligence, the intelligence of the rational mind, which is what intelligence tests measure, and the intelligence of the experiential mind, which can account for both practical intelligence and emotional intelligence. Most important, as is demonstrated in the remainder of this book, the concept of experiential intelligence and its manifestation in the form of automatic constructive thinking can provide the key to understanding and improving both practical and emotional intelligence.

Chapter 3

Constructive Thinking:
The Intelligence of the
Experiential Mind

People delight in observing that someone who is very bright intellectually is unable to lead his or her life sensibly. The highly intelligent person may be unable to hold a job, fail to establish satisfactory relationships with spouse and children, make foolish comments at group meetings, and may be all thumbs when it comes to solving simple practical problems. "College boy," they say, "and he can't get along with anybody and doesn't even know how to check the oil in his car!" They then ask, "How can it be that someone can do really difficult things, like solve problems in calculus or be a computer whiz, and yet be unable to solve practical problems in everyday living? Why do smart people think dumb?" As you learned in the previous chapter, intellectually smart people don't actually think dumber, on average, than others when it comes to solving practical problems; it is just that they don't necessarily think smarter. The violation of our expectancy that they should be better than others at solving practical problems in living makes us think they do worse. Many people who do not have high IQs also do very poorly with solving practical problems in living, as witness the divorce rate, but we pay no special attention to such people because they do not violate our expectancy.

If there were only one cognitive system, people would apply the same system to solving abstract problems as to solving practical problems, and people who were smart in one would be smart in the other. The answer, then, as to why people who are smart in the abstract realm may be dumb in the practical one is that people operate by two minds, a rational mind that is well suited for solving abstract problems and learning from books and lectures but is not particularly good at solving practical problems and an experiential mind that has just the opposite advantages and disadvantages. The result is that being good at one kind of endeavor has little to do with being good at the other. In research on this issue, we have found that the correlation between the two types of intelligence is zero. This means that people can have high intelligence in both of their minds, in neither of their minds, in one but not in the other, or vice versa. The rational mind that equips us to learn from books and lectures does not ensure that we will draw practical lessons from experience anymore than the experiential mind that learns from practical experience ensures that we will be good at solving abstract problems. The two kinds of ability are simply independent.

The degree to which the automatic thinking of the experiential mind is constructive corresponds to the intelligence of the experiential mind. More precisely, constructive thinking can be defined as the degree to which a person's automatic thinking—the thinking that occurs without deliberate intention—facilitates solving problems in everyday life at a minimum cost in stress. Examples of good constructive thinking are viewing situations as challenges rather than as threats, considering failures and rejections as unfortunate but not the end of the world, and seeing the positive side of things, but not to an unrealistic degree. Examples of poor constructive thinking are dwelling on negative events, thinking in extremely categorical ways, overgeneralizing, worrying needlessly, and thinking in ways that increase unhappiness without accomplishing anything worthwhile. The following three components of the serenity prayer sum up very well good constructive thinking: accepting what cannot be changed, changing what can be changed, and knowing the difference between the two.

It is not enough to just talk about constructive thinking. If one wishes to examine it, it is necessary to have a means for measuring it. To this end I developed the Constructive Thinking Inventory (CTI), a questionnaire to which people respond by indicating their characteristic constructive and destructive automatic thoughts and ways of viewing themselves and the world. The scores on this test, when compared to IQ, led me to conclude that the intelligence of the experiential and rational minds are unrelated. Of further interest, when scores on the CTI and intelligence tests were compared in terms of how strongly they related to various criteria of success in living, including work success, school success, social success, emotional adjustment, and physical health, a most revealing pattern emerged. CTI scores were more strongly related than IQ to all the criteria, with one exception. The exception, as you no doubt guessed, was school success, for which IQ was the better predictor. The CTI is described in detail in the next chapter, and you will be presented with a modified version that you can use to test yourself. In later chapters, more detailed evidence is presented that attests to the important role constructive thinking plays in emotional intelligence, social intelligence, and practical intelligence. In this chapter, I mainly want to introduce you to the concept of constructive thinking and to give you a feeling for how it operates.

In a class I have taught for several years on coping with stress, I have found that one of the most effective exercises for illustrating the constructive and destructive operation of the experiential mind is to have everyone in the class indicate how he or she would respond to situations that fellow students report. Following is an example. As you read it, think of how you would emotionally react in the same situation and of the automatic thoughts that would precede your emotional reaction. Consider how constructive or destructive the automatic thoughts are by judging how they would make you feel at the moment and what their long-term consequences would be. Finally, consider how changing your automatic thoughts would change the emotion you would experience.

The background for the following incident is that the student's parents were getting divorced, and both of them were trying to gain his sympathy and convince him that the other one was at fault. Both accused him of siding with the other parent. On this occasion, the student, whom we shall call Robert, came home to pick up some warm clothes for the approaching winter. To his dismay, the doors were all locked and his mother, who was the only one in the house, would not let him in. She yelled out the window that he deserved such treatment because he sided with his father.

The exercise requires the narrator to report what his or her strongest emotional reaction was, followed by a description of the thoughts that preceded and followed the emotion. Robert said his strongest emotion was anger, and his thoughts preceding the emotion were that his mother had no right to treat him that way, that she was being unfair because he had not sided with his father, and, in any event, that's no way for a mother to treat her son. He added that he was sure that everyone would be angry in such a situation. Following the emotion, his thoughts were that her inappropriate anger at him was her problem. His only problem was to get the clothes he needed. He decided to call the police, and they escorted him into the house and waited for him to gather up his clothes.

The second part of the exercise is to have students in the class indicate how they would react in the same situation. A show of hands indicated that ten of the fifteen students in the class said they would react with anger, two with sadness, one with fear, one with sympathy, and one with cool detachment and perhaps even amusement. Robert was absolutely amazed when he heard that not everyone would react with anger. The angry reaction was so natural to him that he could not imagine anyone reacting differently. As you read about each of the following thoughts, evaluate how constructive or destructive you believe them to be.

One of the women who reported she would be sad described her automatic thoughts preceding the emotion as follows: "I would feel pretty worthless if I were treated that way by my own mother. I would think I must have done something to deserve it, like not being a loving enough daughter." She said that her thoughts following the emotion would be that she should leave immediately and get by as best she could when the weather turned colder by borrowing clothes from other students until she could afford to buy her own at a clothing exchange.

The woman who reported that fear would be her strongest emotion said her thoughts preceding the emotion would be that her mother was acting like a crazy woman. She would be concerned that her mother would do other things to hurt her, possibly even attack her physically. She would want to get out of there immediately and would let the clothing issue go for the moment.

The student who reported she would feel sympathy said she would think that someone would have to be very upset to behave so unreasonably. She would wonder what was bothering her mother and what she could do to help. She would leave and call her mother later, after her mother had a chance to calm down. She would then offer her emotional support by listening sympathetically and telling her how much she loved her.

The student who reported he would react with cool detachment and possibly amusement said it would strike him as somewhat funny that a grown-up person could behave so ridiculously and get herself worked up in a way that would not be good for her health and would estrange her from her own son. He said that rather than take the situation personally, he would realize that people act crazy when they are emotionally upset and that the best thing to do is to leave and to discuss the situation by telephone after his mother had a chance to calm down.

The students in the class invariably listen very attentively to each other's responses. They are intrigued with the different ways people automatically think and how particular ways of thinking predictably lead to certain emotions. They observe that some people tend to be consistently better constructive thinkers than others, but that everyone has weak points, or sensitivities. They note that the woman who said she would blame herself reports the same reaction in many other situations, but particularly when she is faced with the possibility of rejection. Given that she is so prone to think in terms of self-blame, it is no wonder that she often is depressed and that her report of the most negative emotion of the day is often sadness. The woman who said she would feel sympathy appears to be a genuinely thoughtful and concerned person who likes and respects herself and others and to whom others respond in kind.

Through observing the constructive and destructive automatic thinking of their classmates, it dawns on the students that their own, presumably "natural" way of thinking is not the only way to think and that if they could make their automatic thinking more constructive, not only would they be more effective people, but their emotional life would improve. Before, they had grasped this intellectually from my lectures and their readings, but it had not penetrated to their experiential mind and therefore was not emotionally compelling. Now, after witnessing how their classmates think differently in response to the same situations, their intellectual understanding is buttressed by meaningful experience, and they seriously consider trying to make their own thinking more similar to that of someone whose thinking they admire. In other words, it becomes apparent to them that some ways of automatic thinking are constructive and others destructive and that it is to their advantage to cultivate the constructive ways.

In teaching the class on coping with stress, it has become evident to me that it is very common for otherwise capable people to think in surprisingly self-destructive ways Following are some examples:

A young man named Joe did unexpectedly well on an examination he thought he had failed. Yet when he told the story to the class, he expressed little enthusiasm about his success. When questioned about this, he admitted that he generally derived little satisfaction when good things happened to him because he was sure they would be balanced by equally bad things. No matter how much people praised his performance, he "knew" he would do terribly the next time. No amount of argument could shake him of this conviction, which not only prevented him from enjoying the fruits of his accomplishments but also dampened his enthusiasm for new tasks.

Paula worried so much about upcoming examinations that she was unable to study. To alleviate her anxiety, she often went to the movies before an exam, which only ensured the outcome she feared. In a vicious cycle, her failure convinced her that her fears were justified. Paula could not solve this problem with rational thinking because the source of the problem was in her experiential mind, which she did not even know existed.

Brian was sympathetic and understanding when others made mistakes but showed no mercy toward his own imperfections. When he faltered, he severely castigated himself, saying, "You stupid fool, how could anyone be so incompetent!" When questioned, he said he believed that attacking people for their mistakes was a poor way to help them improve. "Then why do you attack yourself?" I asked him. With passion in his voice, he replied, "Because I really am no good, and it would be dishonest to pretend otherwise."

It is amazing to what lengths the rational mind will go to defend the experiential mind's beliefs as rational—beliefs that were not arrived at by rational thinking in the first place. But what else is the poor rational mind to do when it doesn't even know the experiential mind exists?

The destructive thinking that I observed was not always pessimistic or self-negating. Some students were what I call naive optimists, as in this example:

Stan drifted through school assuming that things would always work out well. As a result, he failed to plan ahead. He usually got away with this because his upbeat manner endeared him to his classmates, who would often "cover" for him—for instance, by letting him study with them just before an exam. The consequences were more serious, however, when Stan assumed that the business career he envisioned would simply fall into place after college. He was so optimistic that he neglected to lay the groundwork by taking the necessary courses. Graduation brought a rude awakening when he failed to land a good job.

Would telling him to be responsible make any difference? Of course not. Stan was intelligent enough to figure it out himself. Besides, many people—including, of course, his parents—had warned him what would happen if he did not shape up and take responsibility for his life. These warnings accomplished nothing except to irritate him ("Stop lecturing me—I know that!"). Stan needed to be reached at the level of his experiential mind, not his rational mind.

I routinely observe similar patterns of self-defeating thought both in my clinical practice and among people I know personally or professionally. I recall Herb, for example, a client who had a very high IQ but was not a good businessman. His mind was not well disciplined, with the result that his wishful thinking often overpowered his better judgment. At one point, he bought a neighborhood restaurant based on the owner's assurances that the restaurant was very profitable. Herb wanted so much to believe in this once-in-a-lifetime opportunity that he could not bring himself to take a close look at the restaurant's books. "Books can always be faked," he said. Furthermore, he told me, whenever he went by the restaurant, it was always crowded.

When I pressed him for details, such as how many times he had observed the restaurant and whether he had taken actual counts, he became annoyed. If I was not going to trust his judgment, he did not want to discuss the matter further. In the end, he lost a great deal of money. What is it that makes an otherwise intelligent person behave so foolishly? In Herb's case, he was a naive optimist. He allowed his experiential mind to interpret situations in a way that gave him good feelings right away rather than good results later on.

Monica and Ralph had been married for five years. Both had graduated with distinction in their respective fields, Ralph as an engineer, Monica as an artist. Ralph, who prided himself on his ability to think logically, was regarded as having a mind like a steel trap. Monica, with equal justification, took pride in her intuition and creativity. Although they both excelled at solving problems in their respective professions, they were a disaster at solving problems with each other.

Ralph would typically try to reason carefully with Monica, which to him meant pointing out the weaknesses in her thinking. This simply infuriated Monica, who would frustrate him by becoming even more illogical. When, in defense, he would fall back even more on logic, she would accuse him of being a robot with a brain and no heart. Each had contempt for the other's way of thinking, and each felt compelled to protect his or her self-esteem by putting the other down. These are perfectly understandable human reactions, but when they turn a household into an armed camp, it is clear that they represent a failure of constructive thinking.

At the other end of the spectrum, here is an example of a good constructive thinker. Elizabeth was a small, slightly pudgy woman of about average intelligence for a college student. She had a ready smile and was quick to laughter. When she made comments about other people's presentations, they were invariably made in a friendly, sympathetic manner. She criticized the reports, but never the person. When her own reports were criticized, she appeared genuinely appreciative of the advice and did not exhibit a need to defend herself. Yet, she could assert herself when she disagreed with a criticism, and it was evident that she had a mind of her own. I was most impressed by her ability to learn from experience, which was probably related to her lack of defensiveness. She very quickly caught on to what the class was about and immediately began to implement what she learned. Unlike many of the other students, what she learned was more important to her than the grade she received. I don't know how successful Elizabeth will be in terms of conventional criteria, such as income and status, but in terms of achieving happiness and rewarding relationships, she is already highly successful. Elizabeth was lucky that, based on a fortunate combination of heredity and experience, her automatic thinking developed in a highly constructive manner. Nevertheless, it was far from perfect, and she eagerly went about applying what she learned in class to making it better.

The most impressive constructive thinking that I witnessed was many years ago when I observed that of a five-year-old African-American boy, whom I shall call John. To fulfill a course requirement in developmental psychology, I had to observe a child in a nursery school over the course of a semester and then write a report on the child's personality. I selected John to study because he seemed to be a particularly competent child who was well liked by the other children as well as the teachers, and I wanted to see exactly how he did it. The school was located in a poor neighborhood of Brooklyn, New York, and although his family did not have much to give him in terms of material wealth, they apparently had a great deal to offer in whatever is necessary for the development of self-esteem and social competence. Following are some examples of his behavior that particularly impressed me.

On one occasion, the bully of the class, who was an older, larger, and I suspect retarded child, made a point of kicking down the other children's block constructions. John was busily engaged in building the highest tower he could when the bully approached him. Looking up to see the bully eyeing his tower, John immediately grasped what was up. He said, "You sure are big and strong. I wish I was as strong as you."

"Yeah, you bet," said the bully. "I can beat you up and kick down your blocks and make you cry."

"I hope you won't," John said. "I've got it real high, and I want to build it to the sky."

With that, the bully laughed and launched a mighty kick that sent the pieces flying. He then laughed again and said, "See, I told you."

I expected John to cry or protest or threaten to tell the teacher. What he did instead was to join in the laughter. "Wow," he exclaimed, "you really sent them flying all over the place!"

After the two of them had a good laugh, John admired the bully's strength once more and invited him to play blocks with him. The two boys sat down together, and before long they were engrossed in building a tower that was higher than the first. Not only that, but they were doing it under John's direction. John would ask the bully to get one of the blocks from across the room, and the bully would scurry to carry out his request.

Shortly thereafter, the teacher, who had been out of the room, returned and blew her whistle to call the children together for a juice break. One of the children held up his glass and said, "Look at my glass. It's a great big one." Bedlam broke loose as children began to scream, "I want a big glass like James'!"

The teacher was having a difficult time trying to quiet the children when John held up his glass and yelled, "Everybody look at the cute little glass I have." Several other children then imitated him, saying, "I have a cute little glass, too." Peace once again reigned in the nursery.

This episode was typical of many that I observed with John. He had a warm, engaging smile and was quick to laugh. Nothing seemed to faze him. He enjoyed playing with the other children, and they with him. He also got along well with the teacher, who was genuinely fond of him and appreciated his helpfulness in creating a good atmosphere in the class. I often wonder what became of John. I don't know if he is rich or famous, but I suspect he is happy and successful according to his own standards.

Does John seem too good to be true? Only if we fail to grasp the difference between constructive thinking and the kind of intelligence measured by IQ tests. If five-year-old John had an IQ of 120, then his mental age was no greater than six. Yet he was a much better constructive thinker than many adults who have vastly higher mental ages. He kept his head, did not react emotionally to threats or dwell on setbacks, and saw each new challenge as a problem to be mastered. We adults might well say to ourselves, "If I could react and think the way that kid did, if I could be that poised and resourceful, my life would be a lot better." Put John's experiential savvy and mental agility into the head of an adult who does have the necessary knowledge base, and you have a winning combination.

From getting the class bully on your side to mastering the stock market, decisions about the basic directions of your life require a blend of experiential and rational thinking. When it comes to choosing an educational or career path, succeeding in business, deciding on a mate, buying a house, selecting a school for your children, evaluating different treatments for a serious illness, or seeking to have an impact on your community, the issues at stake cannot be reduced to a set of cold calculations. You often must find an answer by drawing upon your life experience.

Most people are not so fortunate as to react in such a spontaneously constructive way as John. All of us, however, can improve our constructive thinking by training and disciplining our experiential minds.

WHAT YOU WILL FIND IN THIS BOOK

Thus far in Part I you have been introduced to the idea that there are two minds, experiential and rational, each with its own form of intelligence. You were informed that the intelligence of the rational mind is measured by IQ tests and that the intelligence of the experiential mind, which is referred to as constructive thinking, provides the key to understanding emotional intelligence. It is measured by a test that I developed called the Constructive Thinking Inventory (CTI). You were given examples of people who exhibited good and poor constructive thinking. In the next chapter you will have an opportunity to take a version of the CTI specially constructed for this book and to obtain a more detailed understanding of constructive thinking. The remainder of Part I explains in greater detail how the experiential mind operates and why effective performance requires the harmonious operation of the two minds.

Part II illustrates in detail how constructive thinking leads to success in living—in career, in personal relationships, and in mental and physical well-being. Part III explores how constructive thinking is developed and maintained, with emphasis on how parents can teach their children to be constructive thinkers. Part IV gives you techniques—experiential as well as rational—for understanding, assessing, and developing your experiential mind and thereby improving your constructive thinking. An epilogue considers broader applications of constructive thinking with respect to social and environmental problems and sums up the principles presented in the book.

HOW TO READ THIS BOOK

There are three ways to read this book. First, if you wish to get the most out of it, you should read it thoroughly and do all the exercises. Second, you can skip the most demanding exercise that requires you to keep daily records of your emotions and automatic thoughts and substitute the less demanding one that is provided as an alternative. Third, you can read the book as if it were not a self-help book. Rather than doing the exercises, you can simply read them to get an idea of what they demonstrate. This book could well have been written as something other than a self-help book, as what is most important in it are the ideas it presents. If you understand the principles of how the experiential mind operates and the manner in which it influences the rational mind, you will have gained important knowledge about human behavior in general and about emotional intelligence in particular. At least you will have this knowledge in your rational mind, which is of considerable value in its own right. However, if you want to change your behavior and emotions, intellectual knowledge is not enough. Rather, you will have to supplement it with experiential knowledge. This means you can either wait a long time for experiential learning to occur as you interpret your everyday experiences from the perspective of your newly acquired intellectual understanding, or you can hasten the process along by doing the exercises. As you might expect, you will get out of this book what you put into it. I promise you no magic. Rather, this is meant to be a thinking person's how-to book, not a set of simple steps that can be thoughtlessly applied.

Chapter 4

Testing Your
Constructive Thinking

Testing your constructive thinking is very different from taking the usual kind of test. Here we are not concerned with whether or not you can figure out the "right" answer. Rather, we want to find out how you typically think, feel, and act in real life.

How can we measure how effectively a person copes with life? The test you are about to take, the Constructive Thinking Inventory (or CTI for short), was developed and refined over a considerable period of time. I searched for examples of constructive and destructive thinking in the work of other researchers and therapists who had studied the influence of thinking on behavior. Among the categories of destructive thinking I came up with were overgeneralization, categorical or black-and-white thinking, perfectionism, and catastrophizing (making mountains out of molehills). I made up items to represent these categories. When I found myself or others thinking in a particularly constructive or destructive way, I made up additional items for the questionnaire.

By far the major source of items, however, was the records kept by my students in a class I taught on emotions. To meet the course requirements, they had to record the most pleasant and unpleasant emotion they experienced each day for thirty days. Included in their records were descriptions of their automatic thoughts. By collecting thousands of these reports over several years, I came up with over 200 items that described the full range of destructive and constructive thoughts that the students reported.

I constructed the CTI by standard psychometric procedures. By a procedure called factor analysis as well as conceptual considerations, the items were grouped into the following six main categories: emotional coping, behavioral coping, categorical thinking, esoteric thinking, personal superstitious thinking, and naive optimism. Using statistical procedures, the poorer items were eliminated, and the better ones retained. This procedure converted the six categories into six reliable scales that constitute the main body of the CTI. Each scale is divided into several subscales that provide a more detailed picture of how a person obtains a particular score on a main scale. For example, behavioral coping is divided into the subscores of action orientation, positive thinking, and conscientiousness. As all the main scales, with the exception of naive optimism, are significantly correlated with each other, they are combined into a composite global scale. Thus, the CTI provides scores at three levels of generality, a global scale and six main scales that are further divided into subscales. Through extensive research that will be reported later, the CTI has been demonstrated to be a reliable and valid measure of the constructive and destructive thinking in which people tend to automatically engage. It is important to recognize that, unlike tests of emotional coping that some authors have hastily put together off the top of their heads, the CTI has been administered to large samples of people and constructed according to recognized psychological principles of test construction.

I never thought the CTI would work as well as it has, as I thought that people would be unaware of, or unwilling to admit, their maladaptive automatic thoughts. The CTI works because people are very much aware of some of their experiential mind's reactions. Even if they don't understand how that "second mind" works, they know that they have certain habitual ways of thinking that keep them from managing their lives as successfully as they might. People are always saying things like, "How is it that I can't sleep at night just because someone insulted me? Even when I believe it reflects more on them than on me, why can't I just let it go?" That's the kind of thing you need to know about yourself to take the CTI.

THE CONSTRUCTIVE THINKING INVENTORY

Here is a version of the CTI that, although brief, still captures the basic ingredients of constructive versus destructive thinking. By doing this exercise, you will familiarize yourself with the components of constructive thinking and learn your strongest and weakest points.

Important! Take this test before reading further, as what you read can influence the results.

Answer each item by entering a number from 1 to 5 in the space to the left of the item, according to the following scale:

1 = completely false

2 = mainly false

3 = neither true nor false, or undecided

4 = mainly true

5 = completely true

Do not try to give the "correct" answer. Instead, give the answer that best describes how you typically react. Remember, the purpose of the test is to find out how you typically think, not whether you know how you "should" think.

1. __ I don't worry about things I can do nothing about.

2. __ I am the kind of person who takes action rather than just thinks or complains about a situation.

3. __ I feel that if people treat you badly, you should treat them in kind.

4. __ I have found that talking about successes that I am looking forward to can keep them from happening.

5. __ If I do very well on an important test, I feel like a total success and that I will go very far in life.

6. __ I believe in astrology.

7. __ I don't let little things bother me.

8. __ If I have an unpleasant chore to do, I try to make the best of it by thinking in positive terms.

9. __ There are basically two kinds of people in this world, good and bad.

10. __ When something good happens to me, I believe it will be balanced by something bad.

11. __ I believe that people can accomplish anything they want to if they have enough willpower.

12. __ I have at least one good-luck charm.

13. __ I don't feel that I have to perform exceptionally well in order to consider myself a worthwhile person.

14. __ I look at challenges not as something to fear, but as an opportunity to test myself and learn.

15. __ I think that there are many wrong ways, but only one right way, to do almost anything.

16. __ I believe in good and bad omens.

17. __ I think everyone should love their parents.

18. __ I believe that ghosts exist.

19. __ I tend to dwell more on pleasant than unpleasant incidents from the past.

20. __ When I am faced with a difficult task, I think encouraging thoughts that help me do my best.

21. __ I tend to classify people as either for me or against me.

22. __ I sometimes think that if I want something to happen too badly, it will keep it from happening.

23. ___ If I was accepted at an important job interview, I would feel very good and think that I would always be able to get a good job.

24. ___ I believe some people have the ability to read other people's thoughts.

25. ___ I don't take things personally.

26. ___ When faced with upcoming unpleasant events, I usually carefully think through how I will deal with them.

27. ___ I am very judgmental of people.

28. ___ I've learned not to hope too hard because what I hope for usually doesn't happen.

29. ___ I believe that if I do something good, then good things will happen to me.

30. ___ I believe there are people who can literally see into the future.

SCORING YOUR TEST

When I developed the CTI, I wanted to measure not just constructive thinking in general but also the various dimensions or components of constructive thinking. I wanted to find out what specific ways of thinking are especially constructive or destructive in people's daily lives. At first, I grouped the 200 items of the CTI into eighteen homogeneous categories. These included such patterns as positive thinking, negative thinking, self-acceptance, self-rejection, worrying, dwelling on past injuries, grandiose thinking, positive overgeneralization, and negative overgeneralization. (The last two refer to generalizing inappropriately from favorable or unfavorable events.)

With the aid of statistical procedures, I was able to consolidate the eighteen categories into six basic patterns of constructive and destructive thinking. In the scoring sheet that follows, the questions you answered are rearranged into these six categories. To score your test, simply enter beside each item the same number you assigned to that item when you did the inventory. Then add up the numbers for each scale and record the totals in the spaces provided. Don't worry now about what the six categories mean. That will be explained in the next section. It should be evident, though, that the first two categories stand for constructive ways of thinking, while the last four represent destructive ways of thinking.

Emotional Coping

1. ___ I don't worry about things I can do nothing about.

7. ___ I don't let little things bother me.

13. ___ I don't feel that I have to perform exceptionally well in order to consider myself a worthwhile person.

19. __ I tend to dwell more on pleasant than unpleasant incidents from the past.
25. __ I don't take things personally.
_____ Sum

Behavioral Coping

2. __ I am the kind of person who takes action rather than just thinks or complains about a situation.

8. __ If I have an unpleasant chore to do, I try to make the best of it by thinking in positive terms.

14. __ I look at challenges not as something to fear, but as an opportunity to test myself and learn.

20. __ When I am faced with a difficult task, I think encouraging thoughts that help me do my best.

26. __ When faced with upcoming unpleasant events, I usually carefully think through how I will deal with them.

_____ Sum

Categorical Thinking

3. __ I feel that if people treat you badly, you should treat them in kind.

9. __ There are basically two kinds of people in this world, good and bad.

15. __ I think that there are many wrong ways, but only one right way, to do almost anything.

21. __ I tend to classify people as either for me or against me.

27. __ I am very judgmental of people.

_____ Sum

Personal Superstitious Thinking

4. __ I have found that talking about successes that I am looking forward to can keep them from happening.

10. __ When something good happens to me, I believe it will be balanced by something bad.

16. __ I believe in good and bad omens.

22. __ I sometimes think that if I want something to happen too badly, it will keep it from happening.

28. __ I've learned not to hope too hard because what I hope for usually doesn't happen.

_____ Sum

Esoteric Thinking

6. __ I believe in astrology.

12. __ I have at least one good-luck charm.

18. __ I believe that ghosts exist.

24. __ I believe some people have the ability to read other people's thoughts.

30. __ I believe there are people who can literally see into the future.

_____ *Sum*

Naive Optimism

5. __ If I do very well on an important test, I feel like a total success and that I will go very far in life.

11. __ I believe that people can accomplish anything they want to if they have enough willpower.

17. __ I think everyone should love their parents.

23. __ If I was accepted at an important job interview, I would feel very good and think that I would always be able to get a good job.

29. __ I believe that if I do something good, then good things will happen to me.

_____ *Sum*

Global Constructive Thinking

You can calculate your score for global constructive thinking by combining your scores for all but one of the categories. (Naive optimism is not included for reasons explained later.) Your scores for the categories that indicate *poor* constructive thinking must be reversed, which is done simply by subtracting those scores from 30. To obtain your score for global constructive thinking, add up the following numbers:

—Emotional Coping (sum)

—Behavioral Coping (sum)

—30 *minus* Categorical Thinking (sum)

—30 *minus* Superstitious Thinking (sum)

—30 *minus* Esoteric Thinking (sum)

—Global Constructive Thinking score (overall sum)

INTERPRETING YOUR SCORES

The purpose of scoring yourself on constructive thinking is to familiarize you with the basic components of constructive thinking so you will know what is involved in being a good constructive thinker and to give you an idea of your strengths and weaknesses so you will know where to concentrate your efforts in order to improve.

The first step in interpreting your scores is to plot them on the following chart. For each category, circle the range in which your score falls. For example, if you scored 15 on emotional coping, circle the numbers "11–16" in the column marked "Emotional Coping," which will inform you that your score falls in the average range. The classification of the ranges is based on the responses of over 700 people. A classification of "average" places you among the middle 50% of this group. A classification of "high" places you in the upper 25%, and a classification of "very high" in the upper 5% of this group. Classifications of "low" and "very low" correspond to the lowest 25% and 5%, respectively.

It is important to be aware that your results will be accurate only to the extent that you were completely honest when you took the test.

Your Constructive Thinking Inventory

	Emotional Coping	Behavioral Coping	Categorical Thinking	Personal Super-stitious Thinking	Esoteric Thinking	Naive Optimism	Global Constructive Thinking
Very High	>19	>23	>18	>20	>22	>23	>99
High	17–19	21–23	16–18	17–20	19–22	21–23	89–99
Average	11–16	16–20	10–15	10–16	11–18	15–20	74–88
Low	8–10	13–15	7–9	6–9	7–10	12–14	63–73
Very Low	<8	<13	<7	<6	<7	<12	<63

Here, at a glance, you can see your current profile of constructive thinking. Remember, it is desirable to be *high* on global constructive thinking, emotional coping, and behavioral coping and to be *low* on the other scales.

You may want to make photocopies of the profile chart before you have filled it out in order to plot your improvement as you continue to apply the principles in this book. For now, note which of your scores fall into the high and very high or low and very low regions and pay particular attention to these. Go back over the scoring key and note the kinds of items that appear under the categories in question. Refer to your own responses to see the exact items on which you did well or poorly. Where they signify a high level of constructive thinking, congratulate yourself. Take pleasure in your strengths and take every opportunity to exercise them. Where they indicate destructive thinking, alert yourself to the specific patterns of destructive thinking that you reported. Consider the advantages and disadvantages of these ways of thinking (as outlined in the remainder of this chapter). Attend to such thoughts as you go about your everyday affairs. In Part IV you will be given a program for changing those automatic thoughts that you wish to change. For the time being, just be alert to them. Get to know the situations in which they occur and what they do for you at the moment and later. Ask yourself the following questions:

- In what ways do they make me feel good?
- In what ways are they useful to me?
- In what ways do they make trouble for me?

Before proceeding to interpret your record, here is some background information that can help you put things in perspective:

1. *The questionnaire in this chapter is not the "official" CTI.* The thirty questions you have answered represent a simplified version of the official CTI, the latest version of which has 108 items and a more complex scoring key as well as methods for detecting dishonest or inappropriate responses. The full CTI cannot be included in this book without making it invalid for professional use. However, assuming that you have taken the test honestly, this abbreviated version should be sufficient for indicating how generally adequate your constructive thinking is and in what areas you most need to improve.

2. *Your scores on the CTI are not set in stone.* The CTI is not a test of "objective" abilities but of your opinions about yourself. The attitude with which you take the test can therefore influence the results. But even if the test does not give you hard evidence of what you are "really" like, it *can* tell you how your view of yourself compares with those of hundreds of other people who have taken the same test. You may even find that, relative to other people, you are a more constructive thinker than you thought you were.

3. *Don't take your exact scores too seriously.* Just as your car's speedometer is never precisely accurate, so every questionnaire has a margin of error. In this version of the CTI, the margin of error is fairly large. For this reason, you should not attach any great importance to specific numerical scores. Instead, note where you fall on the broad classifications: very high, high, average, low, or very low.

To assist you in observing and understanding your habitual patterns of thought, here are some brief descriptions of the six main characteristics of constructive and destructive thinking and of the overall global trait of constructive thinking, which they combine to produce.

Emotional coping. Emotional coping and behavioral coping are the two most important components of constructive thinking. Together they encompass the ability to deal effectively with the inner world of feelings and the outer world of events.

Good emotional copers are particularly effective in dealing with negative feelings. They are characterized more by peace of mind and low levels of stress than by peaks of joy. They are calm and centered, and they experience less stress in living than others. Taking things in stride, they "do not sweat the little stuff." In particular, they do not take things personally, are not overly sensitive to disapproval or failure, and do not worry about things that are beyond their control. They are not overly critical of themselves or others, and they do not overgeneralize from, or overreact to, unfavorable events. They neither dwell on past misfortunes nor worry needlessly about future ones. Whereas a poor emotional coper might conclude, "I failed to put across this deal, so I guess I'll never amount to anything," a good emotional coper would realize it is only a single incident and that one can learn from the experience.

Behavioral coping. While emotional coping consists mainly of the ability to avoid falling into negative, self-defeating thoughts and feelings, behavioral coping has a more positive emphasis. It is *action-oriented thinking.* People who are good behavioral copers think in ways that promote effective action. Their optimism allows them to take on challenges and risks, as they have the confidence that things will work out well. Good behavioral copers do not hold grudges or dwell on failures and past injuries but let bygones be bygones, accept people as they are, and focus their energy on carrying out their plans. Instead of worrying about deadlines, they get right to work. Instead of punishing themselves for a mistake, they figure out how to correct it. They circumvent obstacles and compensate quickly for setbacks so as to regain momentum and control.

People who are good behavioral copers are more accepting of others, more optimistic, and more action-oriented than those who are good emotional copers. Good emotional copers, on the other hand, are more self-accepting, take things less personally, and are less distressed when things don't go their way. Each form of coping has its advantages, and they are not mutually exclusive. Although people are often better at one form of coping than the other, those who are above average on one usually are above average on both. These are people who are good overall constructive thinkers.

Emotional coping and behavioral coping contribute directly to constructive thinking; the following four maladaptive patterns describe the *opposite* of constructive thinking.

Categorical thinking. People with high scores on categorical thinking are rigid thinkers. They view issues in black-and-white terms, without acknowledging shades of gray. They view people who disagree with them not simply as having a different opinion but as being in error. Judgmental and intolerant, categorical thinkers tend to classify people as good or bad, "for" or "against" them, "winners" or "losers." They assume there is only one right way to do anything, and it happens to be their way. Because decisions appear very clear-cut to them, it is easy for them to take action. Incidentally, men tend to score slightly higher than women on categorical thinking, which implies that men tend to be more opinionated and rigid in their thinking.

Personal superstitious thinking. As used in the Constructive Thinking Inventory, this term does not refer to traditional superstitions but to personal superstitions, or the mental games people play to prepare themselves for disappointment. One example is the belief that if something good happens to you, it will be balanced by something equally bad. Or that if you talk about something you are hoping for, it will not happen. Constructive thinkers, in contrast, are not likely to believe that talking about the prospect of success will prevent them from succeeding.

Esoteric thinking. Esoteric thinking, as distinct from personal superstitious thinking, refers to beliefs about unusual and paranormal phenomena and standard superstitions. These beliefs cannot easily be verified by objective evidence, and scientists are accordingly skeptical about them. They include believing in traditional superstitions (breaking a mirror, walking under a ladder, having a black cat cross your path), good-luck charms, astrology, ghosts, extrasensory perception, and mind control.

This is another category of constructive thinking on which gender does make a difference: women typically score slightly higher than men. Unlike personal superstitious thinking, esoteric thinking does not tend in a pessimistic direction, but it is equally unrealistic. Up to a point, a high score on esoteric thinking may simply suggest an openness to new ideas. A very high score, on the other hand, points to a lack of mental discipline and a failure to use one's critical faculties. It is not surprising, therefore, that very high scores are associated with poor constructive thinking and high levels of stress.

Naive optimism. Naive optimism refers to a tendency to jump to conclusions after a positive outcome, as if a single success guaranteed that things would always work out the way one liked. To the naive optimist, one high grade in an exam, one successful job interview, one instance of requited love, is a blueprint for a secure, untroubled future. Naive optimism is also expressed in convictions that are too simpleminded to be a helpful guide in the real world—for instance, that everyone should love their parents or that people can accomplish whatever they wish if they have enough willpower.

Naive optimists are positive thinkers to the point of being Pollyannas. They have all the proper ideas, endorse conventionally accepted beliefs, and do not think things out too thoroughly. They like people, are liked by others (everyone loves an optimist), and feel that all is right with the world. Unlike the more realistic optimism that is part of behavioral coping, naive optimism carries positive thinking too far. The danger for naive optimists is that they will fail to plan and take proper precautions for the future. Fortunately for them, they are frequently forgiven for their errors.

Interestingly, people who score high on naive optimism tend to overgeneralize from bad experiences as well as good experiences when they get older. Apparently, once they have learned to overgeneralize in a positive way, the tendency to overgeneralize spreads to distressing experiences as well. The naive optimist then becomes someone whose hopes are easily dashed.

Global constructive thinking. The overall measure of constructive thinking includes items from all six categories except naive optimism, which is unrelated to overall constructive thinking because its bad aspect (unrealistic thinking) cancels out its good aspect (positive thinking). People who score high on the global scale are accepting of themselves and others, have a positive outlook on life, and view their lives as having purpose and direction. Although they are positive thinkers, they temper their optimism with considerations of what is realistic. Thus, their optimism does not prevent them from planning and taking reasonable precautions.

Good global constructive thinkers do not overgeneralize from their experience, whether positive or negative. They neither over- nor undervaluate themselves. Instead of resorting to superstition or other forms of magical thinking to explain or control their environment, they have the self-confidence to face the uncertainties and complexities of reality. Their automatic, experiential thinking helps them feel good about themselves and others, handle negative emotions with a minimum of stress and disruption, and take effective action to resolve everyday problems.

An essential characteristic of good constructive thinkers is that they are problem-oriented rather than judgmental. They seek workable solutions, rather than label themselves or others as good or bad people or as deserving to be rewarded and loved or to be hurt and rejected.

Most important, good constructive thinkers are flexible thinkers. They adapt their thinking to different situations and can see the dark as well as the bright side of an issue. However, given equally reasonable choices, they will usually choose the bright side because it makes them and others happier, and because, under most circumstances, it is a more effective and satisfying way to lead one's life.

Why do people become poor constructive thinkers when to do so is obviously self-defeating? Poor constructive thinking is often emotionally advantageous in the short run, even though it exacts a heavy price in the long run. Each of the maladaptive ways of coping has certain benefits. If your life circumstances were such that you experienced the benefits more than the disadvantages, of thinking a certain way, then you naturally internalized those patterns of thinking. Let us consider the advantages and disadvantages of each of the destructive ways of thinking in the CTI.

Categorical thinking gives you a stable, though narrow, orientation to life. By simplifying the world for you, it allows you to act rapidly and decisively, unhindered by the consideration of alternatives. At moments of crisis, categorical thinking is particularly helpful, as there is no time for equivocation.

Categorical thinking allows people to feel righteously indignant and therefore feel better about themselves. The cost, of course, is that it prevents them from learning from experience and growing, as well as from accepting others who are different.

Personal superstitious thinking, too, has its emotional payoffs. To understand why people adopt private superstitions, think about why whole societies adopt certain superstitions. Superstitions and rituals provide a sense of order and predictability. In times of helplessness—say, a drought or a plague—they reduce people's anxiety by offering an illusion of understanding and control. Thus, if people believe that the gods have withheld rain because someone has sinned, they have both an explanation of their plight and something they can do about it: they can punish the sinner and give offerings to the gods.

Individuals, too, may develop superstitions in response to feelings of helplessness. Children raised under conditions where they feel helpless are most apt to create private superstitions. Research has shown that people with private superstitions are prone to depression, which, in turn, is known to be associated with feelings of helplessness.

Why would you want to believe, for example, that if something good happens to you, it will be followed by something bad? That belief, it would seem, would only cause you misery. What can such a belief possibly do for you? It can prepare you for disappointment by accepting unfortunate events in advance. People who think this way pay a high price for this protection, for they are generally unhappy, but they are willing to pay that price in order not to be unpleasantly surprised. They are like someone who spends everything he has on insurance in order to be prepared for any possible disaster. Such a person is more concerned with avoiding painful experiences than with leading a fulfilling life.

Esoteric thinking—believing in ghosts, flying saucers, thought control, astrology, and visits from people from Mars—adds spice to life. So long as you don't take these thoughts too seriously, they won't do any harm. In fact, they can allow you to bypass your rational mind and contact your experiential mind, which in certain circumstances can be advantageous. However, if you become too dependent on such ways of thinking, you risk not using your rational faculties sufficiently to solve problems and accomplish what you need to do. I have found in my research that people who score very high on esoteric thinking tend to experience more stress and to be less successful than average.

Naive optimism, the most extreme form of positive thinking, has an obvious payoff: if you are convinced that everything will work out for the best, you will feel good. Not only that, people will probably like you. At the same time, you will pay a price in poor judgment, and as the consequences of poor judgment pile up, it may be hard to maintain your optimism.

Now that you have an idea of the basics of constructive thinking and have tested your own thinking against those criteria, how do you start to develop and improve your constructive thinking? The first step is to understand constructive and destructive thinking as products of the experiential mind. We are now ready to look into the world of experiential thinking and see how this "second mind" works.

Chapter 5

Evidence for the Existence of the Experiential Mind

The experiential mind operates so smoothly and automatically, and its operation is so well coordinated with the rational mind that most people, except under special circumstances, are aware of having only one mind. However, there are good reasons to conclude that we operate by two minds, including a consideration of evolutionary principles, everyday real-life experiences, such as conflicts between the heart and the head, and formal cognitive research.

EVOLUTIONARY CONSIDERATIONS

Recall that the experiential mind is essentially the same mind by which nonhuman animals operate. Nonhuman animals adapt to their environment by learning directly from experience and obviously not by making inferences by using language and logical thinking. That the experiential way of functioning by learning directly from experience is highly effective is indicated by the survival over many millions of years of many animal species. There are two fundamental capacities animals require to learn from experience. One is a means of making connections between events, including a connection between their own behavior and outcomes, which makes it possible for them to develop a model of the world and their influence on it. The other is to have feelings, which makes possible reinforcement of behavior by reward and punishment. As a result of connecting actions with outcomes and the subsequent pleasurable and unpleasurable feelings that follow, animals acquire an increasingly sophisticated repertoire of responses for achieving what is pleasurable and avoiding what is unpleasurable. Such learning occurs automatically and in the absence of consciousness, as non-human animals, unlike human ones, have no language for representing consciousness. Thus, animals don't think about what they do; they just behave, and their behavior is directed by their feelings. It is important to remember that this is exactly the way the experiential mind works in humans.

The rational mind, in contrast, is a relatively new evolutionary development, and its long-term adaptive value has yet to be demonstrated. With its capacity for conceptualization, invention, and technological development, it is a most remarkable evolutionary achievement. Yet the same technology that has vastly increased agricultural production, provided a cure for many diseases, sent information instantaneously thousands of miles through the air, and sent people to the moon can obliterate an entire city in the flash of a bomb. It remains for the future to determine whether the ultimate effect of the rational mind will be to promote human existence or to destroy it.

Given the long-term proven adaptability of the experiential mind, it is unthinkable that the hard-won gains achieved in the evolution of the experiential mind would be surrendered with the development of a new, insufficiently tested rational system. A much more reasonable assumption is that both systems are operative. That this is undoubtedly the case is supported not only by logical considerations concerning evolution but by a great deal of evidence in everyday life as well as by psychological research.

EVIDENCE FROM REAL-LIFE SITUATIONS

Although the two minds normally work in such close harmony that it creates the impression that people operate by only a single mind, there are situations in which the operation of two distinct minds becomes apparent. Included are the different ways we react to pictures and words, the irrational fears that people have despite recognizing they are irrational, the conflicts people have between their hearts and their heads, the difference between learning from experience and learning from books and lectures, the difference between insight and intellectual knowledge, the prevalence of superstitious thinking, and the ubiquitous appeal of religion throughout history.

Pictures versus words. As the experiential mind represents events primarily in the form of images, it is more responsive to pictures than to words. Look at a cigarette advertisement. Which part of it do people respond to more strongly—the health warning expressed in words or the pictorial images of the enjoyment and emotional fulfillment associated with smoking? Clearly, the tobacco companies are playing to the experiential mind with an image of a person's life as the person would want it to be. Next to that, what impact can an abstraction about the person's health have? The tobacco companies might think twice about running their ads if they had to include a picture of a person near death in the hospital surrounded by his distressed relatives.

Irrational fears. Some people are afraid to travel by air, even though they know that, statistically, it is safer than riding in a car. All the statistics in the world, all the arguments of well-meaning friends, and all the inconvenience a person suffers by refusing to fly make no difference. The experiential mind assesses the situation as dangerous, and the person acts on the basis of that assessment, no matter what the rational mind thinks.

Conflicts between the heart and the head. Have you ever found yourself caught between competing priorities? You want to do what "feels" right, what will satisfy your romantic side, but you "know" you should choose the more practical option, the one that will work out better in the long run. "The Miata won my heart, but practicality argued for the Civic wagon." The conflict is actually between two different ways of processing and acting on information—that is, two different kinds of thinking. One considers emotional consequences, which are experienced immediately, while the other uses facts and logic to calculate long-term payoffs.

We acknowledge this inner conflict when we say, "I didn't feel like going to work today, but I made myself do it." It is as if we were referring to two people within ourselves. When we say, "I made myself do it," we cast the rational self in the role of a stern taskmaster, the experiential self as a wayward child. We realize that the experiential self often needs correction but also that all work and no play can make for a very dull rational self.

Learning from experience. The famous psychologist Jean Piaget, who studied child development, had children practice hitting a target with a tether ball. With the ball whirling in a circle, the trick was to let go of the string at just the right moment for the ball to hit the target. With practice, the children learned to release the string when it was at a right angle to the target. However, when asked to tell other children how to do it, only children above a certain age were able to give the correct explanation. Younger children incorrectly stated that they let go of the string when it was pointing at the target. If they were really doing that, of course, the ball would go off in the wrong direction. In fact, the children's experiential minds learned to solve the problem, but their rational minds did not know how they did it.

This example demonstrates clearly how our two ways of knowing sometimes work at cross-purposes. A great deal of learning occurs in this way. Children routinely learn to keep their balance when riding a bicycle or skiing. For the most part, they do not do so by following step-by-step instructions. According to Timothy Gallwey, in his books on the "inner games" of tennis and other sports, we can best learn complex forms of motor coordination by suspending rational thought and simply mimicking the movements of someone who is experienced at the activity. Trying to analyze the components of the physical process may actually interfere with the experiential mind's efficient, intuitive mastery of the task.

Insight versus intellectual knowledge. Psychotherapists emphasize a distinction between intellectual knowledge and insight. If intellectual knowledge were all that were necessary to correct deep psychological problems, then it would be a relatively simple matter for therapists to effect cures by understanding their clients' problems and telling them what to do to solve them. Yet, such a procedure is usually ineffective because it reaches only the rational mind, and effective change requires changes in the experiential mind. The difference between intellectual knowledge and insight is that intellectual knowledge is general knowledge that reaches only the rational mind, whereas insight is associated with personal significance and emotional involvement and therefore reaches the experiential mind. As an example of the development of insight in the course of psychotherapy, consider the following case.

A client I was seeing in psychotherapy was extremely passive. He did whatever people told him to do and then resented their domination. We discussed the part he played in such interactions, but it did nothing to change his behavior. Then one day he asked if it would be all right if he missed the next appointment, as he was invited to go on an expense-paid vacation with a wealthy relative. I said, "No, it isn't all right. You have too much to do right here." As I anticipated, this made him angry. He complained, "I knew it, I knew it! Up to now, I thought you were different. Now I see you are just like the rest. You enjoy bossing me around just like they do. I made a reasonable request, and you denied it." I asked him what he could learn from this about why people boss him around. "Nothing," he said, "except that you are as bossy as the others." "What role did you play in it?" I asked him. "None," he said, "I just asked a question." I responded, "At our last meeting you complained that your brothers were bossy because they told you to bowl last. Did you ask them when you should bowl?" "Yes," he said, "I asked them." Then, in an excited tone of voice, he added, "Golly, I guess I always ask people, and that's why they always tell me! I shouldn't ask if I will resent their answer." He decided he had better stop asking so much and make up his own mind more often. In our next meeting he proudly announced that he had been asserting himself more than ever before, and although it was a bit scary at first, he found, to his surprise, that people accepted it and even liked him more for it. He learned something from this personal, emotionally involving experience in therapy that helped him to change his behavior in a way that his previous intellectual understanding had failed to accomplish.

Superstitious and magical thinking. The prevalence of superstitious and magical thinking provides striking evidence that the human mind does not process information by reason alone. Superstitious and magical thinking develops according to the rules of the experiential mind, which means it is often the result of arbitrary associations that have been emotionally reinforced. A young business executive was very nervous before meeting the CEO of a large company from whom he hoped to obtain a lucrative contract. All went well, and he secured the contract. Later he became aware that, in his nervousness, he had put on one black and one brown shoe. From then on he made a point of always wearing one black and one brown shoe before important business meetings. Was this foolish? Not necessarily, for it put him in a positive, confident mood that reduced his nervousness and improved his performance. He simply took advantage of his automatic experiential processing.

How prevalent is superstitious and unrealistic thinking? In a recent Gallup poll, 1,236 adults were interviewed about their superstitions. One in four reported believing in ghosts, one in six said they had communicated with someone deceased, one in four that they had telepathically communicated with someone, one in ten that they had been in the presence of a ghost, one in seven that they had seen a UFO, one in four that they believed in astrology, and one-half said they believed in extrasensory perception.

In my own research on superstitions and magical thinking, more than half of college students reported having at least one superstition, and 72% reported having a good luck charm. Of particular interest, superstitions were reported to be more frequent in adults than in children. This can be explained by adults having had more opportunity to experience arbitrary associations, as in the case of the man with the black and brown shoes, than younger people. It also provides strong additional evidence that people operate by two minds, since if there were only one mind, adults should be more rational and less superstitious than children.

Religion. The ubiquity of religion throughout history provides perhaps the most impressive evidence of all that there are two fundamentally different ways of thinking. Few societies, if any, have not developed some form of religion. For many individuals, rational, analytical thinking fails to provide as satisfactory a way of understanding the world and of directing their behavior in it as does religious teaching. The reason for this is that religion is better suited than analytical thinking for communicating with the experiential system. It does so by using music, singing or chanting, group cohesiveness, mythical explanations of the creation of the world, and rituals for coping with critical events in life, including birth, marriage, and death. Of course, every religion regards its own myths as reality, while considering the beliefs of other religions as unrealistic myths.

RESEARCH EVIDENCE FOR TWO MINDS

In the formative years of psychology, both Pavlov and Freud independently introduced theories that emphasized two fundamentally different ways of processing information. For Pavlov, the distinction was between what he referred to as the "first signal system" and the "second signal system," the former being associated with conditioning, and the latter with thinking in more complex ways that are dependent on the use of language. For Freud, the distinction was between the "primary process" and the "secondary process," the former illustrated in the associative thinking in dreams, and the latter in analytical, conscious thinking.

Within the past two decades, a "cognitive revolution" has occurred in psychology. From a wide variety of disciplines in psychology, including cognitive psychology, clinical psychology, developmental psychology, and social psychology, the view that there are two different systems for processing information has been independently proposed. Although they differ in details, the theories are in essential agreement that there are a primitive mode of thinking that is automatic, preconscious, rapid, and effortless and a more evolutionary-advanced mode that is deliberate, conscious, and more effortful. Almost all of the theoretical positions are supported by extensive research programs that provide evidence of the operation of two different cognitive systems. The scope of this research is far beyond what can be summarized here. Instead, I shall focus on selected studies from the research program conducted by my associates and myself.

A particularly important development for my research program was a series of investigations by cognitive psychologists Amos Tversky and Daniel Kahneman and others on the ways in which people think nonrationally. Before this research was conducted, economists and others constructed models of human behavior based on the assumption that people are essentially rational creatures who behave in ways that maximize their gains and minimize their losses. It is now apparent that this model is seriously flawed. Human thinking is neither mainly conscious nor rational. Most of it occurs automatically, below the threshold of awareness, and follows nonrational principles that, although usually adaptive, are maladaptive in certain situations.

I will present three kinds of research evidence for the existence of two fundamentally different ways of processing information: research with specially designed vignettes for probing particular mental processes, research using a unique experimental situation for examining conflicts between the two ways of thinking, and the investigation of individual differences in the two ways of thinking.

EVIDENCE OF TWO MINDS IN SPECIALLY DESIGNED VIGNETTES

One way in which cognitive psychologists have studied how people think is to have them respond to vignettes, or scenarios, that probe particular thought processes. My associates and I used similar vignettes, but unlike other researchers, we had people respond from three perspectives: how they believe most people would react if they were in the situations described, how they themselves would react, and how a completely logical person would react. As you will see, most people believe that they and others respond according to the principles of the experiential mind but that a completely logical person responds according to the principles of the rational mind. Thus people are intuitively aware of the two systems I propose.

As you read each of the following vignettes, consider what your own responses would be from each of the three perspectives and what the differences suggest about the nature of two different modes of processing information.

Reactions to Arbitrary Events

The following events all involve arbitrary outcomes that are beyond the control of the protagonist. The research reveals that although people are well aware that it is irrational to assume that one has control over such events, they nevertheless report that they and others would behave as if they were responsible for the outcomes. Why? The answer is that the irrational thinking is attributable to the operation of the experiential mind, which operates by association, not by logic.

Off the beaten path. Mr. Jones was involved in an accident when driving home after work on his regular route. Before leaving work, he had thought about taking another route for a change in scenery but decided against it. Mr. Green was involved in a similar accident when driving through a similar neighborhood on a route that he took only when he wanted a change in scenery.

In both cases an oil drum fell off a truck in front of them and hit their front wheels. It caused each of their cars to crash into a telephone pole. In each case, the car suffered $1,000 worth of damage.

Who do you think was more upset, Mr. Jones, who took his usual route, Mr. Green, who changed routes, or neither?

Your answer from the perspective that Jones and Green are average people _____

Your answer from the perspective of how you would most likely react _____

Your answer from the perspective of Jones and Green being completely logical _____

When a miss is not as good as a mile. Mrs. Roberts and Mrs. Smith were scheduled to leave the airport at the same time on different flights. They were on their way to important business meetings. Each drove the same distance to the airport, was caught in a traffic jam, and arrived at the airport thirty minutes after the scheduled departure of her flight. Mrs. Roberts learned that her flight had left on time, half an hour ago. Mrs. Smith learned that her flight had been delayed and left just a few minutes ago. Both had dawdled ten minutes before leaving home.

Who do you think was more upset about her dawdling, Mrs. Roberts, whose flight left on time, Mrs. Smith, whose flight was delayed, or neither?

Your answer from the perspective that Roberts and Smith are average people _____

Your answer from the perspective of how you would most likely react _____

Your answer from the perspective that Roberts and Smith are completely logical_____

The burden of choice. Mary chose the most convenient place to park her new car in a parking lot that was half empty. As luck would have it, when she backed out after shopping, another car backed out at the same time from the space opposite hers. Both cars sustained damage of $1,000.

Jane parked her new car in the same parking lot in the only space that was available at the time. As luck would have it, when she backed out after shopping, another car backed out at the same time from the space opposite hers. Both cars sustained damage of $1,000.

Who do you think was more upset about where she parked, Mary, who chose her space, Jane, who had no choice, or neither?

Your answer from the perspective that Mary and Jane are average people _____

Your answer from the perspective of how you would most likely react _____

Your answer from the perspective that Mary and Jane are completely logical _____

Bad luck is no accident. Three young men, Jones, Cooper, and Smith, are told by a rich benefactor that if each throws a coin that comes up heads, he will give each of them $100. Jones and Cooper both throw heads. Smith, who is last, throws a tails. The rich benefactor gives them another chance, only to have the situation repeat itself.

Answer the following questions from the three perspectives by entering a number from 0–5, where 0 = not at all, 1 = slightly, 2 = moderately, 3 = considerably, 4 = very, and 5 = extremely.

How guilty does Smith feel, assuming he is an average person? _____

How guilty would you probably feel if you were in his place? _____

How guilty would a completely logical person feel? _____

How angry at Smith do the others feel, assuming they are average people? _____

How angry at Smith would you feel if you were in their place? _____

How angry would a completely logical person feel? _____

Now assume that Jones and Cooper have been planning a gambling vacation at Las Vegas. They have agreed to pool their money and share their wins and losses. Before the incident with the rich benefactor, they had been thinking about inviting Smith to join them.

From the three perspectives, rate the likelihood that they will now invite Smith. Use a scale in which −3 = definitely will not, −2 = highly likely will not, −1 = probably will not, 0 = about 50–50, 1 = probably will, 2 = highly likely will, 3 = definitely will.

From the perspective that they are average people _____
From the perspective of your being in their place _____
From the perspective that they are completely logical people _____
Give your reasons from the three perspectives of why Smith will or will not be invited _____

This vignette was presented under two conditions. Half the participants were told that the amount of money at stake was $100 per person, and the other half was told that it was $1 per person. Do you think that the amount of money affects the responses? Would you change your ratings if only $1 were at stake?

What these vignettes tell us. The outcomes of the events described in the preceding vignettes were all chance occurrences. From a logical perspective, most people agree that none of the characters was responsible for the outcome, and therefore neither they nor others should hold them accountable for the unfortunate outcomes. Yet, from the perspective of how the average person would react in the position of the protagonists, as well as how they themselves would react, most said that they and the average person would be more upset about their behavior in one of the conditions described in the vignettes that contrasted two situations than in the other. In the vignette about the coin tosses, most said that the average person and they themselves would feel guilty in Smith's position and angry in the position of his partners but that a completely logical person in Smith's position would not feel guilty and in the position of his partners would not be angry at him.

As these results show, people are intuitively aware that, in the kinds of situations described in the vignettes, they operate by two minds, a rational mind and an associationistic mind that corresponds to the experiential mind I described.

Here is how most people answered the questions from the perspective of how most people and they themselves, but not a logical person, would respond if they were in the situations described in the vignettes and what their answers reveal about the experiential mind:

Off the beaten path: Mr. Green, who changed routes, would be more upset than Mr. Jones, who took his usual route. Generally we have a more intense reaction in our experiential mind to an arbitrary negative outcome after we do something unusual than after we do something the customary way.

When a miss is not as good as a mile: Mrs. Smith, who barely missed her flight because it was accidentally delayed, would be more upset than Mrs. Roberts, who missed her flight by a longer period because it left on time. Generally, we have a more intense reaction in our experiential mind after an arbitrary near miss than after an arbitrary miss by a wider margin.

The burden of choice: Mary, who chose her parking place, would be more upset than Jane, who had no choice. Generally, we have a more intense reaction in our experiential mind after we freely choose to do something that arbitrarily has a negative outcome than after we act in a way over which we have no control.

Bad luck is no accident: Mr. Smith would feel guilty, and he would feel more guilty when $100 was at stake than when $1 was at stake. His two partners would feel angry at him, and they would be more angry when the stakes were higher. They will not invite him on a gambling vacation because "he is a loser." When tested for their knowledge about probability, many endorsed the gambler's fallacy, which is the mistaken belief that after a particular outcome, like losing, has occurred a number of times, the probability is higher that the opposite will occur. You might think that those who believed in the gambler's fallacy would be eager to invite Smith to join them, as it is about time he started winning. However, being viewed as a loser apparently takes precedence in the experiential mind over belief in the gambler's fallacy. From a logical perspective, most participants said they would not be angry at Smith, and they would invite him to join them on the gambling vacation. As to how they themselves would react, most said they would be more rational than the average person, but less rational than a logical person.

What do these experiments more generally reveal about the operation of the experiential mind? First, they indicate that most people, at least in the kinds of situations described in the vignettes, can be made aware of the two systems if they are asked to respond from different perspectives, which they normally would not do. Second, they indicate that the experiential mind operates by association rather than by logic. It associates outcomes with whatever precedes them, and it does not consider whether the relation is a cause-and-effect one, or simply arbitrary. If A precedes B, the experiential mind reacts as if it believes A causes B. In certain situations, this can lead to serious errors in judgment, such as developing a dislike for someone who delivered bad news. Third, the responses to the vignettes reveal that in most situations the experiential mind is adaptive. It has learned from previous experience that it is more dangerous to do something unusual than to stick with the tried-and-true, that a near miss should be taken more seriously than a far miss, and that one should be more concerned about actions over which one has control than about those over which one has no control. These beliefs are automatically applied in a highly general way, usually appropriately, but sometimes inappropriately, as when logical distinctions are required (e.g., the deliverer of bad news is not necessarily a bad person). Fourth, the responses indicate that the greater the emotional involvement (as when the stakes were raised in the gambling vignette), the more extreme the experiential response.

Automatic Experiential Processing Is Often Followed by Corrective Rational Processing

Our initial reactions to situations are often maladaptive, and we then correct them by thinking more rationally. This sequence of thoughts suggests the operation of two different modes of thinking—one that is rapid, preconscious, automatic, and nonrational and another that is slower, conscious, deliberate, and rational. Why do the maladaptive thoughts occur in the first place? By what principles do they operate? We sought answers to these questions by conducting research in which we examined people's immediate and delayed reactions to a variety of situations. The research revealed, as anticipated, that the initial reactions usually follow the principles of the experiential mind whereas the delayed reactions often follow those of the rational mind. Following are examples of two vignettes used in these investigations. Respondents were asked to list the first three thoughts that occurred to them when they considered how they would react in the situations described.

Blame it on Joe. Imagine you bought a lottery ticket where the winner receives a new car. After you were given a certain number, you asked if it could be switched to another that corresponded to your lucky number. The person was about to do so when your friend Joe, who is very rational, gave you a lecture on how foolish it is to decide things by lucky numbers. He said that since the probabilities are absolutely identical for all numbers, you might as well stick with the first one. You decided to listen to your friend. As luck would have it, the number you wanted to switch to was the winning number.

A typical first reaction was as follows: "My damn friend and his stupid advice. He always thinks he knows best. I'll never listen to him again." By the third thought, the person realized that the outcome was not his friend's fault as it could just as well have gone the opposite way.

Crime and punishment as viewed by the experiential mind. One group of participants was given the following vignette:

Imagine you and your four-year-old son Robert visited a rich relative who has very expensive antiques in her living room. You carefully explained to Robert that he must be very careful and not run in the living room. When your attention was distracted, Robert and your relative's little girl began to chase each other in the living room. Before you could stop them, Robert knocked over a small vase that crashed to the floor. Your hostess looked horrified and said, "Oh, my God, that vase is irreplaceable!"

A second group was given a version of the vignette in which the vase was described as a cheap item about which your hostess was not at all concerned.

A typical first reaction to the version with the expensive vase was that the parent would be very angry and would severely punish Robert. A typical third thought was that Robert was just a child who could not appreciate the value of the vase and that he should be reprimanded but not severely punished. There was less of a difference between the first and third thought in the second version, where the parent's first thought was to moderately reprimand Robert for breaking the inexpensive vase, and the third thought was to mildly reprimand him for his disobedience.

What these vignettes reveal about the two minds. In addition to providing support for two different modes of thinking, the responses to these vignettes suggest that the experiential mind operates in a rapid, automatic manner and judges events by association rather than by logical considerations of responsibility and cause-and-effect relations. The results also reveal a relation between the intensity of the emotion that is experienced and the balance between experiential and rational processing. The greater the emotion, the more the balance shifts toward a dominant influence by the experiential mind.

The Notorious Linda Vignette

Linda is described as a thirty-one-year-old woman who is single, outspoken, and very bright. In college she was a philosophy major who participated in antinuclear demonstrations and was concerned with issues of social justice. Rank the following possibilities by assigning "1" to the most likely and "3" to the least likely: Linda is a feminist; Linda is a bank teller; and Linda is both.

If you responded like most people, you ranked Linda as being both a feminist and a bank teller ahead of Linda's being just a bank teller. In doing so, you made a conjunction error, because, according to the conjunction rule, two things cannot be more likely than only one of them. The interesting thing about the Linda problem is that although the conjunction rule is one of the simplest and most fundamental rules in probability theory, nearly everyone violates it, including people who are sophisticated about probability theory. The reason for this is that most people engage in a different kind of reasoning from rational, analytical thinking when it comes to the Linda problem. According to Tversky and Kahneman, who introduced the Linda problem, people engage in a natural, simplified form of reasoning when responding to the Linda problem. From the viewpoint of CEST, this natural, simple form of reasoning corresponds to the reasoning of the experiential mind. People make conjunction errors in the Linda problem because the experiential mind reacts to context in a very concrete way. Unlike the rational mind, which operates largely by abstract, situation-free generalizations, the experiential mind reacts concretely to behavior in specific situational contexts. Presented in the context of a personality problem, the experiential mind believes the solution requires a match between Linda's personality and her behavior, as this is the way problems in this context are usually solved. Given the personality information provided, most people therefore decide that there is a better match between Linda's personality and being a feminist and a bank teller than just being a bank teller. That context is the determining factor is indicated by asking people whether it is more likely that a person will win both the firemen's lottery and the sweepstakes or will win just one of them. Virtually no one makes conjunction errors with this latter problem because lotteries suggest probability problems, not personality problems. What we learn from the Linda vignette in addition to the situation-specific, concrete thinking of the experiential mind is that the experiential mind is likely to be adaptive in natural contexts, where solutions are consistent with past experience, and it is likely to be maladaptive when problems are presented in contexts that are unnatural in the sense that they differ from expectancies based on past experience with similar problems.

Conflict and Compromise between the Two Minds

Imagine that you are presented with two trays of jelly beans, a larger one that has 100 jelly beans, 10 of which are red and the rest white, and a smaller one that has 10 jelly beans, one of which is red and the rest white. You are told that on every trial in which you pick a red jelly bean you will receive two dollars. Before each trial, the jelly beans are scrambled, and an opaque screen is placed in front of them so you cannot see what you are picking. From which tray would you choose to draw, and how much, if anything, would you be willing to pay for the privilege of having a choice of trays, rather than having the choice made for you by the flip of a coin?

When we described this situation to people, most said that it would make no difference to them, "as 10% is 10%," and they would not pay a cent for the privilege of having a choice between two equal probabilities. However, when we asked them how they thought most people would react, they said that most people would prefer to draw from the large tray and would be willing to pay something for the privilege. This suggests that at some level people are aware of the greater appeal of the tray with more red jelly beans, or else why would they think that most people would select it? They apparently like to think of themselves as more rational than others, so they deny they would behave that way. Of yet greater interest, when people were put in a real situation in which they actually received two dollars on every trial in which they drew a red bean, most decided to draw from the large tray, and they were willing to pay ten cents for the privilege. Many spontaneously commented that they know it is foolish to pay to choose between two equal probabilities, but somehow they felt they had a better chance of getting a red bean when there were more of them. An even more impressive finding was that when we made the probabilities uneven by always offering a 10% probability in the small tray and smaller probabilities, ranging from 5% to 9%, in the large tray, more than half of the participants selected the 9% over the 10% probability, and fully a third selected the 5% over the 10% probability.

How are such strange findings to be explained? "Numerosity," or frequency information, is one of the most fundamental cognitive abilities and has been demonstrated to be present in nonhuman animals and preverbal human infants. It is therefore clearly within the domain of the experiential mind. An understanding of probability ratios, on the other hand, except in its most rudimentary form, lies exclusively within the domain of the rational mind. The jelly bean experiments place these two sources of reaction in conflict with each other. Some people who are highly rational always make the most optimal choice. However, most indulge their experiential reactions to some extent, which results in compromises between the two processing modes, in which they select the 8% or 9% probability, but not the 1%–7% probabilities, in the large tray over the 10% probability (with fewer red jelly beans) in the small tray. In studies with children, we have found that those who have not yet learned about ratios prefer the 2% (2 out of 100 red jelly beans) over the 10% probability (1 out of 10 red jelly beans). Children who understand ratios prefer the 5–9% probabilities, but not the 2–4% probabilities, in the large tray over the 10% probability in the small tray.

What the jelly bean experiments teach us is that people have two different ways of processing information, a more primitive, spontaneous way that can understand numerosity but not ratios (except, as other research teaches us, in the most rudimentary form) and a more rational way that is influenced by formal knowledge of ratios. Behavior represents a compromise between these two ways of processing information, experiential and rational. With maturity, the rational mind becomes increasingly dominant over the experiential mind, but never completely so. Most people, despite "knowing better," prefer to follow their experiential mind to some extent. Others value rationality so highly that they always try to make rational decisions. This introduces us to the next topic, individual differences in the use of the two minds.

Individual Differences in People's Use of Their Two Minds

We all know people who pride themselves on their rationality and look askance at others who consider themselves intuitive. We also know people who exhibit the opposite pattern. That there are such individual differences supports the view that there are two fundamental ways of thinking, experiential and rational. This raises some basic questions, such as whether the two ways of thinking are opposite ends of a single dimension or are independent. In the former event, if people are high in one way of thinking, they must be low in the other. In the latter event, their standing on one dimension has no bearing on their standing on the other: they can be high on both dimensions, low on both, or high on one and low on the other. Other questions of interest are how the two ways of thinking are related to various personality characteristics and adjustment. Who is better off, people who are primarily rational or people who are primarily intuitive?

To answer these questions, my associates and I located a questionnaire that provided a measure of degree of interest and engagement in rational thinking and constructed another that measured degree of interest and engagement in experiential thinking. Some typical items in the questionnaire on rational thinking are "I prefer to talk about international problems rather than to gossip or talk about celebrities" and "I would rather do something that is sure to challenge my thinking abilities than something that requires little thought." Some typical items in the questionnaire on experiential thinking are "I believe in trusting my hunches" and "I am a very intuitive person." We found that the scores on these two measures are independent, which supports the assumption that there are two fundamental ways of thinking that operate by different principles. We also found that degree of rational, but not experiential, thinking is related to adjustment. Insofar as good adjustment is concerned, one apparently cannot afford to be irrational. However, there is considerable latitude in which one can be experiential. So long as one is reasonably rational, one can be high or low in experiential thinking and still be well adjusted. Rational and experiential ways of thinking each have their advantages and disadvantages. High scores on rational thinking are associated with superior IQ, superior college grades, and various measures of adjustment, including low anxiety, low stress, and low depression. High scores on experiential thinking are associated with establishing secure relationships with others. Thus, those who are best off, who are well adjusted, perform well academically, and establish rewarding relationships with others are those who use both of their minds to advantage. It appears that there is a price to be paid for cultivating one of the ways of thinking at the expense of the other.

The Intelligence of the Two Minds

I noted in Chapter 1 that if there are two minds, each must have its own form of intelligence. I further noted that the intelligence of the rational mind is measured by IQ tests, and the intelligence of the experiential mind is indicated by the constructiveness of a person's automatic thinking that underlies the experience of emotions. This theme was further developed in Chapters 2 and 3. In Chapter 4 you took the Constructive Thinking Inventory, a measure of automatic constructive and destructive thinking. Now, it follows that, if reliable, independent measures of two kinds of intelligence can be constructed, there must also exist two different minds or modes of thinking that are the source of the two kinds of intelligence. In other words, the very fact that my associates and I were able to construct the CTI and that it was then found to be independent of IQ is in itself support for the view that there are two different minds, or mental systems, that operate by their own rules.

A great deal of research has been conducted with the CTI that demonstrates that it measures practical abilities, including the ability to lead a rewarding and successful life. The point in discussing the CTI in this chapter, however, was only to indicate that it provides support for the conclusion that there are two different minds. The more specific findings with the CTI that demonstrate its reliability and validity are discussed in a later chapter.

WHY PEOPLE OVERLOOK THE EXPERIENTIAL MIND

If the evidence is so overwhelming that people operate by two minds, how come everyone is not aware of it, psychologists included? This is a most fascinating issue that I have often pondered. Once one is aware of the difference between the two minds and observes their operation day in and day out in oneself and others, it is almost incomprehensible that not everyone sees this self-evident truth. There thus must be very strong reasons that people are not aware of it. Perhaps the strongest is that the two minds operate in such well-synchronized harmony with each other that except in special circumstances, such as when conflicts arise between the heart and the head, people are aware of only a single, smooth-functioning process. We are aware of the rational mind because it operates in our consciousness. As the experiential mind, on the other hand, operates automatically and does not require our conscious attention, we usually are oblivious of its operation. It is so much a part of our natural functioning that we don't notice it, just as we don't notice the double vision of everything in our line of sight on which we are not focused. As Carlyle said in one of his essays, if a fish had an inquiring mind, the last thing it would discover is water.

In addition to its smooth, automatic functioning at a preconscious level, there are the following reasons people are unaware of the experiential mind.

People can rationalize their experiential processing. People like to believe they are consciously in charge of their day-to-day behavior. They tell themselves that they know why they do what they do and that their reasons make good sense. What they do not realize is that, behind the scenes, their experiential minds direct their conscious thinking as well as their feelings and behavior. As an example, without realizing it you may favor a political candidate because you like the way that person looks or because he or she reminds you of someone else. If you do that, your behavior is being driven by your experiential mind, which is closely tied to your feelings. Yet you may well justify—rationalize—your vote by saying that you favor the candidate's principles or policies. Do not underestimate the human capacity to rationalize. Your rational mind likes to take credit for governing your actions even when it does not, and it is clever enough to convince you that this illusion is a reality.

People prefer to leave well enough alone. There is the story of a centipede who, when asked which of his many feet he moved first, got so confused that he was unable to walk. You may fear that this will happen to you if you try to become more aware of how your mind works. After all, if nature programmed you to do most of what you do without thinking about it, why do you need to be aware of everything you do or think? Indeed, it may be more comfortable to accept your view of reality than to question it. But then you will be stuck with the consequences of haphazard past experiences. Things don't always go "well enough" when they are left alone. Even if they are going well, why not make them go better?

People wish to avoid responsibility. People tend to assume either that they have complete conscious understanding and control of what they do or that their behavior and understanding are influenced by a deep, dark, unconscious mind over which they have no control, with nothing in between. As a result, they fail to gain control of the thinking that produces their everyday emotions. It is easier to say, "The way he acted made me angry" than, "I am angry because of the way I interpreted his actions." Such self-absolution may be more rewarding—and surely less threatening—in the short run than the promise of gaining control of your emotions by owning up to your automatic interpretations. If you allow yourself to become aware of the automatic interpretations that give rise to your feelings, then you won't be able to blame your emotions exclusively on external events. You might even find there is something you can do to train your emotions.

Not long ago a young relative asked me what courses I was teaching. When I told her about my course in which I have students record their daily experiences and relate the stress they felt to their interpretations of those experiences, she said she wanted to do the same. But after a few days of recording her experiences, she stopped. "Why did you quit?" I asked.

"Because it kept me from acting the way I wanted to," she replied. "It made me aware that I use my emotions to manipulate people. By crying or getting angry, I can get people to do what I want. When I observed my automatic thoughts, I saw how they influenced my emotions, and I realized that I could feel differently if I wanted to. If I continued with the exercise, I wouldn't be able to let myself get away with using my emotions that way, and I like being able to do it."

This was an honest admission that her experiential mind, as it had developed "naturally" for her, was furnishing short-term rewards that she was unwilling to give up. Still, would she not be better off in the long run if she kept up the exercise until she gained control of her "natural" habits of thought and feeling? Certainly, that would empower her in much more effective ways than by attempting to control people with emotional displays.

People believe that irrational behavior requires an esoteric explanation. The unconscious seems to many people to be a deep and mysterious region of the mind that only psychoanalysts can understand. They believe that such an unconscious is necessary to account for the strange behavior of human beings who, despite being capable of rational thinking, often behave irrationally, even against their own welfare. Surely, some strange, incomprehensible source of influence must be behind such thinking and behavior! Having made this implicit assumption, it is difficult for people to believe that the experiential mind, which is so easily understood by anyone who takes the trouble to seriously consider it, can account for humankind's pervasive irrationality. Yet the experiential mind can account for everything that Freud and Jung attempted to account for with their esoteric views of the unconscious and can do so in a scientifically more defensible manner. Unlike these other conceptualizations of the unconscious mind, the principles of operation of the experiential mind are consistent with evolutionary principles and modern cognitive theory and research, and, since the experiential mind can influence the rational mind, the mechanism is clearly present by which it can induce irrational behavior.

SUMMARY AND CONCLUSIONS

Logical considerations and evidence from three different sources support the position that human beings operate by two different minds that correspond to the experiential and rational minds. First, based on evolutionary principles, it was deduced that humans must retain a mental system that is essentially the same as that employed by other higher-order nonhuman animals in adjusting to their environments. Such a system would necessarily be based on learning directly from experience rather than on the use of language and logical inference and would be associated with the experience of emotions, which would serve as a source of motivation and reinforcer of learning. With the advent of language and the development of a larger cerebral cortex, a second way of information processing based on logical inference became exclusively available to human beings. Second, a wide variety of evidence in everyday life indicates that people do not operate solely by their rational minds. Examples of the operation of two minds in everyday life include conflicts between the heart and the head, the greater appeal of pictures, narratives, and specific examples than abstract verbal statements, the prevalence of unrealistic fears despite people's awareness of their irrationality, the greater effect of insight than of intellectual knowledge on changing behavior, the prevalence of superstitious thinking in people who are otherwise rational, and the prevalence of religion despite the development of science. Third, many psychologists from various persuasions using different research approaches have independently arrived at the conclusion that most information is processed automatically, without conscious awareness, by principles that differ from rational reasoning. I provided examples of such research from an extensive program my associates and I conducted to elucidate the principles of information processing in the experiential mind.

In response to the question of why people are not normally aware of their experiential mind, I proposed the following reasons: (1) the experiential mind normally operates in such close synchrony with the rational mind that it gives us the impression that we operate by only a single mind, (2) although the experiential mind constantly influences our conscious thinking and behavior, we are good enough at rationalization to deceive ourselves into believing we are in conscious control of almost everything we think and do, (3) we prefer to react naturally and not burden ourselves with trying to understand our thinking and, relatedly, we prefer not to take responsibility for our emotions, and (4) we assume that complicated thinking and behavior require complicated explanations, and we therefore conclude that the idea of an experiential mind is too simple and easily understood to provide an explanation of humankind's pervasive irrationality.

Given the compelling logic and evidence that I have presented for the existence of an experiential mind that operates by its own principles and influences the rational mind, there are two very important conclusions that follow. One is that if we wish to be truly rational, it is necessary for us to be in touch with our experiential mind, for only by knowing it can we compensate for its influence. In the absence of such self-knowledge our intellectual understanding is bound to be biased by our experiential thinking. The other is that it is no less important to train our experiential mind than to educate our rational mind.

Chapter 6

How Your Experiential Mind Thinks

I began to pay close attention to the workings of the two minds after watching a heated discussion of rape on television. The participants were two men who were on parole after having served sentences for violent rape, a psychologist who specialized in treating rapists, and an audience of mostly women.

In response to questions from the talk-show host and from the audience, the rapists challenged some common stereotypes. One of the men was asked, "How did you pick the women you decided to rape? Did you find them especially attractive?"

"No," he replied. "I just was mad and decided I was going to rape the next woman I saw. It was her bad luck that she was next."

"You must be very desperate for sex. Do you have any sexual relations with other women?"

"Oh, yes, I have a girlfriend."

"Is she unattractive, then?"

"No, she's more attractive than the women I raped."

Hearing things that confounded their expectations, many in the audience became frustrated and angry. "I don't believe you're sorry," they said. "You're sorry only because you got caught, not because of what you did!" They could not accept the idea that anyone who could feel sorry afterward could commit a rape in the first place. The rapists maintained that in their normal state of mind they could not comprehend what they had done, but they knew they would do it again if they were in the same angry state that had preceded their violent acts. As one of them put it, "I'm scared out of my mind that I could do these terrible things again and end up back in prison."

That was all the audience needed to hear. "Then you should be kept in prison for the rest of your lives. That should be the law!" one woman said.

At this point the audience applauded enthusiastically, and a number of women shouted their agreement.

"Wait, think of what you're saying," the psychologist interjected. "If you pass laws like that, then these men aren't going to admit that they could rape again. They won't seek treatment because that might be used against them, and then when they're released, which they would be eventually, they'll be just as likely to do it again. Wouldn't it be better to try to understand what causes them to do it and then work to prevent it?"

This calm, logical explanation was greeted with silence. A man in the audience who identified himself as a policeman commented that he had absolutely no sympathy for rapists. To the cheers of the audience, he said that anyone who could rape should be kept off the streets for life. The psychologist reiterated that this policy would be counterproductive from the victim's viewpoint as well as the rapist's, as the penalty for rape in many states would then exceed that for murder. A rapist would then be more likely to murder his victim, often the only witness to the crime.

Again, the women in the audience grew impatient with the psychologist's cool detachment. One woman, expressing the sentiments of the group, yelled at one of the rapists, "You're just saying these things to make excuses for yourself. You're just a brute who has no respect for others. All you think of is your momentary gratification. I'll bet you wouldn't rape if the punishment was severe enough. What would happen if you knew there was a death sentence for rape?"

"Lady, it wouldn't make a bit of difference," he replied. "I wish it would, but it wouldn't. Because when I'm in that mood, it's as if I'm in a different world. All I can think of is my anger at women and how I want to take it out on the next woman I see. It never occurs to me to think about what the consequences may be for me or what's happening to her. The death penalty, any punishment, would make no difference."

I watched, fascinated, as the participants talked past one another, as if they were talking different languages. The women, possessed with ready-made, emotionally driven answers, were not open to explanations or proposals that ran counter to their preconceived views. Their unwillingness to consider long-range consequences as they rushed to an emotionally compelling solution was not so different from the rapist's automatic leap from feeling to action.

It was increasingly apparent to me that the people in the television program were not communicating because some were reacting mainly with their rational minds, while others were reacting mainly with their experiential minds. Being a psychologist, I identified with the psychologist's approach and even felt proud that he was a member of my profession, so good was he at keeping things in perspective. Yet, I might well have shared the audience's outrage had a member of my family been recently raped. Then I might have been shaking my fist at the television and identifying with the women's outrage. Remember, when beliefs are based on experiences, particularly emotionally intense ones, the experiential mind tends to become dominant.

What were you thinking as you read this story? Which way did your sympathies go? Did you have "mixed feelings"? Did you perhaps experience a growing irritation, even indignation, at the cool detachment of the psychologist? It is a natural, "human" way to react. The women in the audience had good experiential reasons to say the things they did. Some may have come to the studio that day because they themselves had been raped. All women are threatened with the possibility of rape. For some, it is an ever-present fear; for many, it necessitates continuous caution and a sense of not being fully free. That they would feel frustrated and bitter about it is perfectly understandable.

Yet it seems most sensible and beneficial in the long run to combine this experiential motivation with a rational focus on results. What better way can there be to reduce the fear and outrage women experience about rape than to reduce the incidence of rape? However, even at the rational level, there are many questions to be asked before we decide how best to deal with rapists. First, even if we accept as honest the report of the two rapists that they "couldn't" control their behavior, if we take what they said at face value, we may give license to others to use such excuses cynically. With people now routinely identifying themselves as having this or that behavioral disorder, we may be contributing to a loss of personal responsibility if we accept too readily a person's claim to have been powerless to resist an overwhelming impulse or to have had an abusive childhood.

Second, there may be considerable value in the expression of emotions such as indignation. Taken to an extreme, of course, the attitude of the television audience screaming for retribution would lead to lynch mobs. Yet Albert Einstein pointed out the danger of going to the opposite extreme when he wrote that a society is in serious trouble if it thinks it can deal with such horrors as the Holocaust or the threat of nuclear devastation through rational discourse alone. Once people lose the capacity for emotional indignation, Einstein warned, terrible things will follow. This advice from a man regarded as the epitome of scientific rationality reminds us that we cannot trust to reason alone.

THE "LANGUAGE" OF THE EXPERIENTIAL MIND

The experiential mind interprets experience and directs behavior automatically, effortlessly, and almost instantaneously. It evolved over millions of years. Its primary task is to process information and interpret events with great rapidity so as to initiate quick, decisive action. Operating effortlessly, without deliberation, it must produce an immediate sense of assurance and motivation to act. It does so through emotions and by directing behavior in ways that maximize good feelings and minimize bad feelings.

How does the experiential mind function in order to serve these general purposes? Through an analysis of everyday behavior and the kind of research I described in the previous chapter, I have identified thirteen specific characteristics of the experiential mind, which I describe by contrasting them with the corresponding features of the rational mind (See Figure 6.1). Although these are differences in degree rather than absolute differences, they are clearly observable if you know what to look for. As you familiarize yourself with these characteristics, you will be better able to recognize them in your own thinking.

1. *The experiential mind learns directly from experience.* This is the crucial distinction between the two minds, from which all other differences follow. For the most part, the rational mind learns from words, numbers, diagrams, and so forth. This abstract communication is essential for solving engineering problems or writing history, but it is not as helpful in coping with emotions or getting along with people. To do those things we need to use the experiential mind, which learns primarily from emotionally significant experiences. The stronger the emotions an experience arouses, the stronger the impression it makes on your experiential mind. What you learn from being rejected by a loved one—and the way you learn it—is a far cry from what you learn by seeing the demonstration of a mathematical proof.

Your experiential mind learns from imaginary experience as well as from real experience. Thus, you can influence your experiential mind by using your imagination. If you vividly imagine a frightening scene, your heart will accelerate, your breathing will change, and your nervous system will react just as surely as if you actually had a threatening experience. By the same token, if you imagine a happy or a calm scene, you can calm your physiological reactions. As you will see in Part IV, imagination can be a powerful tool for influencing your experiential mind and, through it, your emotions and bodily states.

2. *The experiential mind is action-oriented and thinks and acts quickly.* Its simplifying strategies enable it to reach quick decisions, which, although sometimes inaccurate by the standards of rational analysis, are right much of the time. In contrast, the rational mind works slowly and thoroughly. It is capable of delaying gratification, weighing alternatives, and making long-range plans.

3. *The experiential mind thinks in holistic terms.* If you had to jump out of the way of a car bearing down at you at high speed, you wouldn't be calculating the speed of the car, reading its nameplate, or studying its trim. In order to process information rapidly and act expeditiously, your experiential mind sacrifices analysis and detail to size up the overall picture. This holistic assessment has another big advantage as well: it can keep you

Figure 6.1
How the Experiential and Rational Minds Work: A Point-by-Point Comparison

Experiential Mind	Rational Mind
1. Learns directly from experience	Learns from abstract representations
2. Thinks quickly; primed for immediate action	Thinks slowly, deliberately; oriented toward planning and consideration
3. Holistic	Analytic
4. Thinks in terms of associations	Thinks in terms of causes and effects
5. Closely connected with emotions	Separates logic from emotions
6. Interprets experience and guides conscious thoughts and behavior through "vibes" from past experiences	Interprets experience through conscious appraisal of events
7. Sees the world in concrete images, metaphors, and stories	Sees the world in abstract symbols (words and numbers)
8. Experienced passively and automatically (as if we are seized by our emotions)	Experienced actively and consciously (as if we are in control of our thoughts)
9. Experiences its beliefs as self-evidently valid ("experiencing is believing")	Requires justification by logic and evidence ("give me proof")
10. Pays attention only to outcome	Pays attention also to process
11. Thinks in terms of broad categories	Thinks in terms of finer distinctions and gradations
12. Operates in different modes corresponding to specific emotional states	Highly integrated and more internally consistent
13. Changes slowly (with repetitive or intense experience)	Changes rapidly (with the speed of thought)

from losing the forest for the trees. But there is a corresponding disadvantage: sometimes you may think the trees are all alike when they are not. Moreover, a single vivid detail can determine a person's holistic impression, as when someone decides not to like you because of the color of your skin or the sound of your accent. Such generalizations, under the direction of the experiential mind, contribute to prejudice.

4. *The experiential mind thinks in terms of associations.* Let's say your father often beat you when you were a child. Your experiential mind will become sensitized to people like your father. As an adult, when you meet someone who looks or talks like your father, you may well become irrationally angry or frightened in the person's presence. You may then search for a reason for your reaction, and, searching hard enough, you are likely to find one, which will convince you that your reaction is rational.

Whereas your rational mind makes logical connections between cause and effect, your experiential mind makes arbitrary connections between things that have similar features, typically external features that are quickly and easily identified.

Still, the experiential mind is not as foolish as it might seem. In fact, it sometimes makes essential discriminations long before the rational mind would awaken to an opportunity or danger. Maybe people who sound gruff and nasty really do tend to be harsh; the experiential mind knows that such people have been unkind in the past and expects them to be so in the future. Most of the time you are right to avoid encounters similar to those that have felt bad in the past, since such feelings often are harbingers of issues important to your well-being. A sound intuition can protect you from getting involved with someone who might harm you. That is why the experiential mind is still in business after all these millennia of evolution.

5. *The experiential mind works hand in hand with emotions.* Your experiential mind not only interprets events but also seeks to manage the emotions you feel. Its fundamental purpose is to maximize pleasure and minimize pain, to produce pleasant feelings and avoid unpleasant ones.

Your experiential mind is connected with emotions in another way as well. The more emotionally aroused you are, be it severe stress, frustration, fear, anger, or even ecstatic pleasure, the more you come under the sway of your experiential mind. For example, if you are tense, you are more likely to interpret another person's defensive behavior as threatening and as calling for an aggressive, rather than a sympathetic, response. For this reason, you need to be especially conscious of your experiential mind and to monitor carefully the way it works whenever you are emotionally aroused.

6. *The experiential mind interprets experience and directs action and conscious thoughts through "vibes."* The intimate connection between your emotions and your experiential mind is most evident in the way your ex-

periential mind makes the links between past and present situations by activating feelings, or "vibes," associated with memories of past experiences. I use the word "vibes" reluctantly because of its association in the 1960s with trusting feelings to the exclusion of intellect. However, I have not been able to find a better word. Vibes, as I use the term, refer to subtle feelings of which people are often unaware. Such feelings guide thought and behavior far more than people realize. As a result, it is extremely helpful to become aware of your vibes in different situations as a way of improving your constructive thinking.

I can best make clear how vibes work to influence behavior by describing an incident that occurred in a large lecture course I taught. One of the students often snickered during my lectures. I therefore asked her to come to my office, where I questioned her about what it was in my lectures that she found so objectionable. The student looked astonished. She said that she had no idea she was snickering; in fact, she said she liked and admired me and enjoyed my lectures. Apparently, she was completely unaware of the negative feelings she was projecting.

I then suggested that while the positive things she was telling me came from her rational mind, her experiential mind might be making a different judgment about me. I explained that unlike her rational mind, which attempted to size up people reasonably, her experiential mind reacted in an automatic way.

"When you come into a new situation—say, being in this class," I told her, "your experiential mind wants to figure out how to respond to it. So it scans its memory bank for similar situations that happened in the past. If it finds one, it activates the feelings associated with the memory of that past situation. Those feelings may be strong emotions of which you are aware, such as anger or anxiety, or vague sensations of which you are unaware, as may be the case here. If you remember the past experience as pleasant and fulfilling, you will experience positive vibes in the present. If you remember the past experience as painful or threatening, you will experience negative vibes in the present. Either way, those vibes will influence the way you think and act. Although you *think* you are reacting directly to the present situation, your experiential mind may really be reacting to a past situation. So when you snicker at me without being aware of it, you may really be snickering at someone you knew previously."

I then asked the student if she would be willing to try an experiment in which she would monitor her vibes during my lectures. The idea of an experiment appealed to her, and she agreed. Two weeks later she returned, eager to share her observations. She said that at first she had difficulty detecting her vibes, but with practice she learned to do so. She discovered that she had feelings of discomfort and hostility whenever I described my research. At those moments, she said, I reminded her of her father, whom she resented deeply for being so involved in his work that he had little time for her. Once she made that connection, she realized that her reaction was inappropriate in the present situation. Her experiential mind had identified me with her father because I seemed very much involved in my research, but her rational mind realized that I was also very different from her father in that I always had time for my students. Her bad vibes, once made conscious and looked at critically, disappeared. After that, there was no more snickering, and the student became attentive in class and friendly toward me.

This incident shows how important it is to be in touch with your vibes, as well as to react constructively when someone else's vibes appear to be disrupting your relationship with that person. Imagine what would have happened if I had taken offense at this student's snickering and publicly embarrassed her by confronting her in class. The student would then have had an objective reason to be hostile to me, and the conflict could well have escalated into an ongoing feud. Such conflicts occur all the time between spouses, parents and children, and employees and their supervisors.

Most people have no inkling of how much their conscious thinking and behavior are influenced by their vibes. They come up with rational explanations for conscious thoughts and behavior that are actually triggered by vibes. The result is that if you are unaware of these subtle feelings, they will dominate you without your having any idea of what is happening. By becoming aware of your vibes, you can gain greater control over your life.

7. *The experiential mind thinks about the world in concrete images, metaphors, and stories.* It is said that a picture is worth a thousand words. This is so because pictures speak mainly to the experiential mind, whereas words and numbers speak mainly to the rational mind. Words and numbers break things down into components through rational analysis; pictures enable an entire tableau to be perceived at once. By relying mainly on concrete, nonverbal imagery, the experiential mind can process information holistically and with great rapidity. (Compare the time it takes to read a novel with the time it takes for the same story to unfold in a movie.)

Although they speak different languages, the rational mind and the experiential mind are each capable, to some extent, of understanding the language of the other. The rational mind can use pictures for rational analyses, as with maps, diagrams, and medical illustrations. Conversely, emotionally laden word pictures and metaphors can be an effective way of reaching the experiential mind. To say that a flooded river is like a raging beast carries a very different message from saying that it crested 3.53 feet over its banks. The Bible uses images, metaphors, and stories to reach the experiential mind. So do politicians. Ronald Reagan, "the great communicator," was recognized for his ability to shape national opinion with word pictures, just as Winston Churchill and Franklin Roosevelt had done in their time. Poetry, painting, music, and drama all require the artist to use both minds in a coordinated way, combining experientially instigated inspiration with careful planning to create rich experiences for others. In Part IV you will learn how your rational mind can speak to, as well as learn from, your experiential mind through the medium of fantasy and imagery.

8. *The experiential mind is experienced passively and automatically, as if it were not under our control.* We experience our rational minds consciously and actively. We know what we are thinking, and we believe that we are in control of our thoughts. This, to some extent, is an illusion, for, as we have just seen and as will be further demonstrated later, vibes triggered by the experiential mind can influence our rational thinking. With regard to our experiential minds, we harbor the opposite illusion. Because the experiential mind operates automatically and unobtrusively at a preconscious level of awareness, we normally don't know that it exists. Unaware of the active interpretation that goes on all the time in the experiential mind, we assume that our emotions are direct reactions to external reality rather than to our automatic interpretation of that reality. In other words, we feel as if we are "seized" by our emotions and that what we think has nothing to do with what we feel.

When we express the angry feeling that "So-and-so is an SOB," we do not realize that we have anything to do with creating the feeling. Coming, as it were, from outside us, the feeling takes on a reality and a validity of its own. "I wouldn't feel so strongly if it weren't true," we say to ourselves. "I'm so angry that my judgment must be right." Others then react the same way. "Look how aroused she is," they say. "Something really serious must have happened to get her so riled up." Thus our feelings often become their own justification, in others' eyes as well as in our own.

The credence we give to "sincere" emotional displays can be exploited by people who feign or exaggerate their emotions, thereby giving themselves or their positions an air of authenticity. For example, people who are insecure about their ability to influence others rationally or to hold their own in a discussion sometimes find that they can put others on the defensive by becoming indignant. Instead of asking why the person is being unreasonable, people too often fall for this tactic, thinking, "If she feels so strongly, she must have a good reason. What have I done to offend her?" Imagine how much better we could resolve conflicts if we took responsibility for the role of our interpretations in our emotional reactions instead of assuming that they are automatically triggered by external events.

9. *The experiential mind's beliefs are experienced as self-evidently valid.* According to the experiential mind, experiencing is believing. We say, "You can't really understand this unless you've experienced it." This is in marked contrast to the rational mind's beliefs, for which we demand proof by logic and evidence. We do not say, "This solution to this math problem is correct because I've experienced it in my heart." We say, "Give me objective proof." Information produced by the rational mind is considered provi-

sional; it can easily be replaced by new information backed up by more convincing evidence. The same is not true for the kind of information produced by the experiential mind, for there is nothing more convincing than experience itself.

Along with other characteristics of the experiential mind, self-evident validity motivates people to engage in rapid, decisive action. When you feel something strongly, by God, you *know* you are right, and you can act with conviction. Unfortunately, however, the fact that experiential beliefs are inherently convincing does not make them valid. Nor does feeling something more strongly make it more true. The "vibes" we get, which are based on past experience, may not apply to the present situation. But the experiential mind is not equipped to make such discriminations. Thus, the self-evident, powerfully convincing nature of experiential beliefs may lead to inappropriate conclusions and actions that, at best, fail to achieve their goals and, at worst, are the source of destructive behavior. The women who screamed for draconian punishments for rapists and the man who bought a restaurant without looking into its finances felt no need to evaluate their beliefs critically, but they would eventually have to reckon with the consequences of acting on those beliefs.

This tendency to treat experiential thoughts as self-evidently valid gives us insight into difficult social problems. For example, prejudice persists so stubbornly, in part, because people feel no need to question their opinions. It is simply something they strongly *feel*, and therefore they assume it is right. How can you argue with convictions based on strong feelings? Those who seek to convince people of the need to change established policies must reckon with the fact that "experiencing is believing." You cannot expect to get much reaction to a rational assessment such as this: "If we run all our existing nuclear power plants for 100 years, there is a 5% likelihood that one serious accident will occur that will kill 100,000 people and leave a lot of cancer-causing chemicals in the air." But let one real mishap such as Three Mile Island happen, one not nearly as bad as the projected disaster, and suddenly people are aroused to action.

10. *The experiential mind pays attention to the outcome, not the process.* When I took a calculus course in an army training program for engineers, I thought I had done well in the final exam. Imagine my chagrin when I found I had gotten a zero on one of the big problems. Looking more closely, I was outraged at the way I had been graded. After figuring out the whole problem correctly, I had carelessly copied the answer incorrectly on the line where it was to be filled in. I protested to the instructor:

"Does it make sense to grade somebody just on the answer, and not credit their understanding?"

"Yes, it does," he said. "Let's assume you are an engineer who builds a bridge. The bridge collapses, and you go through your song and dance about knowing how to design bridges and about how you simply made a careless error. How convincing would that sound? In the Army Engineers, where lives are at stake, there is no room for careless errors."

I had to agree with him. There are clearly times when the outcome is all that matters.

Good outcomes produce good feelings, and the experiential mind makes a chain of associations back from a good feeling to a good outcome to the action that preceded the good outcome. It does not stop to ask whether the action logically caused the outcome. Unlike the rational mind, it does not have the capacity to do so. Likewise, if the outcome is bad, the experiential mind looks for acts, decisions, or people to blame. Most of the time, this crude process works reasonably well. However, it can also be a source of inappropriate beliefs, feelings, and behavior.

Being actively aware of this focus on outcomes and critically evaluating the misinterpretations it can lead to are useful steps in improving your constructive thinking and understanding others' destructive thinking. Still, before you relegate your experiential consciousness to the status of mere irrationality, think again. You do not have time to go through a reasoned calculus about everything you do, and you have little else but outcomes to guide you in situations where the process is too complicated to analyze. Sometimes your experiential mind is right, and sometimes it is wrong. It is up to your rational mind to know the difference, and to be able to do so, it is helpful to know how the experiential mind operates.

11. *The experiential mind thinks categorically instead of making fine distinctions.* Whereas the rational mind is capable of fine gradations of thought, the experiential mind thinks more crudely, dividing the world into a limited number of categories. This is what I described in Chapter 2 as "categorical thinking." In order to make quick decisions and take rapid actions, the experiential mind cannot be bothered with fine discriminations. People are judged to be friends or enemies—if not the one, then the other. At times of strong emotion, especially in a crisis, there is no middle ground. Unfortunately, this tendency to lump things together without making finer distinctions can lead to large blunders. In particular, categorical thinking is a major source of prejudice.

The television documentary "Who Killed Vincent Chin?" described how an unemployed automobile worker clubbed a young Chinese-American man to death after a quarrel in a bar. Blaming the Japanese for the loss of his job, the assailant saw anyone who looked Asian as a sinister competitor. This tragic incident dramatically illustrates the way categorical thinking sweeps aside important distinctions. The killer assigned all Asians to one category, which, in his experiential mind, was associated with feelings of frustration and resentment. Note also that the killer thought and acted as he did at a moment of heightened emotionality and when the operation of his rational mind was impaired by his drinking. Categorical thinking, like other ways of thinking characteristic of the experiential mind, is intensified when strong feelings are aroused, and controls are reduced.

12. *The experiential mind is divided into "multiple personalities" that emerge in different emotional states.* The rational mind is highly integrated and tries to be internally consistent. In contrast, the experiential mind takes on different personalities associated with different emotions. These emotional states are like modules that program the experiential mind to perceive, interpret, and act in certain ways. In particular, they put the individual's mental and physiological state into a few basic crisis modes: one for attack, one for flight, one for withdrawal, and one for increased engagement in the world. Thus, a person who is angry sees and hears differently, thinks differently, remembers different kinds of events, and acts differently from a person who is frightened, sad, or happy. In effect, the person is a different person when in a different emotional state.

The documentary film *The Thin Blue Line* relates the way many people in a Texas community went into a particular defensive mode in response to their anger at the killing of a policeman. The police department and the local government experienced this act as a threat to their sense of order, authority, and power—a threat they felt could be assuaged only by executing somebody for the crime. They chose to prosecute Randall Adams, presumably because he was from out of state and was old enough to be executed, even though the evidence pointed to another suspect, David Harris. Initially sentenced to death, Adams served more than a decade in prison before the error was exposed. What is noteworthy about this case is that it was not just one person reacting at one instant, but an entire law enforcement system that stayed in an irrational anger and attack mode at first and then in a defensive mode, over a period of years. It also illustrates the seeking of targets by the experiential mind, giving it something against which it can take immediate action.

13. *The experiential mind is slow to change.* Although the experiential mind assesses situations and initiates action more rapidly than the rational mind, the opposite is true when it comes to changing existing beliefs. The rational mind can adapt to new information with the speed of thought or verbal communication. Present new evidence or a better argument, and the rational mind can instantaneously change its opinion. Simply explaining the solution to a mathematics problem can produce instant learning.

Now think of a child who learns, by burning his hand on the stove, that the stove is too hot to touch. That lesson, learned from experience, must be unlearned by experience. Try telling the child, "Don't worry about touching the stove now; it is cool." Even if the child knows this, he will still flinch because the experiential learning is more powerful than the verbal knowledge. It will take a lot of trials of touching the stove to put aside the anticipation of a painful experience.

You cannot just talk people out of their fears. It does little good to say to someone, "Why are you afraid of talking in front of a group? It's stupid; it's irrational." Such experiential beliefs can change over time, however, when the person has given enough well-received speeches. If you are going to change the experiential mind, you must do it through experience or through special techniques that accomplish the same thing, which you will learn about in Part IV. Even though intellectual understanding of an irrational fear can occur quickly, the person will likely need to reexperience the feared situation (in reality or in imagination) a number of times without its feared consequences before he or she will be convinced experientially.

Addictions are a prime illustration both of the persistence of experiential beliefs and of how they can be changed. After all that has been invested in medical treatments for addiction, we are now learning that people get into, as well as out of, addictions chiefly as a result of accumulated life experience. The experiential mind solidifies and maintains habitual behavior— bad habits as well as good. People usually *know* that the long-term effects of smoking, overeating, or drug and alcohol abuse are harmful, but at the time of the behavior, they *experience* the short-term positive rewards, not the long-term negative ones. As long as the habit is supported by positive vibes, it will be difficult to break, especially when alternatives to the habit (such as grappling with difficult problems in life) have negative vibes attached to them.

Normally, beliefs held by the experiential mind change only after repeated experiences that run counter to those beliefs. Thus, in most cases, it takes considerable time for a person to be convinced that an addictive habit no longer is as rewarding as it once was and that other ways of living (such as taking care of one's health, working productively, having good relationships with people, and staying out of trouble with the law) can be more rewarding. However, a single experience can also produce change if it is of sufficient emotional intensity to dislodge existing experiential beliefs. Thus, some ex-addicts speak of "epiphanies," moments of heightened self-revelation, that caused them to give up their habits instantaneously. Typically, though, these dramatic moments are best understood as a culmination, or crystallization, following a long period of experiential learning that has prepared the person (consciously or otherwise) to move on.

Chapter 7

Why We Do What We Do: A New Understanding of Human Behavior

Understanding how your experiential and rational minds work opens up a whole new way of thinking about human behavior. The two minds are a centerpiece of this new approach, which I refer to as *cognitive-experiential self-theory* (CEST).

You are already familiar with a major part of CEST—namely, the attributes of the experiential mind, as presented in Chapter 6. Building on this detailed portrait of your "second mind," CEST will give you a radically new picture of how the unconscious mind influences your everyday actions, feelings, and conscious thoughts. With this knowledge, you should be able to understand human behavior in a more meaningful way than ever before.

As explained in the last two chapters, people continually interpret reality through the automatic, unconscious workings of their experiential mind, which operates by its own rules. CEST explains how and why this happens. For each of us, the interpretations made by the experiential mind add up to a model of reality. The foundation of this sense of reality is a set of implicit, basic beliefs that give us a picture of what we and the world are like. We construct this model automatically to make our lives as emotionally satisfying as possible.

Four basic beliefs are the cornerstones of our picture of reality. Depending on the kinds of experiences we have had, these beliefs may be either constructive or destructive; that is, they may either help or hinder us in satisfying four basic needs that are related to them and are essential to our well-being. Knowing the four basic needs and beliefs will give you a broad understanding of yourself and others that you can use to identify sources of stress, frustration, and conflict.

Keep in mind this all-important principle of CEST: our unconsciously held beliefs are mainly generalizations derived from experience. Sometimes experience leads us to make faulty generalizations, so that we try to satisfy our needs in ways that are not effective and may, in fact, be very costly. For example, we may expend a lot of energy avoiding experiences we have learned to fear instead of creating new experiences to teach ourselves that our fears are no longer appropriate.

A NEW VIEW OF THE UNCONSCIOUS

When I emphasize the influence of unconscious processes on our thinking and behavior, Freud's name immediately comes to mind. In fact, CEST does not contradict Freud's insights so much as put them into a new perspective and draw attention to an important source of unconscious thinking of which Freud was unaware. According to CEST, Freud was right when he said that much human behavior is unconsciously driven; he just emphasized the wrong unconscious. The deep, dark unconscious that Freud depicted, seething with primitive passions that are inaccessible to the conscious mind, is not nearly as important as Freud made it out to be. CEST acknowledges its existence, but only in limited realms such as dreams and psychotic delusions and hallucinations.

There is no need to resort to a deep, dark unconscious to explain the irrationalities of everyday life, for the real source of much of our irrational behavior lies much closer to home. The experiential mind, which automatically interprets reality and influences our feelings, behavior, and conscious thoughts, does operate unconsciously, but it is not so mysterious or inaccessible as the unconscious that Freud depicted. I therefore use the term *preconscious* to describe the realm in which the experiential mind operates.

The preconscious mind is not as far removed from consciousness as is the unconscious mind. It is more directly connected with reality, more adaptive, and easier to access and communicates more readily with the conscious mind. Freud referred to the preconscious as merely a way station between the conscious and unconscious minds. I see it, on the contrary, as the key to most human functioning. For this is the middle ground—not conscious and rational, yet not utterly detached from consciousness and rationality—in which the experiential mind interprets reality and directs our responses to it.

As we saw in the last two chapters, experiential thinking is not always adaptive; it does not always lead us in constructive directions. But it is often adaptive and certainly more adaptive than the unconscious thinking Freud described—and easier to modify as well, since it can be brought to conscious awareness by paying careful attention to it. The prospects for therapy and self-improvement, then, are more hopeful than in Freud's somber scenario. You really can redirect your experiential thinking, and you don't need years of psychoanalysis to do it.

Paradoxically, Freud's ideas may have gained such wide acceptance, in part, because people are so accustomed to believing that they act rationally in their own interest. When forced to acknowledge behavior that is unconsciously driven, people assume that only some bizarre, irresistible force could make them act that way. Thus, we have embraced Freud's image of repressed primitive impulses, of an unconscious mind driven by sexual and aggressive impulses that constantly threaten to burst through the fragile constraints of civilized life.

If Freud portrayed the unconscious in overly stark, negative terms, some mainstream psychologists err in the opposite direction by disregarding the unconscious altogether. They still believe that most human behavior is under conscious control. Actually, Freud and the traditionalists are both making the same mistake. They are ignoring the evolution of the experiential mind over millions of years.

Unlike lower animals (such as insects), whose behavior is "hard-wired" in the form of instincts, higher animals adapt to their environments by learning from experience. The experiential mind directs the behavior of the tiger that hunts for food and the dog that tends the sheep. This mind has continued to evolve in human beings who, with greater brain capacity, can use it in more complex and powerful ways. Human beings also have developed a rational mind that makes use of conventionally agreed-upon signs and symbols and rules of logic and evidence, but this mind has evolved over a much shorter period of time.

The first humanlike creatures are believed to have appeared on the earth more than 4 million years ago. By the most liberal estimate, the rational mind as we know it today, with its use of writing, mathematics, formal logic, and scientific thinking, has been in operation for no more than 5,000 years. That's 5,000 against 4 million. It would be strange, indeed, if an experiential system that has stood the test of time for 4 million years were abandoned in favor of a rational system that has been in existence for less than 5,000 years. Nature does not give up its hard-won gains so easily. Moreover, the rational mind is not an unmitigated blessing. It may yet be the destruction of all living things on earth.

Apparently, it is our existential fate to have two selves, one derived from our biological past, the other from our cultural and social conditioning. Unless we learn to harmonize them, they are destined to chafe against each other. Freud failed to consider that an unconscious mind that was responsible for the survival of living creatures for so long could not simply harbor primitive sexual and destructive passions, but must have an intuitive wisdom of its own.

Freud believed that we would be conscious of all our thoughts if we did not resist awareness of the ones that are threatening (usually because they have to do with sex or aggression). Modern cognitive psychology, on the other hand, has recognized that it is natural and adaptive to be unaware of most of our thoughts. We are normally unaware of the operation of the experiential mind, not because it contains unacceptable thoughts that we would just as soon not know about but because it operates automatically, and there is no reason for us to be aware of it. Consciousness is the exception rather than the rule. How could we function if we had to think consciously every time we crossed the street or greeted someone?

When I say that we are who we are because of how we automatically think and what we believe, I acknowledge a substantial debt to such cognitive therapists as Aaron Beck, Albert Ellis, Donald Meichenbaum, and Martin Seligman, who emphasize how our automatic, preconscious interpretations of reality influence our feelings and behavior. If you went to a cognitive therapist, he or she would seek to bring to the surface your illogical, automatic, self-defeating thoughts, so that you could see how those thoughts contribute to whatever problems in living you are having. You could then learn to correct those biased, maladaptive ways of thinking.

Although current cognitive therapies are based on sound insights about the way we think, feel, and act, their scope is limited. They recognize some of the rules by which automatic thoughts operate but do not consider how they are organized into an overall system. These therapies, effective as they are, are mainly pragmatic approaches to dealing with specific emotional and behavioral problems. CEST provides a more general theory and expands the application of cognitive-therapy techniques to the whole range of everyday life problems.

Furthermore, unlike the cognitive therapies, CEST recognizes that the experiential mind has a wisdom of its own and that it can teach the rational mind as well as learn from it. For this reason, the self-help and therapeutic techniques made possible by CEST are not limited to cognitive ones. Rather, they encompass the range of procedures used by practitioners of various therapies and original ones as well, including intuitive and imagistic procedures that address the experiential mind in its own terms.

YOUR PERSONAL BELIEF SYSTEM

According to CEST, the job of your experiential mind is to construct a model of the world that permits you to live as emotionally satisfying a life as is possible under the circumstances. If you did not have a preconscious model of the world, your life would be completely chaotic. You would be paralyzed by disorganization and overwhelming anxiety and unable to function.

Your model of the world includes the following four basic implicit beliefs, which develop in association with four basic needs.

FOUR BASIC BELIEFS AND FOUR BASIC NEEDS

The four basic implicit beliefs are associated with the fulfillment of the following four basic needs: (1) to obtain pleasure and avoid pain; (2) to make sense out of your experience; (3) to have satisfying relationships with others; and (4) to think well of yourself. Most well-known theories of personality emphasize one or two of these needs. CEST, on the other hand, takes all four into account and regards them as equally important. Each has the capacity to dominate the others.

Understanding your four basic needs and the four basic beliefs associated with them is helpful in becoming a better constructive thinker. These basic needs and beliefs indicate what your experiential mind is trying to accomplish and how successful it is in doing so.

Here are the four basic needs and the beliefs directly related to their fulfillment:

Need 1: To maximize pleasure and minimize pain.

Belief Dimension 1: That the world is benevolent versus malevolent.

It is hard to imagine a more fundamental need than the need to seek pleasure and avoid pain. Consider the time and expense people expend on pleasing their stomachs with enticing foods and their ears with pleasant music. Consider people's willingness to sacrifice their health, fortune, good name, and freedom to experience pleasurable feelings or to escape from unpleasant ones through the use of alcohol or drugs. Think of the millions of dollars society spends on medications such as analgesics and decongestants that reduce physical pain, as well as on tranquilizers and antidepressants that reduce mental pain. Think of the power of the sex drive. Throughout history, people have risked their reputations, fortunes, careers, and even their lives in order to satisfy this drive.

For a long time Freud thought the "pleasure principle" was the key to all human behavior. So did modern learning theorists, who used rewards and punishments to reinforce behavior. Human beings as well as other animals have pleasure and pain centers in their brains. A rat will press a lever until it drops with exhaustion, just for the reward of having its pleasure center electrically stimulated.

To maximize pleasure and minimize pain, it helps to believe that the world is benign rather than malevolent. Within reasonable limits, good constructive thinkers look at life in optimistic terms. If you believe that the world will reward you more than it punishes you, if you experience the world as smiling on your desires and aspirations, your confident outlook will help create the opportunities and outcomes you desire. That does not mean you should be naively optimistic. Someone who is so convinced of the world's perfect benevolence as to take foolish risks, such as exposing oneself to AIDS, may find that the world can be quite malevolent after all. On this as well as the other three dimensions of belief, it is not necessarily best to be at the optimistic extreme. Rather, it is adaptive to have beliefs that allow for flexible coping with situations. There is a time to be optimistic, and there is a time to be pessimistic.

Need 2: To maintain a coherent, realistic set of beliefs that allows one to operate effectively in the world.

Belief Dimension 2: That the world is predictable, controllable, and meaningful versus chaotic and meaningless.

In the depression of the 1930s, a man who had worked hard and sacrificed for years to save money lost all but fifty cents in a bank failure. Handing his two young sons a quarter each, he said bitterly, "Go buy yourselves ice cream cones. That'll teach you what you get by saving." This man was profoundly disillusioned, for he had just seen some of his most strongly held beliefs invalidated, such as "It is better to save than to spend" and "Sacrifice will be rewarded." Think of all the people in the United States who have seen the verities they grew up on challenged by unprecedented economic and social dislocations: high inflation, the loss of jobs in traditional industries, the sexual revolution of the 1960s, the women's and gay movements. Think of the "true believers" in communist countries who had to come to terms with the cataclysmic repudiation of Marxist–Leninist ideology. Such shocks to a person's belief system can lead to bitterness, anxiety, mistrust, and sometimes suicide. It can also lead to personal growth and a constructive reformulation of ones belief system.

People will often do whatever they can to maintain their belief systems, which are the maps by which they navigate the world. Without a model of what the self and the world are like, of what is true and not true, and of what is right and wrong, a person's life would collapse into chaos and overwhelming anxiety. That is why people, such as religious martyrs and heroes, are often willing to suffer great pain, torture, and even death rather than violate their most cherished beliefs, which is an example of the need for coherence dominating the pleasure principle.

To operate effectively, you need to believe that the world is manageable, predictable, and controllable, at least within certain practical limits. If you wake up every day wondering whether there will be an economic crash or a nuclear war, you will not feel secure enough to solve problems effectively. Many people do have these worries, which arise from the turmoil of our times, not to mention ordinary concerns about losing one's job, having an automobile accident, being mugged, and so forth. Nonetheless, good constructive thinkers can acknowledge real uncertainties and still have sufficient faith in "the order of the universe" to try to understand what is happening in their lives, so that they can act effectively.

Need 3: To have close emotional relationships with others.

Belief Dimension 3: That people are supporting, accepting, and trustworthy versus threatening, rejecting, and untrustworthy.

Infants are dependent on their mothers for life itself, let alone happiness. Infants deprived of love and human stimulation wither away and die despite receiving adequate food and shelter, a condition known as marasmus. Children will sacrifice their need for pleasure, their need for coherence, their need for self-esteem, and they will even willingly suffer abuse to maintain a relationship with a loved one.

It is difficult to fulfill your need for relatedness with others unless you believe that others are worth relating to. Although indiscriminate trust can get a person in trouble, good constructive thinkers regard people, until proved otherwise, as decent and trustworthy. Favorably inclined toward others, they are themselves trusting and helpful, which, in turn, brings them the love and support they desire.

Need 4: To have high self-esteem.

Belief Dimension 4: That one is competent, good, and worthy of respect and love versus incompetent, bad, and unworthy of respect and love.

The next time you find yourself tossing and turning in bed, examine the source of your distress. The likelihood is that it was a blow to your self-esteem. When I have had people keep daily records of the events that produced their strongest positive and negative emotions, self-esteem came up more than any other issue. People are extremely sensitive to assaults on their self-esteem, and they glow with pride when their self-esteem gets a boost. Nearly all of us are concerned with our appearance, our performance, and what other people think of us. Being rejected hurts us deeply, not only because it deprives us of an intimate relationship but because we interpret it as evidence that we are not worthy to be loved.

Insecurities about self-esteem sometimes lead to alcohol, drug, or food addiction. Such insecurities, experienced as a sense of dishonor or disgrace, are a major cause of suicide. Some cultures, such as Japan's, have even ritualized this practice. Self-esteem is apparently a need that can override the need to avoid pain and even to preserve one's life.

You will have high self-esteem if you believe that you are a good person, that you can accomplish worthwhile things, and that you merit the love and trust of others. If you project this upbeat image of yourself to the world in realistic ways, people are likely to respond to you in a manner that helps you maintain your positive self-evaluation.

KEEPING YOUR NEEDS AND BELIEFS IN BALANCE

Good adjustment requires that you keep the four basic needs in balance. We do this all the time, with hardly a thought. Let us say that you are a well-adjusted, married person. You will automatically balance your need for pleasure against your need for relatedness by taking into account both your own desires and those of your spouse. You may decide to stay home with your sick spouse rather than go to a movie because, under those circumstances, you care more about your spouse's well-being than about your immediate pleasure. Under other circumstances, you may assert your own desires. Your flexibility about such choices, deciding when it is reasonable to place your needs first and when to attend to someone else's, is a sign of good constructive thinking. A more insecure person might always sacrifice his or her own desires out of fear of losing the spouse's affection or else might always do as he or she wishes without regard to the other person's feelings.

It is important to recognize that the four basic needs serve as checks and balances against each other. Consider the relation between the need to maintain high self-esteem and the need to maintain realistic beliefs. Normal, well-adjusted people, it has been found, typically think more highly of themselves than is justified objectively—but only to a moderate degree. If you should estimate your virtues *too* highly, your needs to have a realistic and coherent model of the world and to maintain satisfactory relations with others would motivate you to moderate your inflated self-evaluation. The same goes for other forms of unrealistic thinking. If you think you can make a living without doing any work, the pain of an empty stomach will provide a strong incentive to correct your thinking. If you maintain unrealistic beliefs about people that lead people to reject you, your need for relationships will motivate you to question those beliefs. Under normal circumstances, then, the simultaneous operation of the four basic needs serves to keep any one of them from getting out of hand.

Sometimes, though, the balance breaks down, such as when people overcompensate for a need that has been severely threatened. This overcompensation may be part of a temporary, healthy readjustment. For example, after a loved one dies, you may withdraw for a time from normal interactions, thus sacrificing everyday pleasures in living and rewarding contacts with others in order to repair your sense of reality and heal your loss.

There are, on the other hand, times when the overcompensation is more than temporary and escalates into serious maladjustment. Consider the case of a man who has received a terrible blow to his self-esteem, such as being fired from a job or jilted by a lover, and consequently has an intensified need to prove that he is a worthy person. He may become so obsessed with defending his self-esteem that he takes offense at the slightest pretext and alienates others. Then, even more desperate to prove his worth, he may take unreasonable risks and enter into foolhardy ventures that threaten his well-being and that of those who depend on him. Eventually, all his other basic needs may go unmet in the service of attempting to fulfill the one that has been deeply frustrated.

HOW YOU ACQUIRE YOUR BASIC BELIEFS

You acquire your four basic beliefs, like any other beliefs in the experiential mind, mainly through emotionally significant experiences. This learning begins in childhood, with the kinds of repetitive family experiences that will be discussed in Part III. As you grow to adulthood, your basic beliefs are refined and modified through reality testing and new experiences. However, certain early beliefs that were forged in the fire of strong emotion tend to persist in your experiential mind despite disconfirmation by other experiences. As a result, you may have irrational beliefs buried in your experiential mind alongside more accurate beliefs. These early beliefs can be activated by emotional experiences reminiscent of the situations that originally gave rise to them.

Children are prone to misinterpretations, including accepting responsibility for things that were not their fault. Childhood, therefore, is a fertile ground for acquiring irrational beliefs. For example, children do not understand death as an impersonal act of nature. A child who misbehaved shortly before a parent's death may believe that the parent died as punishment for the misbehavior. A child who was angry at a parent shortly before the parent's death may believe that he or she killed the parent. These beliefs often persist in a person's experiential mind even in adulthood, when the person's rational mind knows better. As a result, the person may be at a loss to understand the irrational, unremitting guilt he or she feels at the later death of a loved one.

HOW YOUR BASIC BELIEFS CHANGE

Because the four basic beliefs are the foundation of your understanding of yourself and the world, changing any of them will significantly alter your personality. Moreover, since the four beliefs are interrelated, changing any one of them will often change the others as well. Such changes can pose a threat to one's stability. It is natural, therefore, to resist even positive changes. You may fear that, if any of your basic beliefs is invalidated, your accommodation to reality may fall apart like a house of cards from which a foundation card has been pulled. (That is what happens, for example, to people who suffer from acute psychotic breakdowns following unexpected distressing experiences.) Understandably, then, people will go to great lengths to create experiences that confirm their basic beliefs. This can explain why people keep repeating self-destructive behavior.

When basic beliefs do change, it is usually the result of repeated experiences over a period of time. For example, a young person may emerge from a cruel or neglectful family into a loving one or from a crime-ridden neighborhood onto a college campus. An adult may be released from a political prison or concentration camp to a community that treats him with respect or from a psychologically punishing marriage into a nurturant one. Even then, it may take a long struggle for the person to relinquish old beliefs that had proved right in the past.

As a rule, only extremely potent events can produce *sudden* changes in basic beliefs. Such experiences may be traumatic, leaving a person (temporarily or permanently) broken and embittered. Or they may produce a positive transformation, as in the case of a love relationship that gives a person an important new source of relatedness, happiness, and self-esteem.

A wonderful story of a transforming experience of love is told in Victor Hugo's novel *Les Misérables*. The protagonist, Jean Valjean, had known only a life of brutality. He had learned to trust no one and to look out only for himself. After escaping from prison, he was befriended by a priest, who gave him food, shelter, and, most important, trust and respect. Valjean responded to these acts of kindness and support by stealing the priest's silverware. He was soon apprehended by the police, who did not believe him when he said the priest gave him the silverware. They brought him to the priest to identify the stolen goods. The priest, greeting Valjean warmly, chastised the police for not believing the poor man's story. Valjean could not believe what he was hearing. He was shaken to the core, for there was no room in his belief system for such behavior. Yet, he could not deny what his eyes had seen and his ears had heard. The result was a dramatic change in a basic belief. Valjean emerged from the experience a transformed person who knew for the first time the significance of love.

SENSITIVITIES AND COMPULSIONS

A fighter pilot named George flew missions escorting bomber fleets in World War II. On one of those missions, while he was scanning the sky on his right (the direction from which enemy fighters were expected), a German plane dove out of the sun on his left and nearly shot his left wing off. He bailed out and was fortunate to escape with his life. From then on, recollection of the situation repeatedly intruded into his daytime thoughts and even into his dreams. When he went on missions, he found himself automatically searching the sky for enemy aircraft on his left. In the instant when he spotted anything on the left, whether it was a bird, a weather balloon, or a friendly aircraft, he had a strong impulse to fire at it. George knew full well that by being overly attentive to attacks from the left, he was making himself vulnerable to attacks from the right. This knowledge, however, did not rid him of his *sensitivity* to objects appearing on his left and of his *compulsion* to fire on them. The reason, of course, was that his objective knowledge was in his rational mind, whereas the thinking that automatically guided his feelings and behavior was in his associationistic experiential mind.

I use the term *sensitivity* to refer to an exaggerated belief that certain kinds of experiences are dangerous or threatening. Sensitivities are sore spots; they refer to situations or individuals that "get to you," that "bug you," that your friends recognize they must avoid if they wish to keep you from getting upset or angry. I use the term *compulsion* to refer to behavior that is driven and inflexible and that serves, momentarily at least, to prevent or reduce anxiety. Sensitivities and compulsions often come linked in pairs. The sensitivity automatically produces anxiety, and the compulsion is an automatic response that reduces the anxiety.

Sensitivities and compulsions evolved because in primitive situations they promoted survival. When an animal, such as a rabbit, has a threatening experience, such as being pursued by a hawk, it experiences anxiety. From that point on, whenever a hawklike creature appears, the rabbit automatically does whatever it did before that removed the danger and anxiety such as running under a bush. Obviously, this is highly adaptive.

We, too, become automatically sensitized to situations that have evoked anxiety in us in the past; the greater the anxiety, the greater the sensitivity. Furthermore, the greater the anxiety, the more the sensitivity spreads beyond the original situation to others that remind us of it. Like other animals, we are driven to make responses that have successfully reduced anxiety in the past. *Compulsion*, in this sense, means something much broader than the private rituals, such as compulsive hand-washing, that psychologists have identified as abnormal behaviors. As I use it here, the term refers to a much broader range of behaviors that are maladaptive but not necessarily abnormal, as they are very common.

Sensitivities alert us to danger, and compulsions give us tried-and-true ways of reducing the anxiety following the perception of danger. However, when a particular threat has been very great, the person may become so obsessed with it that he or she becomes insufficiently attentive to other threats, as in the case of the combat pilot. Sensitivities and compulsions can be maladaptive in another, more common way as well—namely, when they are generalized to situations that are not realistically threatening or when they persist, even though the person is no longer exposed to the original threat.

Ralph, for example, feels threatened by authority figures because he had a very authoritarian father. As an adolescent, he rebelled against his father's domination and developed into a highly independent young man. This way of behaving was advantageous under many circumstances. However, Ralph now has trouble advancing in his career because he antagonizes his superiors. No matter how reasonable they are, he interprets their actions as attempts to dominate him, and he therefore is less than cooperative. His problem is that he has a sensitivity about taking orders from anyone and a compulsion to be always in charge.

Most sensitivities and compulsions are developed in childhood and are therefore unlikely to be appropriate for the kinds of situations people experience in adult life. They are stubbornly resistant to change because of the emotionally charged circumstances in which they were formed and the habits of thought and behavior that developed around them. As a result, people continue to behave in rigid, counterproductive ways whenever situations trigger their sensitivities and compulsions.

One of the hallmarks of constructive thinking is flexibility. When people react compulsively to potentially threatening situations, their behavior has a driven, inflexible quality. It is in sensitivities and compulsions, therefore, that we find the source of much destructive thinking. Because sensitivities and compulsions are hot spots of destructive thinking, learning to recognize and interpret them can be helpful to you in understanding your own and other people's destructive thinking and in improving your own constructive thinking. With this in mind, let us examine four cases of sensitivities and compulsions. The first two are relatively ordinary, mild cases, and the last two are more extreme.

June Porter: The roots of jealousy. June's sensitivity is to experience jealousy, and her compulsion is to avoid competition at all costs. As a child she felt it was hopeless to compete with her sister, who was a beautiful child. Her parents continually fussed about her sister and ignored June. They would regale visitors with the wonderful things her sister had done, and they would do it right in front of June, as if she were not there. Once June became so distressed that she blurted out, "Mother, why don't you ever say anything nice about me?" Everyone looked embarrassed, and her mother said, "Why, dear, you know that isn't true. We are just as proud of you as of your sister." From then on, June either remained silent or excused herself whenever her parents boasted about her sister. Although she no longer showed it, it hurt her deeply whenever she heard her sister praised. She said she felt as if someone were sticking a knife into her heart.

June developed a sensitivity that remained with her into adulthood. Now, when she hears others praised, she gets unpleasant vibes and feels like attacking the recipient of the praise. She doesn't show her distress, but her jealousy bothers her because she knows it is unreasonable. She would like to be able to enjoy other people's success rather than resent them for it. She long ago gave up competition because she felt she could never win enough to satisfy her, and it hurt too much when she lost.

Mike Smithers: Losing in the clutch. Mike, a professional tennis player, was widely recognized for his unusual talent and great competitive spirit. Although he put his heart and soul into every match, he could not make it into the big time. His problem was that he clutched at the critical moments. His extreme sensitivity to both winning and losing was a direct outgrowth of his childhood experiences.

Mike had a brother who was three years older. Both boys excelled in athletics, but the brother's age advantage enabled him to beat Mike at every sport. The brother would rub in his victories by bragging about his natural superiority. This infuriated Mike, who couldn't wait for the day when the age difference would be to his advantage. One day, after his brother listed all the ways in which he was superior, seven-year-old Mike replied, "You're better only because you're older. But don't feel so smart; you'll be dead first."

Not surprisingly, Mike developed a sensitivity about losing in competition and a compulsion to win. This helped him become an exceptional tennis player. Unfortunately, he would get so "revved up" to win the big matches that his excitement interfered with his performance. Unable to overcome his tendency to clutch at critical moments, he quit tennis and found another, less competitive occupation, in which he was able to do very well.

John Raymond: A dwindling empire. John was a highly successful businessman who made his first million before he was thirty. Ten years later, he lost everything. Try as he might, he was unable to make a comeback. How did it happen? Why did the talent that had worked so well before not work again? The answer can be found in John's sensitivity and compulsion.

John was raised in a family where he felt deprived of his parents' love. His father was a harsh disciplinarian who often beat the children. If they cried, he beat them for crying. Since his mother was much more attached to his sister, John had no one to turn to for support. John grew up determined to depend on no one but himself. He became sensitized to situations that had the potential of making him feel dependent, and he developed a compulsion to take care of himself and be in control all the time. In short, he became a take-charge person: if there were orders to be given, he made sure he was on the giving, not receiving, end. This way of thinking helped him become a successful entrepreneur.

Things began to go wrong for John when his wife divorced him. Tired of being controlled, she had found someone who treated her as an equal. John was devastated. Here was a recapitulation of the rejection he so dreaded. As commonly occurs, the added threat intensified the compulsion. John's reaction was to become even more controlling. As a result, he alienated his best employees, who quit. Their defection further threatened his sense of control, and the more threatened he felt, the more controlling he became. When he met with prospective clients, he no longer listened to them as carefully as he used to. He felt he knew the answers better than they, and he did not hesitate to tell them so. They no more appreciated being controlled than his wife and his employees had, so his accounts dwindled.

John was a highly intelligent, energetic person who had all the attributes of a successful entrepreneur. In many respects he was an excellent constructive thinker. He was confident, optimistic, liked people, and was generally liked by them. He was, however, a terrible constructive thinker in the domain of his sensitivity and compulsion. When this domain became increasingly threatened, his area of poor constructive thinking spread out until it encompassed his whole life.

Joyce West: Too hard to please. Joyce was raised by an overprotective mother. As a young child she was very successful, excelling in school and winning awards for her dancing. Her mother invested herself heavily in Joyce and lavished praise on her for her achievements. Despite being successful and knowing her mother loved and admired her, Joyce was an unhappy child who had a low opinion of herself. The problem was that her mother's love was conditional. To retain her mother's love, she had to do what her mother wanted, not what she wanted. She was living out the Faustus story: she could have everything she desired, but at the price of selling her soul.

Her sensitivity and compulsion arose from these circumstances. The sensitivity was about being loved, which her experiential mind interpreted as dangerous. As desperately as Joyce needed and wanted close relationships with people, she feared them because she equated love with the loss of individuality. Her compulsion was to please others. She believed that people could not love her for herself but only for what she did for them. This belief led her regularly to sacrifice her needs to satisfy others.

After graduating from college Phi Beta Kappa, Joyce married a physician who was attracted to her intelligence and nurturance and appreciated the rapport they had with each other. Still, even with a distinguished career as a teacher and a husband who was deeply devoted to her, Joyce felt neither successful nor loved. Her sensitivity to losing her individuality if she loved anyone prevented her from being able to accept love. Her compulsion to please others kept her from enjoying success because she saw herself as a sham and a failure, doing as others wished rather than fulfilling her own needs.

These examples illustrate several key points to keep in mind as you learn to be more conscious of your own and others' sensitivities and compulsions:

1. *Sensitivities and compulsions are based on generalizations from past experiences.* In this respect they are like any other beliefs and habitual responses maintained by the experiential mind.

2. *Sensitivities and compulsions vary in their breadth.* Those that are narrow in scope have limited and usually not very harmful effects; often they can be dismissed as idiosyncrasies. Those that apply to a broader range of events, however, can have a devastating impact. Mike Smithers, the tennis player, did suffer major frustrations as a result of his sensitivity and compulsion, but by changing careers he was able to put these behind him and get on with his life. But John Raymond's sensitivity and compulsion to control people generalized to all aspects of his life, thereby creating serious problems for him.

3. *Sensitivities and compulsions tend to become more intense and to generalize more broadly when threat is increased.* As a result, sensitivities and compulsions often bring about the very outcomes that the person is attempting to prevent. For example, John felt he had to be in control of all situations in order to protect himself from the rejection he feared. By carrying the control too far, he brought about the rejection—first by his wife, then by his employees, and finally by his clients. Each rejection threatened him in his sensitive area, which led him to intensify his efforts at control (his compulsion). Each such attempt led, in turn, to further rejection, which gave him even less control than before. June Porter's sensitivity to hearing other people praised also backfired on her. By withdrawing and becoming irritable following someone else's good fortune, she alienated people, who were then less likely to admire and compliment her. In line with these examples, see if you can identify situations in which acting out your own compulsions only makes your problems worse.

4. *Sensitivities and compulsions, as instances of destructive thinking, are often associated with rigid, superstitious, and categorical thinking.* To take

one example, Joyce West, who felt helplessly trapped in the pursuit of others' approval, engaged in personal superstitious thoughts such as, "If good things happen, they are sure to be balanced by bad things" and "If you want something too badly, that will keep it from happening."

Categorical, all-or-none thinking can be seen in all four cases. Mike had only two categories for rating his tennis performance: coming in first or being a loser. There was nothing in between. John viewed himself as either fully in charge of events or utterly dependent. For June, when other people were praised, it meant she was nothing. Experientially, she could not accept that she could be considered an admirable, competent person at the same time as someone else was being praised. Joyce, too, thought in either-or terms: either pleasing someone else or pleasing herself. Because she did not think it possible to do both at the same time, relationships with people were always problematic for her.

Since rigid, personal superstitions and categorical thinking are often associated with sensitivities and compulsions, you can use this information to help you locate areas of sensitivity and compulsion in yourself and others. What you should look for are specific subjects that, when touched on, are apt to intensify rigid, personally superstitious and categorical thinking.

5. *Sensitivities and compulsions are pockets of poor constructive thinking that are not necessarily characteristic of a person's constructive thinking in general.* Overgeneralizing about a person on the basis of some sensitivity or compulsion the person exhibits in certain situations is itself a form of destructive thinking that can negatively prejudice your relationship with that person, including your relationship with yourself. It is unwise to form an overall opinion about a person until you see how the person behaves in a variety of situations. Sensitivities and compulsions can be highly specific and not at all representative of a person's usual way of behaving. More important, don't get down on yourself just because you don't think constructively in all ways and all circumstances. Who does?

THE BASIC TASK

Sensitivities and compulsions are extremely important in the therapeutic approach that CEST offers. They account for many of the problems in living that psychoanalysts mistakenly believe are caused by unconscious conflict. Sensitivities and compulsions lie at the root of much emotional maladjustment, destructive thinking, and maladaptive behavior. This way of understanding problems in living is simpler, explains a wider range of behavior, and leads to more hopeful, more effective approaches to therapy than the Freudian notion of unconscious conflict.

Freud saw repression—the forcing of unpleasant memories and unacceptable thoughts into the unconscious—as the key to emotional and behavioral problems. He believed, therefore, that the task of therapy was to lift repressions—to make the unconscious conscious. In contrast, CEST maintains that, since adjustment is mainly determined by the experiential system, adjustment problems must be solved by procedures that reach that system. Making the unconscious conscious is, at best, only a first step; at worst, it merely turns a neurotic without insight into one with insight. George, the fighter pilot, was well aware of what caused his sensitivity and compulsion, but that did not make them go away.

The essential task in much therapy is to eliminate sensitivities and compulsions. According to CEST, problems in living can best be resolved through corrective experiences, either in reality or in fantasy, that modify old experiential beliefs so as to accommodate new, more adaptive ones. In this way, the person's preconscious view of the world is reorganized and the distress caused by contradictory beliefs is relieved. Insight can be helpful in this process, but it is rarely sufficient, and it is not always necessary; people sometimes get better without knowing why.

PART II

Constructive Thinking and Success in Living

Chapter 8

Constructive Thinking and Success in the Workplace

I previously argued that the intelligence of the experiential mind is often more important for success in the workplace than the intelligence of the rational mind. In this chapter, I present the evidence that led to this conclusion.

To illustrate the difference between intellectual intelligence and constructive thinking in the workplace, let us begin by considering the performance of a supervisor who has high intellectual intelligence but is a poor constructive thinker.

Mr. Roberts got to be a supervisor by being intelligent, conscientious, and well organized. But he cannot cope with Mr. Smith. Because Mr. Smith is disorganized and forgetful, Mr. Roberts considers him "a fool and a burden to the organization." If Mr. Smith's job were not protected by civil service, Mr. Roberts would fire him. Since he cannot, he shows his contempt by needling and embarrassing him at every opportunity. Mr. Smith, tense and resentful whenever Mr. Roberts confronts him, now does an even poorer job than before. Mr. Roberts then interprets Mr. Smith's greater confusion and reduced efficiency as further evidence that he is incompetent.

Whatever his IQ score, whatever abstract intelligence Mr. Roberts displayed while rising to his present position, he knows little about constructive thinking. He has adopted a course of action that gives him an emotional release but results in the worst possible long-term outcome. How much more constructive it would be for him to consider what Mr. Smith might be contributing to the organization in spite of his faults and to try to help him remedy his deficiencies or else find a way to use his talents in a less sensitive position.

Obviously, what I call intellectual intelligence (the kind measured by IQ tests) can be an important asset on the job, especially a job that requires complex mental tasks. Without it, Mr. Roberts would probably not have been in a position to mismanage Mr. Smith. In fact, as we saw in Chapter 2, a person's IQ does give some indication of how successful a person is likely to be in the workplace. However, it is far from the only factor contributing to success, and it is often outweighed by other considerations, such as practical intelligence, social skills, and emotional adjustment, all of which are influenced by constructive thinking.

George Vaillant, a prominent psychiatrist, followed up ninety-five Harvard students from their college years to middle age. Those with the highest IQs in college did not earn the most money if they became business executives, and they did not achieve the greatest productivity or recognition if they became professors. That is, a person's IQ did not predict the person's success in work—or, for that matter, in other spheres of life, including mental health, physical health, and family and social relationships. Since most people who go to Harvard are well above average in IQ, the study's findings suggest that, beyond a certain minimum level of intelligence, other factors contribute more to success in highly competitive, demanding occupations.

At the other end of the social and intellectual ladder, Vaillant and a colleague followed up more than 450 disadvantaged inner-city men over a comparable period in their lives. They found that the ones who stayed employed most regularly were not the ones with the highest IQs but the ones who, earlier in life, had exhibited an ability to solve practical problems in living. Thus, practical skills may count for more than intellectual intelligence in bringing about successful performance in low-level as well as high-level jobs.

More recently, researchers at Boston College and the University of Illinois followed the careers of eighty-one class valedictorians for ten years. They found that these top achievers in school had not duplicated their academic success in the world of work, where they were achieving at only an average level. The chief researcher, Karen Arnold, concluded that success at work requires different skills from the ones that are most important for success in school; for example, in work situations it is important to be practical, to control your emotions, to cope adequately with frustration, and to be able to work effectively with people.

You may wonder how these studies, which found no advantage to high IQs in the workplace, can be reconciled with the study I cited by Lewis Terman, in which it was found that children with exceptionally high IQs performed considerably better than average as adults, with a disproportionate number making notable contributions. The reason for the differnce in the findings is that the comparison in Terman's study was between much more extreme groups than in the other studies. The high-IQ group in Terman's study included people in the upper 1% of the population. People who are that bright are, not suprisingly, more likely to make unusual mental contributions than others. Very few of the Harvard students in Vaillant's study or the valedictorians in the study by Arnold and her associates would have made it into Terman's highly selected group. Moreover, Vaillant was comparing Harvard students to other Harvard students, almost all of whom were economically and socially advantaged and above average in intelligence.

The results are somewhat surprising for the study of the valedictorians. However, one should not judge by a few studies. Moreover, in the study with the valedictorians comparisons were made across different kinds of jobs, so it was more difficult to detect differences than if the comparisons had been made within single jobs. By now a great many studies have examined the relations of IQ to performance in specific kinds of work. The overall finding is that IQ is modestly positively related to performance in a wide variety of jobs. However, there are exceptions, with respect to both jobs and individuals. It will be recalled that even among Terman's highly selected participants there were failures. The most reasonable conclusion based on the overall evidence is that a high IQ is advantageous in many jobs but that other abilities and attibutes, including motivation, social competence, practical intelligence, emotional adjustment, and creativity, are often as important, or more important, depending on the nature of the job. As you will shortly see, in the research program conducted by my associates and myself, constructive thinking has been demonstraed to be particularly important, very likely because it underlies several other attributes important for success in a wide variety of positions, including thinking in ways that promote effective action, emotional adjustment, and social competence.

In an article by Bibi Wein on constructive thinking, here is how one couple was described as bouncing back from a business failure:

Maggie and her husband were in their early twenties when their small business failed. Forced to declare bankruptcy, they were left destitute with an infant to care for. Many factors contributed to the failure, including bad luck, bad judgment, and bad advice, and they could have overgeneralized and focused exclusively on any of these factors. They could have blamed themselves and each other, concluded their partnership was doomed and other people couldn't be trusted, and started on a downhill spiral that would soon have ended their marriage. In fact, Maggie's husband took it personally at first, blaming himself for things he could not have controlled, and viewing himself, at twenty-four, as a total failure who would never amount to anything.

As Maggie saw it, however, they'd made some mistakes they would never make again, and they had no time to sit around being miserable. She found clerical work she could do at home while caring for the baby, changed the way they managed their finances, and convinced her husband that in a few years they would be solvent enough to forge new careers—which is exactly what happened.

The difference between Maggie and her husband was not one of IQ. What enabled Maggie to chart a path to success was a combination of positive thinking, realistic adaptation, and resourceful action—all aspects of constructive thinking.

"SUPERACHIEVERS": WHAT MAKES THEM SO SUCCESSFUL?

The concrete payoffs of constructive thinking were well illustrated in a special survey I carried out in conjunction with the magazine *Personal Selling Power*. It came about after the *New York Times* ran an article that featured my research on constructive thinking. The response to the *Times* article was overwhelming; I was besieged with calls and letters requesting further information. One of the calls came from Gerhard Gschwandtner, publisher of *Personal Selling Power*, who proposed that we do a study on the constructive thinking of "superachievers."

Gschwandtner was in touch with about fifty people who had outstanding records of achievement. Many were multimillionaires with national or international reputations. I jumped at the chance to learn how good these extremely successful individuals were at constructive thinking and whether or not they were as successful at the game of life as they were in business. So we compared these "superachievers" with a group of 200 sales and marketing executives selected at random from the readers of *Personal Selling Power*. I call this comparison group "average executives." However, judging from their incomes, they are achieving considerably beyond the average person.

The results of the survey were striking. On all of our measures of success in living, the superachievers rank high—higher, in almost all cases, than the average executives. All are millionaires, with half having a net worth of over $5 million and one-third earning at least $1 million a year. (The average executives have a median net worth of $200,000, and most have an annual income of $40,000–$80,000.) The two groups work equally hard, but the superachievers have advanced more rapidly in their careers, enjoy their work more, and are, understandably, more satisfied with their accomplishments. Part of their success seems attributable to their superior skills in dealing with people, particularly their sensitivity to other people's needs. Although both groups prefer friendly cooperation to aggressive competition, superachievers are more influential, more popular, and better able to command the loyalty of others.

On the personal side, both groups place a high priority on family life, but superachievers spend more time with their spouses and children and are somewhat more satisfied with their marital, sex, family, and social lives than average executives. In addition, they have a generally higher level of emotional adjustment and physical health. In particular, they experience less anxiety and depression and are more adept at managing anger. They have less trouble sleeping and report fewer psychosomatic symptoms, such as headaches, stomachaches, and muscle pains. They also have somewhat fewer illnesses and fewer accidents resulting from carelessness. Overall, superachievers are more satisfied with their health than average executives and more frequently feel exhilarated, "on top of the world," and bursting with energy. They find more meaning in life and have a greater sense that they are fulfilling their potential and contributing to society.

These are significant differences. Bear in mind, though, that only half the people to whom we mailed questionnaires returned them. Although this is better than the usual response rate of about 30%, some of those who did not respond may not have liked what they thought their responses would reveal about them (even anonymously), especially in areas of their lives about which they were less proud than their business success. Most likely, then, the superachievers who sent back questionnaires are better adjusted than superachievers in general; the same is true, although to a lesser extent, for the comparison group, itself composed of individuals who are above average in adjustment and achievement. Obviously, not all multimillionaires are good constructive thinkers. Howard Hughes made a mess of his life, and many other people who have been financially very successful have not enjoyed similar success in the social realm, in their family lives, and in their achievement of personal happiness and fulfillment. Nonetheless, the superachievers who answered the survey give us a useful and inspiring model of effective human beings, people who have attained inward as well as outward success.

How Superachievers Think More Constructively

Given that superachievers get more out of life than average executives, it is of great interest that they are also better constructive thinkers. On almost all scales of the Constructive Thinking Inventory (CTI), the superachievers significantly outdid the comparison group. The largest differences between the two groups were in the three most comprehensive categories of constructive thinking: global constructive thinking, emotional coping, and behavioral coping.

Here is an inside look at how superachievers think, broken down into the six components of constructive thinking measured by the CTI. (You can refer to Chapter 4 for more complete descriptions of these categories.)

Emotional coping (the ability to take failure, disapproval, and negative emotions in stride). Within this broad category, superachievers most outdistance average executives in coping with disapproval and with negative emotions generally. Superachievers have confidence in their decisions and don't worry too much about others' disapproval or rejection. They are also less likely than others to dwell on past misfortunes or future threats over which they have no control. Nor do they overreact or overgeneralize as much as others do when things go wrong.

Behavioral coping (action orientation, reasonable optimism, and planning). The largest difference between the two groups is in action orientation. Although both groups are considerably above average on this trait, superachievers are much more action-oriented than the comparison group. In fact, they are more action-oriented than 90% of the population. More than anything else, their constructive thinking consists of determining how they can solve problems by effective action. When faced with a challenge, they roll up their sleeves and address themselves to the task. If they make a mistake, they correct it as quickly as possible so as not to lose momentum. They tend to let bygones be bygones and move on from there.

Categorical thinking (all-or-none, black-and-white thinking). Here there is little difference between the two groups. Superachievers are relatively free from the rigid, judgmental thinking that makes it hard to get along with different kinds of people, accomplish tasks, and solve problems effectively. They don't think people are all good or all bad, completely competent or incompetent; they recognize shades of gray They make business decisions flexibly and are open to compromise. Average executives are also superior in these abilities; in fact, they are only slightly more prone to categorical thinking than superachievers.

Personal superstitious thinking (mental games by which people prepare for bad outcomes by expecting them to happen). This is another area where superachievers stand out. They are influenced far less by personal superstitions than either average executives or people in general. When something good happens to them, they don't think it will be balanced by something bad. Likewise, when something bad happens, they do not assume that more bad things are likely to follow. Nor do they believe in good and bad omens. They are able to accomplish more than most people do because their thinking is more realistic and less pessimistic.

Esoteric thinking (conventional superstitions and occult beliefs). When it comes to conventional superstitions (such as not wanting an office on the thirteenth floor), superachievers score just slightly better than the comparison group. These garden-variety superstitions have little impact on achievement, except when taken to extremes.

Naive optimism (unrealistically positive expectations). Superachievers are somewhat less naively optimistic than average executives. Interestingly, however, both groups score *higher* on this trait than most people do. Notwithstanding the real risk of bad judgment and unwise decisions, positive thinking apparently is, on balance, beneficial in the business world, insofar as it generates in oneself and others confidence, enthusiasm, energy, and a willingness to take risks.

CONSTRUCTIVE THINKING AND SUCCESS IN A VARIETY OF OCCUPATIONS

To obtain more generally applicable findings about the kind of thinking that makes for success, my associates and I have begun to study successful achievement in different occupations. Thus far, we and others have examined constructive thinking in school administrators, naval cadets, insurance agents, college students in the classroom and in the workplace, and employees at a large state university, including custodians, physical plant people, grounds-maintenance workers, food-service personnel, and clerical personnel.

Constructive Thinking and Stress among School Administrators

School administrators must cope not only with demanding daily schedules but also with the concerns of parents, teachers, and students. They have to prepare budgets based on uncertain resources and represent the school system to the public. What qualities make for success in this demanding occupation?

An extensive study by Michael Green revealed much about how school administrators cope with job-related stress. The administrators reported how frequently certain stressful situations occurred and how distressing they found those events to be. Green found that stress lies largely in the eye of the beholder; what to a poor constructive thinker was a highly distressing event was, to a good constructive thinker, an interesting challenge. For example, budget cuts might stimulate them to reevaluate existing programs and improve efficiency. Again, we see how crucial the experiential mind's interpretations are to the way we react to "objective reality."

The school administrators who were good constructive thinkers experienced less stress, were happier with their jobs, and reported fewer mental and physical symptoms than the poor constructive thinkers. Not only that, but they took on heavier workloads. Good constructive thinkers are apparently able to take on more demanding responsibilities than others do because they find them interesting and challenging rather than distressing.

Among all the components of constructive thinking, the one that best predicted job satisfaction in school administrators was behavioral coping. This makes good sense if you recall that the three main features of behavioral coping are action orientation, reasonable optimism, and purposeful planning. By making work manageable and gratifying, good behavioral coping allows a person to work productively while experiencing less stress than those with poor behavioral coping skills.

Constructive Thinking and Leadership among Naval Officers in Training

Which do you think is most important for success at the U.S. Naval Academy: academic ability, personality, or constructive thinking? This was the question posed in a study conducted for the Naval Academy by researchers at the Center for Leadership Studies. Among a group of upper-level midshipmen, Scholastic Aptitude Test (SAT) scores, which measure academic ability, predicted only classroom grades. Personality traits, as measured by several tests, also had little to do with how the midshipmen performed. Only the Constructive Thinking Inventory (CTI) significantly predicted overall training performance, which included ratings of leadership by senior officers and actual shipboard performance.

Again, among the components of constructive thinking measured by the CTI, behavioral coping predicted performance best. Good behavioral copers learned their academic lessons well enough to pass but were not outstanding students. Their superior skill was reserved for more practical matters: performance in the field, demonstrations of leadership, and establishing satisfactory relationships with others. This is further evidence that standard intelligence tests and the CTI tap two different kinds of ability and that the latter often is a better predictor of success.

Constructive Thinking and Productivity among Insurance Agents

Selling insurance requires a different set of abilities from school administration or military leadership. An impressive series of studies by psychologist Martin Seligman and his colleagues has explored how constructive thinking contributes to those skills. Seligman's Attribution Style Questionnaire (ASQ) tests for an optimistic versus a pessimistic style of interpreting everyday events. Recall that the CTI measures two types of optimism: a reasonable optimism that is part of behavioral coping and an unreasonable ("naive") optimism. Seligman's optimism scale corresponds to the CTI reasonable optimism scale.

Among a group of experienced insurance agents, those who scored in the top half on Seligman's optimism scale sold 37% more insurance than those who scored in the bottom half. When the study was repeated with newly hired agents, not only did those scoring in the top half sell more than those scoring in the bottom half, but less than half as many of them quit or were fired. Consider how much money these findings could save insurance companies in training and turnover expenses. Consider how much time, effort, and grief they could save aspiring agents who are not suited for the job. Selling insurance is a demanding, stress-inducing activity; many who begin do not continue. About three-quarters of all newly hired insurance agents quit during their first three years. Thanks to the component of constructive thinking investigated by Seligman, namely, realistic optimism, we can now predict with some accuracy who will stick it out and turn into effective insurance agents and who will quit or do poorly.

In another study, Seligman's assistants administered the ASQ to nearly 15,000 people applying for sales positions with the Metropolitan Life Insurance Company. Agents who failed the company's own selection procedure but who did well on the ASQ sold as much insurance as those who passed the company's regular selection procedure. Among agents already employed by the company, those who scored high on the ASQ sold much more than those who scored low.

It is evident that different aspects of constructive thinking are more crucial for some endeavors than others. If "positive thinking" is an asset anywhere, it is in sales, where people may have to endure twenty rejections (not all of them polite) for every sale they make. A person who lacks both the emotional insulation and the positive energy that optimism produces will get discouraged before experiencing the necessary taste of success. In addition, an upbeat personality generates enthusiasm in others and thus creates the conditions for success.

"To attain success," Churchill said, "one should be prepared to proceed from failure to failure with undiminished enthusiasm." A salesperson may find that motto inspiring. But to attempt to apply it to achievement in all occupations could lead to disaster. Obviously, there are occupations for which measured caution is more appropriate than unbridled enthusiasm. Among these are military service, police work, surgery, and engineering. You would also want your accountant or legal adviser to temper optimism with caution. Remember, good global constructive thinkers are flexible thinkers. Rather than being inveterate positive thinkers, they adapt their thinking to the situation at hand.

In addition to professors, deans, and provosts who are directly concerned with teaching, research, and administration, a university contains a large number of support personnel. Included are food-service personnel, secretaries, clerical people, grounds-maintenance people, custodial staff, and physical-plant workers. How is constructive thinking related to the work performance of such people, who are probably representative of workers in many large organizations? In order to answer this question, Marissa Nadeau tested a group of 74 volunteers at a large state university. Their age range was 24–64, with a mean age of 41. The information that she obtained included supervisors' ratings of the workers' performance and the workers' responses to several questionnaires, including the CTI, and questionnaires on demographics, work satisfaction and performance, social relations, stress, and physical and emotional symptoms and well-being.

Good constructive thinkers, and particularly those with high scores on behavioral coping and its subscale of action orientation, reported greater job satisfaction and work success than poor constructive thinkers. Of particular importance, they were also rated as more productive than poor constructive thinkers by their supervisors. Whereas productivity on the job was related to behavioral coping, absenteeism was related to emotional coping. Those with poor scores on emotional coping reported more illnesses, more stress, more sleep problems, and more emotional distress than those with good scores, which can account for their higher rate of absenteeism. Good constructive thinkers also reported more satisfactory social lives, more satisfactory intimate relationships, and greater overall life satisfaction than poor constructive thinkers. Constructive thinking was unrelated to the participants' age and education, which suggests that it was also unrelated to their intellectual intelligence.

These results suggest that scores on the CTI can be useful in determining which employees are most likely to be effective in a wide variety of positions. As scores on the CTI are related to productivity, emotional and physical well-being (and therefore absenteeism), and social competence (and therefore ability to cooperate), it is understandable why CTI scores are related to job performance.

Constructive Thinking in College Students: Success in and out of the Classroom

If there is any place where a high IQ should give a person an edge, it is in school. How does constructive thinking compare with IQ in predicting success in school and in the workplace among college students? Petra Meier and I sought to answer this question by testing a large sample of college students. Most of these students held part-time jobs (ten to twenty hours a week) and worked full-time during the summer. As criteria for success or lack of success in work, we included salary, promotions, dismissals, bonuses, and job satisfaction.

Our findings closely paralleled those with the naval officers in training. We found that constructive thinking was related to work performance but not to classroom performance, whereas the opposite was true for IQ. The better constructive thinkers did better on the job, whereas those with high IQs earned better grades in school. As in the study of midshipmen at the Naval Academy, behavioral coping was the component of constructive thinking most strongly associated with success and satisfaction in the workplace. Thus, in both the Annapolis elite and the more diverse environment of a state university, constructive thinking was more strongly associated with "real-life" achievement and IQ with academic achievement.

Although global constructive thinking does not have a strong association with school performance, it plays an important indirect role. We found that students who had low scores on global constructive thinking were unable to perform up to their intellectual potential as indicated by their IQs. Apparently, their poor constructive thinking interfered with the use of their intellectual ability. Clearly, a student who alienates teachers and classmates, who has an overconfident or defeatist attitude, or who becomes emotionally overwrought or even physically ill from stress will be at a disadvantage. Recall our examples from Chapter 3: Paula, who worried so much before examinations that she went to the movies to relieve her anxiety, thus bringing about the failure she dreaded; and Stan, whose naive optimism kept him from taking the courses he needed to succeed.

We found that personal superstitious thinking had a larger impact on classroom performance than any other kind of destructive thinking. Personal superstitious thinkers were particularly likely to perform below their potential as measured by their IQ. This finding is understandable in light of the fact that this kind of superstitious thinking is associated with feelings of helplessness and depression. Seligman, too, found that feelings of helplessness and depression lead to poor school performance. You may recall two examples from Chapter 3: Joe, who could not take pleasure from a successful accomplishment because he was sure it would be followed by a failure; and Brian, who was tolerant of others' errors but unforgiving of his own.

Constructive Thinking and Success in Politics

Our study of college students turned up another interesting finding—students who scored high on naive optimism were more successful than others in the political arena. They were elected to significantly more offices in clubs and organizations than those with lower scores. The same was true of those who scored high on behavioral coping. The lesson to be learned is that if you want to get ahead in politics, you should either demonstrate that you are exceptionally good at getting things done, be a naive optimist, or both. If your record doesn't allow you to claim unusual accomplishment, you may be able to compensate by promising people pie in the sky.

In times of prosperity, you can assure the voters that all is right with the world and that they can go on living as they wish without worrying about the consequences. No matter what the times, you can promise to increase funding for social, environmental, and educational programs without raising taxes. Politics is a kind of salesmanship, and it typically rewards positive thinking.

APPLYING CONSTRUCTIVE THINKING IN THE WORKPLACE

The techniques presented in Part IV for observing and modifying how your experiential mind works are as applicable in the workplace as in life's other arenas. For now, in a more general way, here are some principles of constructive thinking that are useful on the job.

Maintain a problem-solving orientation. In the long run, performing well is the best guarantee of success. It is essential to focus on solving problems—getting things done—and not be diverted by side issues, such as impressing people, protecting your image, or worrying about what others think of you. Research has consistently shown that people who are preoccupied with how well they are doing and how they are viewed by others *are* and *feel* less successful than those who concentrate on the task itself. Remember, the main thing that sets superachievers apart from average performers is that they are more action-oriented. Attention focused on the task, rather than on yourself and what will happen to you if you do or do not get it done, is what gets results.

To promote task orientation in the workplace, good constructive thinkers insist on clear communication about performance criteria and evaluation. People should know what is expected of them. When subordinates do not measure up, a good-constructive-thinking supervisor lets them know exactly how their performance is unacceptable and exactly what they need to do to improve it. For their part, good-constructive-thinking subordinates solicit this information. On both sides of the line of authority, good constructive thinkers take active steps to solve their problems rather than nurse their anger, resentment, disappointment, or despair.

I say more in Part IV about how to develop a problem-oriented approach, as this is one of the most important aspects of becoming a good constructive thinker. With a realistic, nonsuperstitious, task-oriented attitude, you don't have to be brilliant to succeed in life. People of average intellect who are good constructive thinkers are usually more successful in most occupations than people of high intellect who are poor constructive thinkers. A New Hampshire high school principal commented, "I have some kids who are real pluggers and are real kind and work real hard, and I'd put my money on those kids. I'm usually right."

Be a flexible thinker. Different jobs require different skills and attitudes. As noted earlier, a salesperson needs enthusiasm more than caution. The reverse is true of a surgeon, a quality-control manager, or an accountant. An entrepreneur is called upon to take risks more regularly than a midlevel manager, who tends to be rewarded for playing it safe. Still, no one orientation is adequate all the time; both the entrepreneur and the manager must adapt to circumstances and act accordingly. A great military leader— a Washington, a Lee, an Eisenhower—is capable of bold, decisive moves but also knows not to underestimate the enemy and not to neglect essential planning. Naive optimism was the death of General Custer.

This is precisely the advantage of constructive thinking over other highly touted coping strategies, whether in work or elsewhere in life: a good constructive thinker flexibly alters his or her behavior to adapt to situational demands. There is a time for risk and a time for caution, a time for optimism and a time for pessimism, a time to control events and a time to "go with the flow," a time to blame one's behavior and a time to recognize that the situation is responsible.

Pay close attention to interpersonal relationships on the job. Most work (especially in a complex, interdependent organization) involves a subtle interplay of cooperative and competitive relationships. Good management entails regulating these relationships so as to bring out the best in people. If people are working at cross-purposes, if lines of authority are snarled, if communication breaks down into bickering or silence, if certain individuals are bypassed in the process, then good constructive thinking is lacking somewhere along the line.

A good constructive thinker does not label people as good or bad but assesses how to use their skills most effectively and how to make them feel good about themselves and one another. A good constructive thinker takes pains to bolster people's self-esteem rather than threaten it by treating them with disrespect or embarrassing them in front of others. When people are not performing well, the deficiency should be brought to their attention with a view toward improving the work, not demeaning the worker. Mr. Roberts, the supervisor in the story at the beginning of this chapter, would have done well to follow these guidelines in his supervision of Mr. Smith.

Consider a supervisor who has negative attitudes about himself and others. He is an unhappy person who is easily annoyed, so people do not come to him for advice. Indeed, they avoid him. Instead of creating an atmosphere that makes people feel good about themselves, one another, and their work, he looks for someone to blame when things go wrong. As a result, stress throughout the organization is high, morale is low, absenteeism and accidents are high, and productivity is low. No matter how intelligent this supervisor is, no matter how many degrees in business administration he has, and no matter how well he understands the technical requirements of his job, he will be more of a liability than an asset to his firm. His style of management will also be a liability to himself, for it will generate levels of stress that can have a disastrous effect on his mental and physical well-being. Such a person is obviously a poor constructive thinker.

Be alert for illness and absenteeism as signs of stress. Poor constructive thinkers tend to be absent frequently either because they are resentful or because, as you will see in Chapters 10 and 11, they are highly susceptible to stress and, with it, physical illness. Likewise, organizations whose executives are poor constructive thinkers have high rates of absenteeism because of the stress to which their personnel are subjected. It is not enough to say, "Mr. Brown is highly motivated and gets the job done. We need more people like him." If Mr. Brown gets the job done at a high cost in stress, he may show frequent absences and even serious physical illness or emotional burnout later down the line. Furthermore, if he is in a supervisory position, he may provoke absenteeism in his subordinates.

Young people can withstand considerable stress (think of the hospital intern getting little sleep for days on end), but the accumulated effects of stress begin to show when a person gets into his or her mid-forties. The Japanese have been losing so many top executives at an early age, especially from heart attacks, that they are beginning to encourage employees to take more vacations for the sake of the company. It is shortsighted, therefore, for either an individual or an organization to ignore the issue of health and the benefits of constructive thinking as a stress reducer.

Take advantage of serendipity. Life is full of surprises or, if you prefer, random occurrences. If you are receptive to taking advantage of the good things that arise unexpectedly, you will be amazed at how often they occur. Of course, it would be foolhardy to completely count on serendipity, as there is no guarantee it will happen. The point is that you can do too much as well as too little planning. When you try to figure everything out too far in advance, you shut off your openness to new possibilities. Once you become more receptive to the notion that good things may happen unexpectedly, you will feel less stress and have more creative energy. Most important, you will provide space for good things to happen, rather than shut off the possibility.

Chapter 9

Constructive Love

Love is a double-edged sword: it can be a source of ecstatic joy or intense anguish. To love and be loved is one of life's most rewarding experiences. Everyone seeks it, yet it eludes many. For each soul that it warms, it burns another.

Almost half of all marriages end in divorce. Parents lavish devotion on their children, only to have the children turn away from them, complaining they have been unappreciated and unloved. The disappointed spouses and parents then ask, "Where did I go wrong?" They are unable to understand what happened because the source of the difficulty lies not in their conscious, rational mind but in their unconscious, experiential mind.

In this chapter, I try to take some of the mystery out of love. I explain what love is and what it is not and when it is constructive and when it is destructive. I describe the automatic constructive thinking that produces the kind of love that works, and the automatic destructive thinking behind the love that produces frustration and anguish. Love relationships, healthy and unhealthy alike, have their roots in automatic thoughts and feelings conditioned by past experience.

WHAT IS LOVE?

Before we can say what it means to think constructively about love, we need to understand what love is. Everybody thinks love is wonderful, yet what people call love is often a blueprint for a destructive relationship. It is worth some effort, therefore, to look carefully at what a constructive love relationship is and what it is not.

Here, for example, are two relationships, both considered "loving" by the couples involved. Both vignettes have the same beginning:

When Joan and Bob had been going together long enough to consider marriage, they confronted one major issue they had to resolve. Joan, who had grown up in a poor family, wanted a husband who would be a secure breadwinner above all else. She was determined not to spend the rest of her life worrying about how she was going to pay the next month's bills. Bob, on the other hand, was willing to take chances. He was caught up in the adventure and independence of entrepreneurship. Spurning the secure life of working for a steady income, he dedicated himself to a struggling business he had started himself. Joan told Bob that if he wanted to marry her, he would have to get a secure job. She begged him to accept an attractive offer that he had received from a large firm. Bob, visibly shaken by her demand, said he needed time to think it over.

Now, here is the first continuation of the scenario:

When Joan thought further about the situation, she was deeply touched by the realization that Bob was seriously considering giving up his dream so that she could realize hers. It occurred to her that she was looking out only for her own welfare and not considering his. It further occurred to her that if he did as she requested, he would be unhappy and might resent her for using his love to separate him from his dream. She decided she could not do this to him. She would talk it over with him and agree to take the risky course, but only for a limited period that the two of them would agree on. She had a reasonably good job that could carry them through a lean period. If she had to postpone having children for a few years, she would gladly make that sacrifice.

Meanwhile, when Bob thought things over, he realized how much it meant to Joan to be financially secure. He knew she was terrified by the prospect of lifelong hardship. Experiencing a deep feeling of compassion for her, he realized that it was only fair to take her needs into account as much as his own. He decided to ask her if she would be willing to have him pursue the entrepreneurial route for a limited period that they would agree on.

When Joan and Bob shared their views, they deeply appreciated each other's empathy, concern, and willingness to compromise. They now felt more confident that they would be able to count on each other in the future. Each also appreciated that the other stood up, within reason, for his or her needs and would not let himself or herself be pushed beyond a certain point. This was something they admired and respected in each other. Working through this issue made them feel more secure about their relationship, and they set a wedding date in the near future.

Now imagine this second resolution of the story, again beginning after Joan's declaration that she will not marry Bob unless he obtains a secure position:

When Bob thought things over, he realized he would never give up his dream of being an entrepreneur. Since he deeply loved Joan, this posed a considerable problem for him. She was the most attractive woman he had ever known, and he did not want to lose her. The question was how to persuade her to marry him without his having to make a ridiculous sacrifice. He was confident that Joan's concern was ill-founded and that he would succeed in his business venture. He decided on a two-pronged approach. He would work on convincing her that he was a winner and that if she would stick with him, she would not regret it. At the same time, he would shower her with attention and gifts to prove his devotion to her.

From then on, Bob was unfailingly attentive to Joan. At least once a week he sent her roses, and he continually reminded her how much he loved her and that he could not live without her. He assured her that someday he would be very successful and would make her happy by giving her everything her heart desired. All he asked in return was that she show some confidence in him.

Joan, moved by Bob's attentiveness and declarations of love, decided she had been selfish to think only of her own problems. Wasn't Bob right that one had to take some risks to get what one really wanted? If she loved him, she should be willing to put her needs aside for his. What better proof of her love could there be? She imagined a future of great happiness with Bob. She would have everything she ever dreamed about, including an attentive, loving husband who would do anything for her. Thus, Bob's response to their disagreement made Joan feel more secure about marrying him, and she suggested that they set a wedding date in the near future. Bob, ecstatic, sent her a beautiful bouquet with the inscription, "I love you more than ever."

Here we have two couples who are "in love." Which marriage do you think is more likely to succeed? In the first scenario Bob and Joan treat each other with equal respect. Each is concerned about the other's welfare instead of simply trying to get his or her own way. They are willing to sacrifice for each other, but they both also respect their own needs. Finally, they communicate effectively and arrive at a mutually satisfactory resolution that can actually be tested and meaningfully implemented. They not only have a relationship that is grounded in mutual respect, but they have effective procedures for solving problems as they arise.

In the second scenario, Bob gets his way by, in effect, bribing Joan and playing on her guilt. Although Joan believes he will do anything for her, she is clearly mistaken, for when it came to something really important, it did not even occur to him that her desires were as legitimate as his own. Now, if he is not successful in business, will she not feel cheated and betrayed? If he does strike it rich, yet continues to control her subtly by giving her things and appealing to her guilt, how good a bargain is this for her? Is she not being seduced into giving up her autonomy and her capacity for growth—conditions that are bound to reduce her self-esteem? If, in the dim regions of her mind, she senses that he has not been good for her, how is that likely to affect their relationship? My guess is that it will instigate some kind of underground warfare.

Psychiatrist M. Scott Peck, in his popular book *The Road Less Traveled*, defines love as "the will to extend one's self for the purpose of nurturing one's own or another's spiritual growth." Peck's definition "includes self-love with love for the other," since "we are incapable of loving another unless we love ourselves." In fact, he concludes, "not only do self-love and love of others go hand in hand," but "ultimately they are indistinguishable."

Why is this so? People who cannot bestow on themselves the same respect and loving-kindness they give to others (and want from others) are likely to become unhappy or bitter. People who love and respect themselves as well as others, on the other hand, are likely to be happy people, for both self-love and love for others feel good. As I have found in my research, these people also tend to be good constructive thinkers.

According to Peck, constructive love is not so much something you feel as something you *do*. It is an active, deliberate commitment to the welfare of another. What, asks Peck, is the use of having good feelings about a person if you don't do anything to foster the person's well-being? As he puts it, "love is as love does." Peck's concern is that having the right feelings is no guarantee that one will love constructively. When we think of the excesses and abuses that people commit in the name of romantic feelings—jealousy, possessiveness, vindictiveness, violence—we can see that Peck has a point. But I believe his definition is incomplete.

People who act in a way they believe will foster another's welfare without having loving feelings for that person may end up hurting the person they want to help. To take a common example, parents often push their children to achieve in ways that are fulfilling for the parents, not the children. If the child complains, the parents say they are doing it for the child's own good. However, if a parent drives a child to succeed as a business executive or a concert pianist, but this is not the kind of success that brings fulfillment to the child, can the parent be said to have acted out of love? Consider a more extreme example—namely, the medieval inquisitors who killed Jews and heretics, all the while telling their victims, "We're sacrificing your body out of love for your soul." They may have sincerely believed they were acting "for the purpose of nurturing another's spiritual growth," but in the absence of loving feelings almost any behavior can be rationalized as an act of love.

It is not enough to define love by actions alone. Your actions are influenced by the automatic thinking of your experiential mind (of which you may be unaware) and by the feelings it generates. If your feelings are unloving, they may compromise your choice of actions or distort the expression of the actions you choose. You may think rationally that you are acting for the good of another, but the automatic thinking that is actually guiding your behavior may be very different. Quite simply, you may be deceiving yourself.

Let's say you extend yourself for another because you want to be a good person. In that case your good deeds may carry a message (explicit or implicit) such as, "I'm working an extra job to put you through college. That shows how much I love you. And since I'm doing so much for your welfare, dammit, you should show your appreciation by studying very hard." That can have hidden costs for both of you. It puts the other person under a sense of obligation for something he or she may not really want in the first place. Moreover, it can trap you in a joyless task of self-sacrifice as well as leave you frustrated by the other person's failure to appreciate you.

In this way, Peck's notion of "disciplined giving" can become an act of will rather than a spontaneous expression of love. It is admirable to train yourself to behave lovingly no matter what you feel, but it can also be dangerous. You may mean well, but if you derive pain rather than pleasure from giving, the consequences are likely to be destructive. Nobody likes to be hurt, so your experiential mind will play tricks on you if you cause it pain. The result may be that you somehow punish the person for whom you are sacrificing yourself.

The best guarantee that your loving behavior will be constructive is to express it with a loving heart. If you experience satisfaction from observing someone else's happiness and development, you are not going to hurt that person. If you feel that way about someone, your experiential mind will direct you to act constructively on that person's behalf. It is best, therefore, to nurture the automatic thoughts that promote loving feelings as well as constructive actions. As a result, you will enjoy giving and will gain from another person's happiness and well-being, as Joan and Bob did in our first scenario at the beginning of this chapter.

Spinoza, the famous philosopher, wrote that love is "happiness with the object known." He viewed love as an automatic reaction to whatever makes one happy. This is the way your dog or cat comes to love you: feed it, pet it, care for it, and the animal will have loving feelings toward you. For human beings, this way of loving does not necessarily ensure that the love will be constructive. That is why I go beyond that definition to propose this one: *to love is to derive satisfaction from observing the welfare and fulfillment of the loved one.* In place of Spinoza's "I know I love you because you make me happy," I say, "I know I love you because it makes me happy to see you happy."

This feeling for another's well-being is spontaneous and unselfish, and it brings about the loving action that Peck advocates. Instead of "I know I love you because I am aware how much you make life better for me," it says, "I know I love you because when I see you happy and developing in your own right, it brings joy to my heart. Therefore, I will try to further your well-being even if it means taking you away from me." This is the most constructive way to love, even from a selfish viewpoint, because it creates the conditions in which the other person is most likely to have the same feelings toward you.

SOME DESTRUCTIVE FORMS OF LOVING

I now describe some common forms of destructive love that you may recognize in yourself or others. Bear in mind that these manifestations of destructive love are not completely separate and distinct. Often they go together as parts of a complex pattern of maladaptive love relationships

Love as Infatuation

Ann, a senior in college, couldn't get her graduate instructor in history out of her mind. He was so handsome, knowledgeable, and confident in his discipline. One night she woke up after dreaming about him and said to herself, "I know now I'm in love with him." For the next few months she felt as if she were living in "a different world," far above the mundane concerns of school. Finally, overcome with passion, she wrote the instructor a letter confessing her love. He wrote back, "We don't even know each other. Are you sure it is I who has inspired these intense feelings?"

Romantic infatuation is a prime example of the operation of the automatic thinking of the experiential mind. Its power as well as its irrationality are rooted in early childhood experience. Deeply buried in many people's minds is the fantasy of infancy as a Garden of Eden, where one basked in unconditional love. With the passing of childhood, the reality or fantasy of a warm, close relationship with a figure who attended to one's every need is let go with regret, but it remains as an ideal, a wish that one will find someone someday who will fulfill one's dream. The dream may be even more intense and poignant for you if you never really enjoyed such love in childhood, but only imagined it as a possibility and were consumed with unfulfilled longing.

Suddenly, you meet someone who brings the forgotten dream to life, and the world becomes incredibly exciting. He or she is beautiful, intelligent, an image of all you admire. But the image is, of course, illusory, and you soon awake to find a real person with normal human failings. There remains the possibility of developing a partnership that both of you are responsible for maintaining, rather than a ready-made paradise. Whether you realize the potential for achieving a rewarding love relationship depends on what the two of you do to develop it.

In romantic infatuation, we can see the experiential mind supplying the initial energy, the momentum for overcoming personal inertia and making meaningful contact with another person. This initiative can lead to enduring rewards, provided that the rational mind plays its part as well. The evolution from infatuation to stable love is a good example of the two minds working in harmony. It takes the deliberate efforts of the rational mind to direct the journey begun intuitively by the experiential mind along pathways that will open up new vistas rather than lead you over a cliff. If you want a good love relationship, you must work at it with dedication, sensitivity, respect, and discipline in addition to cultivating a loving heart that is the source of deriving happiness from another's well-being.

Love as Need

In *Women in Love*, D. H. Lawrence portrays industrialist Gerald Crich as outwardly successful but inwardly hollow. Carrying on the enterprise his father's ambition had created, Gerald loses his sense of direction after his father's death. For him, life is no more than "a noise in which he participated externally." Desperately hoping to find meaning in life through a love affair, Gerald walks through the night to Gudrun Brangwen's house and enters her bedroom. "I came—because I must," he tells her. "If there weren't you in the world, then *I* shouldn't be in the world, either."

Many people, like Gerald, experience love in terms of need. Their automatic thinking runs like this: "If I need you very much and can't live without you, that proves how much I love you." Such thinking makes an implicit demand on the loved one to fulfill the lover's need to be loved—or else to feel guilty for failing to do so. Love must be earned, even inspired, not demanded. Unmet demands that play upon the partner's guilt feelings promote resentment in the partner, not love. Thus, a desperate need for love that makes implicit demands on another person is its own worst enemy, for it creates conditions antithetical to achieving its aim.

To attain a secure love relationship, one must be secure enough to be willing to relinquish it. Thus, two people who come to a relationship from a position of strength and wholeness can transmit those qualities to each other while maintaining their individual integrity. They can support each other's growth even at the risk that their growth may separate them, for they have their secure selves to fall back on. But when two people come to each other out of a sense of incompleteness and insecurity, they feel compelled to cling to each other, however destructive the consequences, for fear of being thrown back on their inner vulnerability.

Some people, in fact, use love as an all-consuming substitute for a positive engagement with other people and with life itself. As Stanton Peele and Archie Brodsky note in their book *Love and Addiction*, these people love in the same compulsive, driven way that other addicts use drugs, alcohol, or food. They do it for the same reason—because their early childhool experiences did not give them an adequate sense of security, confidence, and self-esteem. Since an addiction is a form of compulsion, CEST helps us understand this driven, love-seeking behavior in the same way we understand other compulsions.

For the emotionally needy person, everyday life events often evoke memories of emotional withholding, abandonment, or cruelty, which trigger feelings of disappointment, frustration, and rage. In the language of CEST, the person has developed a sensitivity to experiences associated with rejection and unfulfilled desire. The experiential mind reacts automatically, directing the person to do things to gain control and thus be protected from the feared occurrences. One person's compulsion may be to plead for verbal reassurances of a lover's devotion ("You don't tell me often enough that you love me"). Another's may be to make sure the lover never goes out alone or makes friends independently.

Does this mean that relationships based on mutually intense needs are doomed? Not necessarily. Given an understanding of their sensitivities and compulsions, such people can control their destructive effects, and, understanding the nature of the experiential mind, they can provide the conditions for mutual growth and appreciation.

Love as Control

The controlling form of love, like the dependent form, arises out of insecurity, but the insecurity is dealt with through an attempt to exercise power. The thinking of the power-oriented lover is as follows: "Because I need you, you have great power to hurt me. I therefore must control you, so you cannot hurt me." Here are three variations on the theme of love as control, three ways in which people exert destructive power over those closest to them. One wonders if Oscar Wilde had such relationships in mind when he wrote the following lines:

> For each man kills the thing he loves,
> By each let this be heard.
> Some do it with a bitter look,
> Some with a kindly word.
> The coward does it with a kiss,
> The brave man with a sword.

Direct control. The controlling lover—in this case typically a man—may exercise outright domination, a practice encouraged by cultural norms that allow for treating women and children as inferior. Sam, for example, is a demanding husband who never lets his wife out of his sight when he is home and insists that he be informed of her whereabouts when he is at work. He dictates how she dresses, how she spends her time, and whom she can see. He explodes with anger when she pays the most trivial attention to another man. Sam values his wife as one might value a prize poodle or a racehorse—as a possession of his, rather than as a worthy, autonomous person in her own right. He masks whatever insecurity he feels with his commanding manner, and he reduces his anxiety by demanding frequent demonstrations of his wife's devotion. If, however, she were to leave him because she could not tolerate being controlled, his vulnerability would be exposed. He would alternately demand that she return, perhaps with threats, and desperately plead for her to come back because "I cannot live without you."

Control through guilt. As noted earlier, a needy, dependent lover may try to keep the loved one tied to him or her with bonds of obligation and guilt. One form of control through guilt is based on desperate need: "I've become so dependent on you that, if you are a decent person, you *can't* leave me, for I'll fall apart without you. Because I'm more needy than you, you should subordinate your needs to mine."

Another variation of the appeal to guilt is "You owe me." Here the lover exercises control by continually being of service to the loved one. "Look how much I've *done* for you," says this controlling lover. "Can't you see how much I love you?" The rest is left unspoken: "I'm doing all this for you, so you should be grateful and give me what I want in return." Charlie, for example, does the chores for his girlfriend while she is at work. As he explains, "I'd madly clean her bathroom for two hours so that she could have more time for herself—anything, *anything* to make her feel loved. So after all this, after cleaning her bathroom down to the last tile, what happens? She explodes in a fit of anger, saying that she has to pay back in guilt the things I've done for her." The girlfriend understandably feels constrained and manipulated by this "love with hidden strings attached."

Imposed dependency. Whereas some controlling lovers bestow lavish favors in order to extort gratitude and guilt from a *stronger* person, others do a great deal to make themselves indispensable in order to keep the loved one weak and therefore dependent on them. This form of destructive love is commonly seen in parents who shower affection and material benefits on their children, with one string attached: "You must fulfill *my* needs." As an example, imagine a parent who desperately wants his or her child to achieve the success the parent never had. The parent, accordingly, rewards the child for developing in the parent's, not the child's, chosen direction. In a Faustian bargain, the parent will do anything for the child, so long as the child becomes the kind of person the parent wants the child to be: "You can have the world; all I ask in return is your soul."

Desperately wanting to be loved, the child faces the dilemma of having to choose between acceptance by the parent and his or her own development toward autonomy and self-fulfillment. The result, all too often, is that the child sacrifices his or her needs and self-respect to please the parent. Ultimately, the child builds up resentment against the parent for robbing him or her of the opportunity to develop into an autonomous, competent human being and may then express open hostility to the parent. This resentment is apt to persist in the experiential mind after the parent has physically left the scene, making it difficult for the child, upon reaching adulthood, to establish secure loving relationships, as love has become a two-edged sword.

THE PARADOX OF LOVE

Love is not a zero-sum game; one person does not win at the expense of another. It is not a traditional business deal in which the object is to get more than one gives. (Indeed, even in business, new approaches are emerging based on the idea that the best bargain is one from which both sides benefit.) If you give love with an expectation of return, you are likely to defeat your purpose. Love with strings attached can be expected to earn resentment, not love. What is destructive for the recipient then becomes destructive for the giver as well.

Likewise, what is constructive for the recipient is constructive for the giver. For when love is given constructively, it creates feelings such as this in the loved one: "I love you and want to make you happy because I deeply appreciate your concern about my welfare, your respect for who I am—not what I do for you—and the encouragement you give me to fulfill my potential. In other words, I know how you are good for me, I love you for it, and I want to be just as good for you."

If you give up the economic calculus ("Why should I do this for you? What will you do for me?"), you can't lose and are likely to gain. If you give without expecting anything in return, then you have nothing to lose by giving, as there is no sacrifice involved. Besides, giving in itself, then, is a source of pleasure. It is as if you were saying, "I will do this for you, and not only is it not taking anything away from me, but I derive enjoyment from seeing you happy." Furthermore, people, by and large, do reciprocate. Getting begets giving, and giving begets getting. Rather than being in competition for a limited resource, you and your loved one jointly "own" a magical resource that returns in greater abundance the more you give it away. Actually, of course, there is nothing magical about the way it works. Most people deeply appreciate relationships that help them grow, and they automatically react with love to those whom they recognize as sources of their happiness and fulfillment. This, then, is the paradox of love: to maximize your chance of a return on your "investment," you do not concentrate on the return. As Joan and Bob discovered in our first scenario, the less you are concerned with getting back what you give, the more likely you are to create the kind of relationship that will give you what you want to get.

This kind of thinking about love exemplifies what good constructive thinking is about. It is problem solving in the best sense of the term because it solves the problem of how to establish constructive love relationships by understanding the problem, as opposed to trying to get what you want by demanding it, offering material or emotional bribes (as Bob did with Joan in our second scenario), or other futile strategies. It is not surprising, therefore, that in the study of college students that I did with Petra Meier (described in the previous chapter), we found that people who were good constructive thinkers had more satisfactory relationships than those who were not.

Having loving feelings helps us thrive and grow. When we have loving feelings, we feel the benefits in the form of enhanced mental and physical well-being. We are happier, healthier, and more accepting and tolerant of ourselves and others and therefore better able to function effectively in everyday life.

CONSTRUCTIVE THINKING IN SOCIAL RELATIONS

Constructive thinking helps us establish better relationships with people generally, not just in intimate love relationships. Everyone wants to be popular, well liked, and respected. Everyone wants to know "how to make friends and influence people." But people often go about it in the wrong ways. Some people think they can win people over by flattery or by giving gifts. As often as not, though, they pick out the wrong gifts because they have not taken the trouble to understand what the other person wants.

With a little constructive thinking, you can come up with a better answer. To have good relationships with people, it is essential to be sensitive to their needs and to work effectively to satisfy them. Recall the four basic needs presented in Chapter 7:

1. To maximize pleasure and minimize pain
2. To maintain a view of the world as predictable, meaningful, and controllable
3. To have close emotional relationships with others
4. To have high self-esteem

If people feel that you are contributing to the satisfaction of these needs (in ways that mean something to them individually), they will feel good in your presence. If they believe that you are creating a good environment for them by making them feel good, showing them respect, and acting in a trustworthy and supportive manner, they will value and esteem you and most will be motivated to satisfy your needs in return.

This all sounds obvious, doesn't it? Many people pay lip service to these precepts, but they are speaking only with their rational minds. Their automatic, experiential thinking runs in a different direction. When people feel insecure about themselves, they view others as potential sources of disapproval or rejection, against which they feel they must defend themselves. They are withdrawn, aloof, or aggressive in the company of others, making others feel uncomfortable in their presence. Instead of building people up (which would be more constructive for all concerned), they put people down to protect their own egos.

To improve their relationships with others, these people need to change their automatic thinking. They need to risk the possibility of rejection in order to gain greater rewards in the long run. They need to realize that many people are as sensitive as they are and that others appreciate (just as they do) someone who is a good listener, is trusting and accepting, is not quick to take offense, and gives them the benefit of the doubt.

If you want people to be more accepting of you, a good place to begin is by becoming more accepting of yourself. With self-acceptance and self-tolerance come acceptance and tolerance of and by others. Study after study has shown that people who are more accepting of themselves are more accepting of others. People are attracted to self-accepting people, not only because self-accepting people are more accepting of them but also because self-accepting people are happy people. People enjoy being with happy people, and they avoid depressed people. People like being with others whose good spirits are infectious. So another thing you can do is develop a positive, optimistic outlook, as long as you don't carry it to the extreme of naive optimism.

There are, of course, general principles of constructive thinking to be considered. If you want to make a good impression on people and be regarded as a valued contributor to social situations, you should be positive toward others, refrain from stereotyping or scapegoating people, view whatever comes up as a problem demanding a practical solution, and be willing to take reasonable risks to attain positive goals. Good constructive thinking is, in part, a social skill—indeed, a composite of social skills.

We should expect, therefore, that good constructive thinkers would turn out to be socially successful individuals. My studies using the Constructive Thinking Inventory (CTI) indicate that this is, in fact, the case. People who score high on global constructive thinking have a more active social life and are more satisfied with the support they receive from others than people with lower scores. Good emotional copers have close, satisfying relationships with people. Good behavioral copers have extensive social networks. Most people who think in personally superstious ways have a limited social life and are unhappy about it. Categorical thinkers have a limited social life but are not distressed about it—perhaps because they are suspicious of people anyway, particularly those who are not "their kind" of people. Over the range of human involvement, from intimate to casual contacts, good constructive thinkers tend to establish more rewarding relationships than do others.

THE RISKS OF LOVE

I have said that constructive love begets constructive love. There is no better insider tip I can give you for investing in human relationships. However, this does not guarantee that, in every single instance, loving others will bring you love in return. It simply says that this is the best shot you have.

Constructive thinking involves a willingness to take risks, but not foolishly, and to learn continuously from the outcomes of the risks you take. Love is no exception. You may offer your love to someone, only to have that person say, "Thank you, but I don't need you. I've found somebody else I prefer." But if you think constructively, you will know that the price of success is the risk of failure. You will be able to take risks and learn from losses without being devastated by them. You will know that not everyone will love you, and that's OK, and you will be prepared to take more risks, confident that some of them will turn out well. In short, you will be a reasonable optimist.

Reasonable optimism is not the same as recklessness. Reckless risk taking might involve making unrealistic choices of partners on the basis of superficial glamour or "come-ons," having so many partners that you are unable to love any of them deeply, or neglecting to take precautions against contracting AIDS. Then, too, if you exercise too little caution, you are likely to meet up with an emotional con artist or someone who is too disturbed to be able to relate maturely to anyone.

It is also reckless to trust another person uncritically. Such unconditional acceptance of another person's behavior is neither to the giver's nor to the receiver's advantage. A constructive love relationship between adults requires understanding, self-respect, discipline, mutual responsibility, and expectations of reasonable behavior. Loving someone may entail challenging the person to acknowledge unpleasant realities, to meet obligations, and to fulfill his or her potential.

That is a far cry from loving someone unconditionally, particularly someone who is emotionally disturbed, irresponsible, or fundamentally incompatible with you. How many times have you heard someone in an unhappy love affair say, "But I thought my love would make him better." This is almost always an unrealistic hope. You have no way of gauging the depth of another person's sensitivities or the tenacity of the self-protective tactics or compulsions the person has developed. If the person lacks the motivation to change his or her destructive thinking, you probably cannot supply it. Even more important, treating someone as a "reclamation project" is itself a disrespectful attitude and is therefore antithetical to a good love relationship, which presupposes mutual respect.

In a relationship between adults, the only person you can reasonably count on changing is yourself. You can work on becoming the kind of person you want to be, and if you change, the other person's behavior may change in response. But don't count on it. You can also respect yourself and your partner and require your partner to treat you with equal respect as a condition for continuing a relationship. That is different, however, from expecting your partner to change in fundamental ways, which will rarely produce anything but disappointment and antagonism.

There is, then, no getting around the need to make prudent assessments of prospective partners in love, just as in business. If you let passion or need overwhelm your judgment, you leave yourself open for emotional or financial exploitation and, at the extreme, physical abuse. To whom can you give yourself safely? You can never know for sure. Nonetheless, as a good constructive thinker you will look to your long-term well-being by taking reasonable precautions to avoid being victimized.

OVERCOMING PAST EXPERIENCE

A person who seems unable to reciprocate constructive love is not necessarily self-seeking and exploitative. The person may, in fact, appreciate the love and want to reciprocate it but may be blocked from giving and receiving love by automatic thinking and vibes derived from past experience that are beyond the person's control. The person may have been hurt repeatedly in love as far back as childhood or even infancy and may have developed a sensitivity that causes him or her to fear rejection or exploitation. As a result, the person may have a compulsion to avoid the risks of emotional involvement. Such sensitivities and compulsions are not usually found in a person who has had satisfying experiences of intimacy early in life. This person, having developed positive vibes about emotional closeness, is free to welcome love that is constructively offered.

Psychoanalyst John Bowlby found that there are three basic patterns of attachment between mothers and infants. In the "secure" pattern, the mother is reliably responsive, and the infant forms a secure attachment. In the "avoidant" pattern, the infant turns away from a mother who is overstimulating, rejecting, or abusive. In the "anxious-ambivalent" pattern, the mother is inconsistent in her responses, and the infant reacts by developing mixed feelings, demanding contact until it is offered and then withdrawing.

These patterns, according to Bowlby, set the stage for the kind of love relationships a person establishes later in life. The secure type, being able to give and receive love in a mutually satisfactory way, is likely to have secure relationships in adulthood. The avoidant type is usually a loner who self-protectively avoids close relationships. The anxious-ambivalent type intensely desires a close love relationship, while fearing it just as intensely. Such a person is likely to be insecure and dependent, continually demanding proof of the loved one's affection, and thereby often alienating the loved one.

Later research, including an extensive study by psychologists Carl Hindy and Conrad Schwarz, confirms the persistence of these three "attachment styles," which strongly influence people's love relationships throughout their lives. So, if you love someone who is avoidant or anxious-ambivalent—someone who never had much love or received it with dangerous strings attached—you may need to be patient and to provide exceptionally convincing demonstrations that your love is different from what the person previously experienced.

The experience that taught me the most about love was a highly personal one—in fact, a life-and-death situation. In Chapter 11, I describe how Alice, my wife, confronted lifelong patterns of destructive thinking that may have contributed to a life-threatening bout with cancer. Alice's life-and-death crisis was also an emotional and spiritual crisis for her and a severe test of our love for each other. We both grew and learned a great deal from this experience, about which I can speak freely since Alice has written in great detail about it in her book, *Mind, Fantasy, and Healing*.

Until cancer struck, Alice and I had what looked like a very good relationship. We had an accommodation that appeared to work well enough over all the years we were together, during which we brought our two daughters to adulthood. It took her illness to bring our relationship to a much more constructive level. To fight her cancer, Alice decided that she had to change the kind of person she was, which meant, in terms of CEST, changing the automatic thinking that had been driving her despairing emotions ever since childhood. Among other steps she took at this time, she began an intensive program of psychotherapy. The test for me and for our marriage was whether or not I could take that journey with her, be as prepared as she was to challenge accustomed beliefs, and willingly accept whatever changes occurred in her and therefore in our relationship.

It became apparent that Alice's childhood experiences, as interpreted by her experiential mind, had led her to develop Bowlby's "anxious-ambivalent" style of attachment. Alice is a prototype of the child who was overprotected and smothered with love—at a price. As a result, no matter how much she was loved, Alice lived in terror that the love would be withdrawn if she dared assert her independence. She didn't feel she could be loved for who she was but only for what she did for others. Even when she was outwardly successful, inwardly she experienced failure, as she felt she was succeeding to please others and not satisfying her own needs.

If this description sounds extreme, bear in mind that these are not the kind of reactions a person can control. The destructive thoughts went on in her experiential, not her rational, mind. Outwardly, Alice was a highly successful person—Phi Beta Kappa in college, much admired as a teacher, well loved as a wife and mother, and highly respected by many. She was elected to important town committees, often becoming chairperson. Using her rational mind, she could relate to people effectively in these roles, and she presented a cheerful, confident demeanor. Inwardly, however, she could not escape the legacy of an overprotective, inconsistent upbringing, the source of the feelings she attempted to suppress by putting up a brave and loving front.

When Alice responded to her cancer by intense self-examination, I faced, along with her, the challenge of assimilating these disturbing insights about our life together. As she became convinced that finding the will to live meant discovering an independent self and going wherever it led (even if it meant leaving me), my love for her was tested in new ways. The largest single test for me was to support her newfound spiritual interests.

Now if there is anything I was not, it was religious or spiritual (although I did have a professional interest in religion and spirituality as they related to constructive thinking). If anything was to test my unconditional acceptance of Alice, this was it. Here she was not being my kind of person. Nevertheless, I learned to take pleasure in the satisfaction she gained from something utterly alien to me. I gave her enthusiastic support: "If this is important to you, go for it. I'll do everything I can to help you go down a path I wouldn't take myself." My supporting Alice's interest in spiritual development not only helped her but gave me a greater appreciation of the value of spirituality and religion. The experience showed me that there are many paths to growth, not all of which are scientifically comprehensible.

This was just one of the constructive changes I experienced by giving unreserved respect and affection to Alice. By losing myself in my desire to help her, I gained as much as I gave. I became a warmer, more open, more giving person which led others to respond to me in kind. This improved feedback from my interactions with people generated positive vibes in my experiential mind, which made me feel better and enhanced the quality of my life. I was then even better prepared to go out and create positive relationships with others. For me, there could hardly have been a more convincing demonstration that love is not a zero-sum game.

In the aftermath of this crisis, my relationship with Alice is closer and more rewarding than ever before. Even though I couldn't put my finger on what was lacking previously, in retrospect I can see the difference. The greater independence, self-esteem, and emotional security Alice has attained have made possible a more genuine and deeper intimacy between us. Love is no longer a double-edged sword for her. She knows she can be loved without having to sacrifice her individuality or think of ways to please me. She knows I admire her for her individuality and would have it no other way. Things are freer between us, with more room to make mistakes or say things that once were points of sensitivity. In our fifth decade together, we have become more trusting, more giving, more intimate, and more affectionate than ever before.

Chapter 10

Better Constructive Thinking Means Better Adjustment and Less Stress

People generally think of emotions as uncontrollable. We want to have good feelings and not have bad ones, but we assume there is little we can do to change our feelings. It seems to us that our emotions have a life of their own, independent of our will. However, as I previously noted, CEST offers a more hopeful view about the control of emotions. As you may recall, according to CEST, emotions are not directly instigated by external events, but by interpretation of events. Logically, it can be no other way. It follows that, by controlling our preconscious interpretive thoughts, we can control our emotions. Since negative emotions are a source of stress, this means that by controlling our preconscious thoughts, we can also control our level of stress. Because this issue is so important, although I have discussed it before, it warrants further discussion with examples to convince your experiential, as well as your rational, mind.

EMOTIONS AND THE THOUGHTS THAT INSTIGATE THEM

When you say, "Kathy made me angry," you are assuming that the emotion resulted directly from an external event—what someone else did. You are aware of the emotion, but not the automatic interpretation. However, feelings cannot arise until the mind takes in what has happened and decides what it means. Thus, when you say, "I am angry because Kathy behaved so irresponsibly," the truth of the matter is that you are angry not simply because of what Kathy did, but more precisely, because you automatically interpreted what she did as bad behavior that deserves some kind of punishment. Had you interpreted Kathy's behavior otherwise, you would have had a different emotion or no emotion at all.

Let us examine this argument further. Consider more closely the way you react to an insult. Without an interpretation of its meaning, an insult is nothing but so much meaningless noise—just sound waves floating through the air and nothing more. If someone insulted you in a foreign language, smiling sweetly all the while, you would probably smile back and think, "What a nice, friendly person." Even if you recognized that a person's words were meant to insult you, your interpretation could lead to a number of different emotions, including anger, fear, sadness, and even happiness or sympathy. Most likely you would automatically think, "He had no right to say that, and he should be put in his place." You would not even have to say those words to yourself. That spontaneous, preconscious interpretation would trigger a feeling of anger. Your anger would be produced by the meaning you gave to the situation ("He did something bad") and by your decision that you would like to attack him.

On the other hand, if you interpreted the same situation as one in which a demented person was attacking you irrationally and might resort to violence, you would likely feel fear. You would feel sad if your interpretation was, "It's too bad that people are so hostile for no good reason. But that's human nature for you, so what is one to do?" Or even happy if you thought, "I'm glad I'm not like that person. When I see people who get upset so easily, it makes me appreciate how well balanced I am." Sympathy could be evoked by an automatic thought such as, "Poor fellow, he must be disturbed to act that way. He needs help." How you think determines how you feel.

Now that you can see how automatic thoughts precede emotions, learning to identify your automatic thoughts can be a first step in gaining control of your emotions. To identify which thoughts precede which emotions, it will be helpful to learn something about the nature of emotions.

The Nature of Emotions

According to Darwin, emotions developed primarily to prepare animals for action, particularly in emergencies. Anger prepares an animal for fighting, fear for fleeing, sadness for disengaging from the environment, and happiness for heightened engagement. In order to have emotions, animals, like people, must interpret the meaning of events. They do not do so in words, of course, but their brains somehow manage to compute the significance of events and what to do about them. If the brain signals "Attack," the body is automatically mobilized to support an attack. Adrenaline and blood sugar are released into the bloodstream, the heart pumps more strongly and faster, and breathing becomes deeper and quicker. The muscles tense, the teeth are bared, and the animal assumes a stiff position that makes it look bigger and more formidable. This preparation for a certain kind of action, the physiological reactions that support it, and the feelings associated with it are all part of the emotion. The animal then may or may not act on the emotion, depending on other factors, such as its realization that the other animal is too ferocious to be attacked without risking serious injury. In this way, an emotion combines cognition, bodily arousal, and behavior in a ready-made formula for responding in line with the way the situation has been interpreted.

Although human beings and animals experience anger, fear, sadness, and joy, there is one big difference in the ways we and they come to feel these emotions. Our interpretations are mainly determined by language. (Observe your self-talk when you experience a strong emotion.) Not only do we interpret events through language, but words themselves create events: you can make yourself angry just by thinking certain thoughts. Of course, occasionally we do get upset because someone did something that affected us physically, such as stomping on our toe. More often, though, we are aroused to emotion because someone said or did something that injured our egos or violated our beliefs about how people should behave. We react to the meanings we assign to the sound waves in the air or to the words on a page, none of which can harm us apart from the meanings we assign to them. The children had it all wrong in their chant: "Sticks and stones can break my bones, but names can never harm me." Names or, more generally, assaults on egos harm people much more often than physical assaults. However, assaults on egos can hurt you only if you interpret them a certain way, whereas the physical assaults hurt no matter how you interpret them. The lesson is that names need not hurt you if you do not empower them with your interpretations, but, unfortunately, nearly everyone automatically empowers them.

The Thoughts Behind Specific Emotions

There are usually three steps in the experience of an emotion. First, an objective event takes place. Second, you automatically interpret the event. Third, the interpretation produces an emotion. The second step actually has two components: your interpretation of what's going on and your interpretation how to respond. First, you assess the nature of the situation: are you being attacked, rejected, or befriended? Second, you assess how to respond: should you attack, withdraw, or be friendly? However, there is often such a strong connection between these two that the first assessment by itself triggers the emotion. For example, if you are like most people, deciding that you have been insulted will automatically make you think you should attack, which will then make you feel angry. If you came to a different decision about what to do, you would have a different emotion. For example, if the person who insulted you happened to be carrying a gun, you would most likely feel fear rather than anger because your brain would instantaneously compute that to attack might not be so good for your health.

With this understanding of the process by which your emotions come about, we can now proceed to identify the automatic interpretations that most often lead people to feel specific emotions, such as anger, fear, sadness, and joy. Each of these four basic emotions is adaptive for some purposes and maladaptive for others—a distinction to keep in mind as you learn to control your emotions.

Anger. The essence of anger is that it facilitates attack. Anger is most commonly instigated by the thought that someone has done something bad or wrong and deserves to be punished or rejected. Related thoughts are that you are right or good and that the other person is wrong or bad. The psychiatrist Eric Berne paraphrased this kind of thinking as "I'm OK, you're not OK."

What Anger Can Do for You:
- Protect your self-esteem
- Allow you to feel secure in the rightness of your beliefs and to defend them by rejecting threatening ideas and the people who hold them
- Motivate you to take decisive action

What Anger Can Do to You:
- Alienate people
- Give rise to prejudice
- Prevent self-questioning (thereby stunting your personal growth)
- Put a strain on your body, particularly your cardiovascular system

Fear. The essence of fear is that it promotes escape, or flight. Fear is evoked when you interpret a situation as threatening and as calling for removing yourself from danger. In warfare, for example, the threat of bodily injury would likely be the most prevalent source of fear. Under normal circumstances, however, the events that elicit fear are more often of a psychological nature. In my research with college students, the threats of failure and disapproval proved to be the most prevalent sources of fear. I also found that fear was instigated by uncertainty, as well as, of course, by anticipation of physical and psychological harm. People have a need to know what to expect. If they do not know what to expect, they have to continually be on guard against possible danger. Not surprisingly, therefore, people who are more frightened than others often have difficulty coping with uncertainty. These are people who worry a lot: "What if Fred is late because he had an accident?" "What if I left the stove on, and the house burns down?"

What Fear Can Do for *You*:

- Promote alertness to realistic threats and lead you to take appropriate precautions
- Motivate accomplishment

What Fear Can Do to *You*:

- Interfere with thinking and action by generating too much tension for effective performance, particularly in tasks that require complex thinking, creativity, or fine coordination
- Divert attention from realistic to unrealistic threats
- Create stress, which serves no useful purpose when the threat is unrealistic and produces misery and wear and tear on your body

Sadness. The essence of sadness is that it promotes disengagement. It is natural to disengage when you feel helpless to cope with a situation more actively. There is a time to step back, lick your wounds, and think through how best to cope with a distressing situation. Sadness typically occurs following thoughts associated with helplessness, loss, and reduced self-esteem. The loss may be of a relationship, job, public position, self-esteem, skill, possession, or hope. In my research, the thoughts that produced depression most often involved ruminations about past events that could not be undone. People are susceptible to sadness or depression when they view a loss as irreversible and feel helpless about doing anything about it. This is especially true when, in the face of a serious loss, a person comes to feel generally inadequate and worthless. Concern about the possibility of a *future* loss, on the other hand, tends to evoke anxiety (a generalized form of fear), not sadness.

What Sadness Can Do for *You*:

- Bring about a state of withdrawal or disengagement—a moratorium or breathing spell for healing wounds, regaining strength, and contemplating the source of your distress and what to do about it
- Motivate you to reevaluate who you are and what you want out of life, thus helping you to develop new ways of thinking (note that this is the opposite of what anger does

What Sadness Can Do to *You*:

- Make you feel awful
- Prevent you from taking realistic, effective action
- Bring about physical consequences (when the sadness is intense and prolonged), such as compromising your endocrine and immune systems and thereby making you more susceptible to illness

Happiness. The essence of happiness is engagement. Some thoughts associated with happiness are that you are a strong, capable person, that the world is a good place in which to live, and that whatever you do will turn out well. Happiness is associated with increased activity based on a heightened sense of security, which encourages risk taking. When an animal is happy, it becomes frisky and runs and jumps for the sheer joy of it. It is all over the place, appears to fear nothing, and loses its sense of caution. Similarly, people who are happy jump for joy, burst into song, or otherwise express their feelings in highly visible and expansive actions. Eager for new experiences and confident of positive outcomes, they are adventurous and willing to take risks.

What Happiness Can Do for *You*:
• Make you feel good
• Promote positive relationships with others (both because it generates positive feelings toward others and because people are attracted to happy people)
• Foster adventurousness and exploring new boundaries

What Happiness Can Do to *You*:
• Reduce caution, which may result in unwise risk taking
• Set up unrealistically favorable expectations that can lead to disappointment and demoralization

CONSTRUCTIVE THINKING AND MENTAL WELL-BEING

"As you think, so you shall feel." Certain ways of thinking are associated with good personal adjustment and life satisfaction, while other ways are associated with maladjustment and misery.

Positive versus Negative Thinking

Research has shown that an optimistic outlook, a belief that one is in control of events, a tendency to interpret events as challenges rather than as threats, and a commitment to long-term goals are all associated with mental health and effective performance. You can interpret most things that happen to you in these positive ways, or you can make the opposite interpretations. Here, in an example taken from an article about constructive thinking by Bibi Wein, is how one woman interpreted events on a particular day:

These are some things that happened to Ellen on a typical day: Her supervisor unexpectedly agreed to a project she'd proposed. Her daughter came home with an A on a math test. Her father, who was recently hospitalized, reported that the doctor gave him a clean bill of health. Her sister turned down Ellen's dinnerparty invitation because of a previous engagement. Her husband suggested they spend the weekend in the mountains.

Would you say Ellen had a good or a bad day? According to Ellen, she had a perfectly rotten day, which is how most of her days are. She was convinced her supervisor said yes only because he planned to back out of a promise to hire more clerical help. Her daughter's high grade infuriated her: it confirmed her feeling that the lazy teacher wouldn't give the child an appropriate challenge. Her first reaction to her father's good news was that he was lying, but she had to accept it when she called the doctor to check. Ellen concluded her day by picking fights with her sister, whose "rejection" hurt her deeply, and then her husband. Why bother going away for the weekend? He'd only go off fishing and leave her stuck with the kids.

As Ellen's reactions illustrate, the way we experience events often has less to do with their "objective" character than with the way we interpret them. No matter how intelligent, talented, and economically well off Ellen is, her destructive way of thinking keeps her mired in misery.

Well-adjusted people, in contrast, are usually upbeat even if it means not being strictly realistic. Research shows that it is actually beneficial to harbor some positive illusions. In fact, under many circumstances, people who are slightly depressed tend to be more realistic than people who are not. Shelley Taylor, an eminent psychologist at the University of California in Los Angeles found this fact so intriguing that she wrote a book called *Creative Self-Deception and the Healthy Mind*. Of course, one has to keep the positive illusions within reasonable limits, or one would end up in a mental institution.

We have seen that optimistic people perform better than pessimistic people on many tasks, such as salesmanship. They have also been shown to be healthier as well as happier. Martin Seligman, the leading researcher on optimism, details these and other benefits in his popular book *Learned Optimism*. Translating his findings into my terminology, I would say that good constructive thinkers do not value accuracy above all else; they equally value maintaining their self-esteem and a favorable outlook. The compromise between the need to be accurate and the need to think positively is to see the world through rose-tinted glasses, but a tint that is light and does not seriously distort the images of the real world.

What about people who interpret events pessimistically? As Seligman and his colleagues have found, both children and adults who are pessimistic are more likely than others to be depressed. Pessimism is only one of several destructive ways of thinking that contribute to feeling depressed. Other ways include believing that one is controlled by events rather than in control of them, interpreting events as threats rather than as challenges, having no commitment to long-term goals, and having a low opinion of oneself. How you think determines not just your everyday emotions but your long-range moods as well.

This does not mean that pessimism is always bad. When my wife had cancer, it would have done us no good to deny the serious threat to her life. Instead, by recognizing the danger we were able to mobilize ourselves to fight the disease.

The Constructive Thinking Inventory and Emotional Adjustment

My students and I found evidence of a close association between constructive thinking and mental health when we tested adults and college students on the Constructive Thinking Inventory (CTI) together with various measures of adjustment. We found that poor constructive thinkers have more negative emotions of all kinds than good constructive thinkers. They are more depressed, more angry, more anxious, more tense, and more disorganized. They also have fewer positive emotions. They are less happy, less affectionate, less enthusiastic, and less energetic than good constructive thinkers.

Breaking down constructive thinking into its components tells us more specifically how constructive thinking is related to mental well-being. We found, as expected, that emotional coping plays an important role in disorders associated with feelings, namely, depression, anxiety, and chronic anger. Behavioral coping is more specifically related to depression. People who are depressed think in ways that make them feel hopeless and helpless. It is therefore difficult for them to get anything done as they believe that what they do will not make any difference. Personal superstitious thinking is also associated with feelings of helplessness and depression. Categorical thinking is more specifically associated with chronic anger.

Overall, the research my associates and I did with the Constructive Thinking Inventory provides compelling evidence that the more constructively you think, the happier you feel, and the better your emotional adjustment. The less constructively you think, the more likely you are to suffer from emotional disorders.

Constructive Thinking and Stress

Imagine yourself having to count backward from 300 by 7s as fast as you can: "300, 293, 286, 279 . . .". Every time you make a mistake, a loud voice calls out, "Error!" and you have to go back to your last correct response. Or picture yourself moving a pencil through a maze, which you can see only in a mirror, as rapidly as possible. Every time you touch the outline of the maze, you hear a voice yell, "Error!" and you have to go back to where you were before you touched the line. Sometimes people get so confused about which way to move the pencil that they are unable to move it at all; instead, they just keep vibrating it back and forth.

These were the stressful tasks that Dr. Lori Katz, a graduate student at the time, and I gave to both good and poor constructive thinkers in a laboratory study. We wanted to see just how the thinking of the two groups differed when confronted with stress and how their thinking was related to their feelings of anxiety. To find out, we asked the participants to report their thoughts at various times during the experiment.

As it turned out, there was little difference between good and poor constructive thinkers in the number of positive and neutral thoughts they reported, but there were large differences in their *negative* thoughts. Poor constructive thinkers worried more than good constructive thinkers. They initially worried about what the experiment would be like, and they worried during the experiment about how well they were performing. No wonder they reported feeling more stress and anxiety during the experiment than the good constructive thinkers. After the experiment they decided that they had, indeed, performed poorly, well below the high standards they set for themselves. They were also concerned about whether the experimenter had formed a low opinion of them. Actually, they had performed as well as the good constructive thinkers, but you would not know that from listening to their reactions.

When asked to describe their thoughts, the good constructive thinkers said they took the situation in stride. They said they did not worry about their performance because it would not affect them in any way. As for what the experimenter thought of them, they believed she was pleased to have subjects participating in her experiment and that she was not concerned about how well they did. It is evident that good and poor constructive thinkers, even when they share the same objective environment, live, subjectively, continents apart.

In real life, unlike a controlled laboratory situation, people do not all experience the same objective sources of stress; instead, they create stress for themselves by the way they live. To demonstrate how poor constructive thinkers bring on stressful experiences by their behavior, Lori Katz and I looked at stressful events as they actually occurred in people's lives. We asked 450 college students to report how frequently they had experienced various stressful events. The events were of two kinds: daily hassles that people could have contributed to causing, such as losing things or not getting along with fellow workers, and events over which the person almost certainly had no control, such as a friend's moving away or the death of a pet.

When it came to stressful events over which they had no control, good constructive thinkers experienced these events as frequently as poor constructive thinkers. The difference was in the stressful events over which they had some control. Most of the stress that poor constructive thinkers experienced turned out to be of their own making. That is, they behaved in ways that brought about stressful events such as failing, being disapproved of, or being treated badly by others. They were "hassled" more by their fellow students and their landlords than were good constructive thinkers because of the way they behaved; their relationships with people were more often unsatisfying; and they had more problems on their jobs.

This and other research has indicated that there are three main reasons that good constructive thinkers experience less stress than poor constructive thinkers:

1. *They behave in ways that produce fewer distressing events in their lives, and they thereby create a less stressful environment for themselves.* As they are better organized, better liked, and more efficient than poor constructive thinkers, they experience less frustration and more support in their daily lives.

2. *They interpret potentially stressful events in less stressful ways.* When possible, for example, they interpret events as challenges rather than as threats. They are also more likely than poor constructive thinkers to interpret setbacks as situationally determined and temporary rather than as permanent and reflecting badly on themselves.

3. *They cope more effectively with situations once they have interpreted them as stressful.*

The overall result is that good constructive thinkers experience less stress in living, while at the same time working harder and exposing themselves to more challenging situations. As a case in point, think back to the school administrators I spoke of in Chapter 8. The good constructive thinkers experienced less stress than the poor constructive thinkers, even though they took on more demanding workloads. These men and women used all three types of constructive thinking listed here: creating fewer stressful events for themselves, interpreting events less stressfully, and coping better with stress. These are all skills people can acquire by improving their constructive thinking.

Chapter 11

How You Think Can Affect
Your Health

You may be wary of the notion that something so intangible as a thought can have an impact on something so solid as the body. Yet this is the whole premise of psychosomatic medicine. Of course, not all illness has a psychological cause; illness can strike you no matter how you think, feel, and behave. Nonetheless, the way you think can affect your health in two well-documented ways. One is by influencing the amount of stress you experience; the other is by influencing your health-related behavior.

In the previous chapter I discussed several ways in which constructive thinking reduces stress; as I show here, less stress means less likelihood of illness. As for health-related behavior, it is evident that if you eat a better diet, exercise more, get enough sleep, avoid tobacco and other harmful drugs, and protect yourself from sexually transmitted diseases, you stand a better chance to stay healthy. If your thoughts influence your health in these two crucial ways, then it follows that improving the constructiveness of your thinking can contribute to improving your health.

HOW YOUR THOUGHTS INFLUENCE YOUR BODY

Why does your heart beat faster when you have to speak in public? Why do you turn red when you are embarrassed? Why do your muscles tense up when someone asks you to do something you don't want to do? For that matter, why does a cat arch its back, bare its teeth, and hiss when its "turf" is threatened?

I gave part of the answer to these questions in the previous chapter when I discussed how particular thoughts set off particular emotions. An emotion, as I explained, includes a physiological reaction in preparation for some kind of activity. When you are frightened, your body is mobilized for flight; when you are angry, your body is mobilized for attack; when you are depressed, your body is mobilized (or demobilized) for disengagement; and when you are happy, your body is mobilized for engagement. Particular muscles are activated to support the appropriate action, and special messages are sent by your brain to your endocrine glands (which control the manufacture and release of hormones) as well as to your autonomic nervous system (which regulates organs over which you have no voluntary control, such as the heart and the stomach).

If you could look into your body when you are frightened, you would see the following all happening simultaneously: your muscles become tense; your heart rate and breathing speed up; your digestion slows down; stored sugar and adrenaline are released into your bloodstream; your blood clots in less time; and your blood flows inward, away from your skin, especially your hands and feet, which is why frightened skiers feel colder than confident skiers.

All of these reactions have developed through evolution to put you on an emergency footing. When you breathe faster, and your heart beats faster, you have a greater capacity for vigorous action. When your muscles tense up, you are ready for intense effort. The release of sugar into your bloodstream provides an immediate source of energy, while the release of adrenaline increases the activity of the other emergency systems. In an emergency your body doesn't need to put a lot of effort into digestion, which supplies long-term energy; you need short-term energy instead. Faster clotting of the blood and the shifting of the blood away from the outside of the body minimize blood loss in case of injury.

The influence of thoughts on bodily processes is so great that you don't need a laboratory with complex equipment to demonstrate it. All you have to do is observe yourself. When you are anxious, such as before giving a speech or taking an important examination, your fingers are likely to feel cold (you can test this by touching them against your cheek), you may break out into a cold sweat, and your throat is likely to become dry (because your saliva has stopped flowing as part of the digestive slowdown). Often you will detect your heart beating more strongly and note changes in your breathing as well. You may also notice that, because of an increase in muscle tension, your fine coordination has disappeared, and you are unable to draw a steady line. All these changes are brought about simply by thinking thoughts that make you anxious. Think differently, and the reactions will not occur.

What better way to demonstrate this power of "mind over matter" than to observe how people master their anxiety when they are engaging in a frightening activity, such as jumping out of an airplane at several thousand feet. Walter Fenz, a psychologist and sport parachutist, and I measured novice parachutists' heart rates on the ground and immediately before they jumped from the aircraft. We found that their average heart rate doubled—from about 70 beats per minute on the ground to 143 beats per minute immediately before jumping. Experienced parachutists, who were unafraid, showed no such increase. When tested before jumping, the parachutists were seated motionless in the aircraft. It would take vigorous physical exercise to bring anyone's heart rate up to the level the novice parachutists reached by simply thinking thoughts such as, "Why did I ever get into this—I'm too young to die" or "What if the chute wasn't packed properly and won't open?"

Thoughts, too, produce intense anger and the physiological reactions that go along with that emotion. When people become angry, their overall tension increases, their movements become exaggerated, their voices become louder, their faces flush, and they may clench their fists and teeth. What has stimulated this mobilization of the body? In all likelihood, it was simply a thought. Someone said something, produced some sound waves that were harmless, until the person who interpreted them had thoughts such as the following: "How dare he say that about me! I'll get back at him if it's the last thing I do." Those thoughts triggered an intense emotion, complete with the physiological reactions that accompany it. Now, if that is how you are in the habit of thinking, you are guaranteed to put a lot of wear and tear on your body and are likely to do yourself far more harm than was done to you by your antagonist.

Blushing is a highly visible physiological reaction that is brought on entirely by thoughts. When you interpret something as "embarrassing," blood rushes to your face. No matter how you try to hide it, everyone knows that you think you have behaved in a way that exposes you to ridicule. The most common cause of blushing, I have found, is the thought of being physically exposed, such as by having your pants fall down. People rarely blush in the privacy of their rooms. It is a social response produced by anticipating other people's reactions.

When people think thoughts or make interpretations that cause them to be sad or depressed, their bodies sag, their movements become slower and less intense, and their speech sometimes becomes so soft and lacking in intonation that it is difficult to understand what they are saying. Here we see the body organizing itself for withdrawal and inaction following thoughts about helplessness, hopelessness, and futility.

THE ROLE OF THE MIND IN HEALTH AND ILLNESS

Given the strong connection between thought and emotion and between emotions and bodily reactions, it would be amazing if thoughts played no role in health and illness.

Evidence in support of a relation between emotions and health has been accumulating over many years. One of the more compelling studies recently reported employed a "meta-analysis," in which 101 studies were combined in a single, overall analysis, a method that produces highly reliable conclusions. The results indicated that chronic dysphoric emotions are a serious health hazard. People with enduring feelings of anxiety, depression, hostility, or general tension were found to have double the risk of suffering from a wide variety of psychosomatic, or psychophysiological, illnesses, including asthma, arthritis, headaches, ulcers, and heart disease. This makes chronic negative emotions no less significant than smoking and elevated levels of cholesterol as a contributor to serious illness.

There is nothing imaginary about the notion of psychosomatic disorders. These are real physical disorders that are caused or aggravated by prolonged stress, which can be produced by maladaptive ways of thinking. Psychosomatic medicine does not deny the effects of other factors, such as heredity, diet, physical stresses, and exposure to toxins and germs, but adds psychological stress as another contributing factor to illness. Like any other contributing cause, psychological factors may have much, little, or nothing to do with a particular person's having a particular disease.

A great deal of research has confirmed that the way a person thinks can affect the person's physical well-being. It is well established that people who are pessimistic, who have a negative image of themselves, who feel that they are controlled by events rather than in control of them, who interpret events as threats rather than as challenges, and who lack significant commitments in life have more frequent headaches, stomachaches, and back pains than others do. People who think in these self-destructive ways also visit health facilities more frequently than others. A link has also been established between hostility and heart disease, and there is also suggestive evidence that psychological factors may be related to cancer, which is discussed shortly.

To find out how a person's way of thinking affects the person's health over a lifetime, Christopher Peterson, Martin Seligman, and George Vaillant kept track of ninety-five graduates of the Harvard classes of 1942–1944 for nearly forty years. The researchers looked at the results of these men's medical examinations between the ages of 25 and 60 in light of the optimism and self-esteem the men showed at age 25. Until these men reached the age of 45, the state of their health was unrelated to their style of thinking, simply because nearly everyone was healthy up to that age. After age 45, however, those who had a negative way of thinking were in poorer health than those with a more self-enhancing way of thinking. Apparently, serious illnesses brought on by destructive thinking may not show up until middle or old age, when people are more vulnerable to illness. Your body may get away with your mind's destructive thinking when you are young and vigorous, but is less likely to do so when you are older.

HOW CONSTRUCTIVE THINKING MAKES FOR BETTER HEALTH

Research using the Constructive Thinking Inventory (CTI) tells us more specifically how people's thinking can influence their health. These studies have nothing to say about major diseases such as heart disease and cancer, which occur infrequently in the college-age individuals who have participated in the research to date. But they do reveal a great deal about the impact of constructive thinking on minor, everyday symptoms. Later in this chapter I show how destructive thinking is also associated with more serious diseases, such as heart disease and cancer.

Good constructive thinkers report fewer symptoms than poor constructive thinkers on a checklist that includes minor ailments such as respiratory infections, skin problems, diarrhea, stomachaches, headaches, constipation, and back pain. Good constructive thinkers make fewer visits to the college infirmary than poor constructive thinkers. They are also more satisfied with their health, have fewer accidents, miss fewer classes due to illness, and have fewer problems associated with overeating and with drug and alcohol consumption—indications that they engage in better health practices.

Not surprisingly, among the components of constructive thinking on the CTI, emotional coping is most closely associated with a person's susceptibility to common physical symptoms. Poor emotional copers report considerably more symptoms than good emotional copers. Personal superstitious thinkers are also especially susceptible to health problems. The explanation here probably lies in the relationship between private superstitions and depression. These findings support the view that the main link between destructive thinking and physical illness is through negative emotions.

Thinking affects health in another way as well—through its influence on a person's lifestyle and health-related behaviors. On the CTI, people who score high on behavioral coping have relatively few symptoms, though not as few as those who score high on emotional coping. However, they do even better than good emotional copers in controlling destructive behavior such as overeating. Poor behavioral copers have problems with overeating because of their poor self-discipline. The same is true for drug abuse. In a study of narcotic addicts in a methadone treatment program, Gernot Gollnisch found that the poorer a person was at either emotional coping *or* behavioral coping, the more drugs the person tended to use. However, behavioral coping was the more crucial factor when it came to fulfilling the requirements of the program and abstaining from further drug use.

This relationship between destructive thinking and poor health practices is readily understandable. People who have low self-esteem, who believe they have little control over what happens to them, or who have little commitment to future goals (examples of poor constructive thinking) do not bother to take care of themselves. After all, if they think that they don't matter or that what they do has no effect, then why bother! People who think destructively may not go to the dentist as often as they should, may not eat nutritious diets, may not get enough sleep, and may not bother to exercise. They are likely to seek short-term pleasures and ignore long-term consequences and therefore to take drugs, smoke, drink alcohol to excess, eat junk food, and take unreasonable risks, such as failing to take precautions in sexual encounters. When they become ill, they may not think constructively about managing their illness so as to maximize the chances of recovery.

The two major pathways from constructive thinking to physical well-being are outlined in Figure 11.1.

HOW CONSTRUCTIVE THINKING AFFECTS HEART DISEASE AND CANCER

The most dramatic evidence of the potential health benefits of constructive thinking comes in the cases of the diseases people fear most, the "killer" diseases, heart disease and cancer. Here we find that different forms of destructive thinking, by facilitating the occurrence of different emotions, contribute to bringing about different diseases. Intense, prolonged anger may increase a person's vulnerability to disorders of the cardiovascular system. Helplessness and depression, on the other hand, may weaken the immune system, thus making a person more susceptible to infectious diseases and possibly to cancer. In both cases, the evidence is mounting that constructive thinking not only can help prevent these diseases but can also be an aid to recovery in some cases.

Constructive Thinking and Heart Disease

You probably have heard about "Type-A" personality, which is characterized by a hard-driving ambition, a competitive and aggressive attitude, and a need to get things done in a hurry. People with Type-A personality were thought to be especially prone to heart disease. Recent research, however, points to anger and hostility as the only components of Type-A personality that really do increase the risk of heart disease. Since anger is associated with a rise in blood pressure and an increase in cardiac activity, prolonged feelings of anger can strain the cardiovascular system. It follows that thinking in ways that promote anger and aggression can be dangerous to your heart.

It is difficult to get conclusive findings on the effects of personality on illness by comparing the personalities of people who are well with those who are ill. Illness may affect people's personalities as well as the other

Figure 11.1
How Poor Constructive Thinking Leads to Physical Symptoms

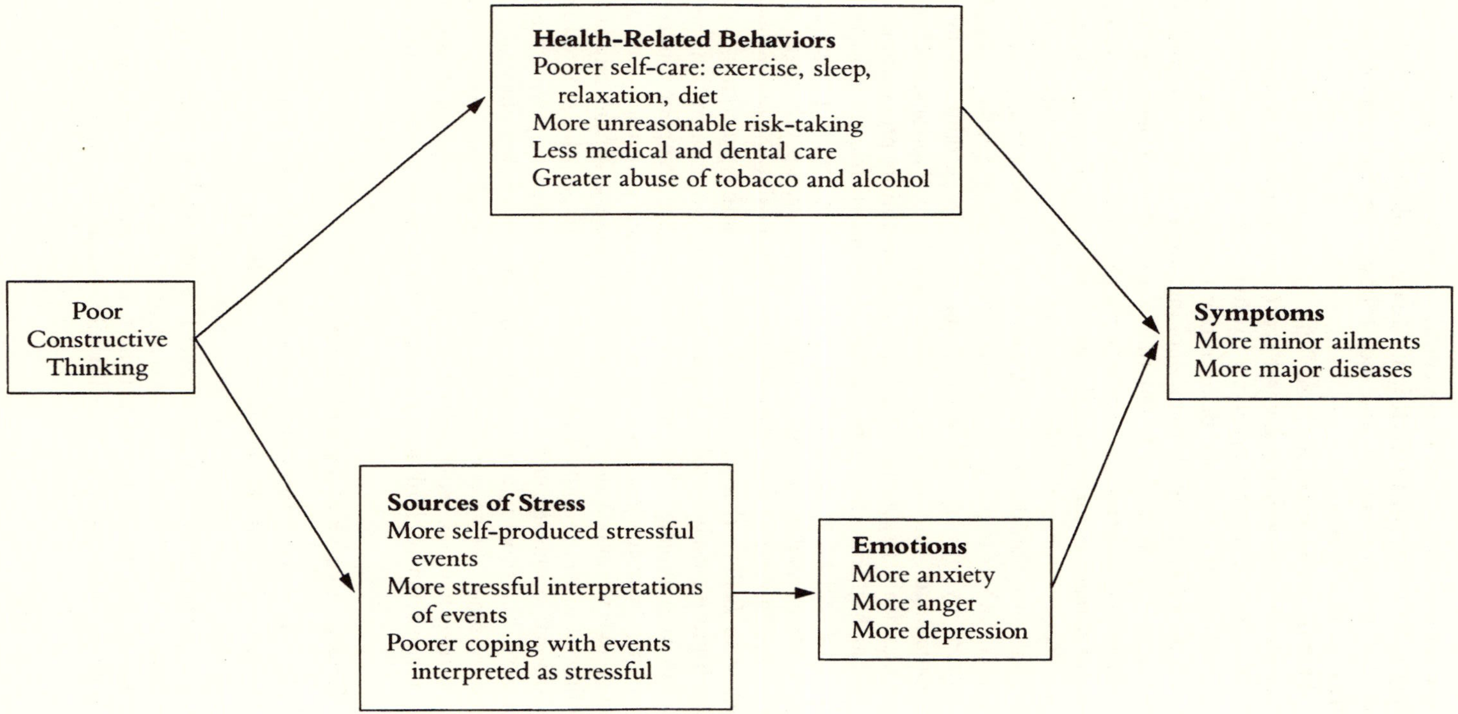

Symptoms
More minor ailments
More major diseases

Health-Related Behaviors
Poorer self-care: exercise, sleep, relaxation, diet
More unreasonable risk-taking
Less medical and dental care
Greater abuse of tobacco and alcohol

Emotions
More anxiety
More anger
More depression

Sources of Stress
More self-produced stressful events
More stressful interpretations of events
Poorer coping with events interpreted as stressful

Poor Constructive Thinking

way around. But what if we could observe people's personalities *before* they got sick, predict which individuals would be more likely to develop heart disease (or cancer), and then follow them for years to see if the predictions were borne out.

That is just what Dr. Redford Williams at Duke University did. He found that physicians with the highest scores on a test of hostility taken many years ago were much more likely to have died by the age of fifty than those with low hostility scores. Being prone to react with anger was a stronger predictor of early death than smoking, high cholesterol, and high blood pressure. Williams also found that a program he designed for reducing anger in heart-disease patients reduced the recurrence of heart attacks. The program teaches fundamental aspects of constructive thinking, including awareness of the early stages of angry feelings, the ability to regulate the feelings once they are identified, and the development of positive, empathic views of others in place of negative, critical views. Similar results have been reported by others, and it is reasonably well established by now that chronic anger, and very likely other dysphoric emotions, such as anxiety, are significant risk factors for heart disease and its progression.

What happens *after* a person develops heart disease? Can the person's thinking make a difference then? Apparently it can, to judge from a study of "dispositional optimism" by Michael Scheier, a psychologist at Carnegie Mellon University, and his colleagues. Dispositional optimism—the tendency to believe that events will have favorable outcomes—corresponds much more closely to what I call "reasonable optimism" on the CTI than to "naive optimism." It is, in other words, a key component of constructive thinking. Scheier's group examined the influence of dispositional optimism on recovery from coronary-artery bypass surgery. Among middle-aged men followed up six months after such surgery, those who scored high on dispositional optimism not only coped more effectively with the ordeal of surgery than those who scored low but also recovered physically at a faster rate, resumed their normal activities more quickly, and were more satisfied with their lives six months later. This was an interesting demonstration of how constructive thinking can aid recovery from a serious illness.

Constructive Thinking and Cancer

Physicians since antiquity have observed that people who are depressed are especially likely to develop cancer. During the past few decades these unsystematic observations have crystallized into the notion of a "cancer-prone personality." A person with this personality appears "too good to be true"—self-sacrificing, more helpful to others than to himself or herself, unassertive in his or her own behalf, but assertive in defending the rights of others. Such a person has difficulty expressing emotions such as anger and fear. Instead, he or she suppresses these emotions in order to put on a happy, cheerful front.

According to Lawrence LeShan, who has made a specialty of treating terminal cancer patients with intensive psychotherapy, a person who is at high risk for cancer often has had a history of neglect or rejection in childhood. The person later establishes a satisfactory relationship with someone, and all seems to be well for a while. The cancer is precipitated when the relationship is threatened or when some other major frustration or trauma reactivates the old sensitivity. For LeShan, a deep-seated despair is at the core of the cancer-prone personality. No matter what outward success such individuals achieve, they feel that life can never give them what they need to feel happy and fulfilled. Of course, LeShan may be seeing cancer patients for whom psychological factors are especially important, as those patients would be the most likely to seek psychotherapy. That is, LeShan's therapy may attract the very people who best fit his description of the cancer-prone personality. Not everyone who gets cancer has a cancer-prone personality.

How can a cancer-prone personality lead to cancer? Cancer is thought to be caused by an impairment of the immune system, which is then unable to combat the cancerous cells that everyone produces. There is also growing evidence that viruses are involved in causing some cancers; this explanation, too, would assign an important role to the immune system. If we could show that the immune system is influenced by a person's psychological state, we would have a link between psychological factors and cancer.

In fact, a chemical called cortisol, which weakens the immune system, has been found at high levels in people with feelings of helplessness and hopelessness. Even laboratory rats, when put into a helpless situation (such as having to swim in a tank from which they cannot escape), lose some of the functioning of their immune systems and become more susceptible to cancer. In studies with human beings, suppression of the immune system has also been observed following an event that touches off feelings of helplessness and depression.

Animals have been shown to be more susceptible to cancer when placed in stressful situations similar to those that people create for themselves by the way they think. Researchers found that they could reduce the number of cancer-prone mice that developed tumors within a year or so after birth from 60% to 7% simply by protecting the animals from the noise and commotion of the laboratory. On the other hand, the incidence of cancer was increased just by rotating the mice on a turntable. Among female mice inoculated with a virus that caused mammary tumors, those who were put through the stress of an electric shock grew larger tumors. Most intriguing was the observation that mice that behaved in an antagonistic, combative manner had smaller tumors. Some human studies have had remarkably similar findings. For example, a research team in England found that women who responded to the diagnosis of breast cancer with feelings of helplessness and hopelessness did not survive as long, on average, as those who showed a "fighting spirit." Unfortunately, this finding has not been uniformly upheld in further research.

The overall findings on the influence of psychological factors on the etiology and course of cancer in humans are, to say the least, confusing. Without going into detail, some studies report positive findings whereas others fail to confirm them. Part of the difficulty is that most studies are retrospective rather than prospective. When differences in personality between cancer and control cases are found after people have contracted cancer, it is not possible to determine whether the differences contributed to the cancer in the first place or are simply a consequence of having the cancer. Among the few prospective studies that have been conducted, the results have been inconsistent. This may be due, in part, to differences in the kinds and stages of the cancers that have been investigated. However, there are sufficient positive findings to make this an important area for further research and to lead one to suspect that, at least under certain conditions, personality factors matter.

A particularly promising recent study on the influence of psychological factors on the progression of cancer was conducted by psychiatrist David Spiegel and his colleagues at the Stanford University School of Medicine. In that study, women with advanced breast cancer were randomly assigned to one of two groups, one of which participated in weekly support sessions while the other did not. In these groups the women "discussed their fears about dying and ways of living the remainder of their lives as richly as possible, improving doctor–patient communication, strengthening family relationships, grieving losses within the group, building a strong sense of mutual support, and using hypnosis to control pain and other somatic symptoms."

The researchers' purpose was to demonstrate that the quality of life could be improved for cancer patients even if the duration of life could not. The researchers did not tell the patients that the support groups might make them live longer because they themselves did not expect this to happen. They were astounded, therefore, by what actually happened: the women who received psychosocial support lived for an average of 36.6 months, as compared with 18.9 months for those who did not. This difference was so statistically significant, and the research so well designed and conducted that the findings stirred up a great deal of interest in the scientific community. In the near future it should be established whether the results can be reproduced. In another, similar study, but with lung cancer patients, no positive results were obtained. This, of course, may simply indicate that lung cancer is less susceptible to psychological influence than breast cancer or that some other difference between the studies is responsible for the difference in findings. Some researchers believe that cancers involving organs associated with endocrine functions may be more responsive to psychological factors than other kinds of cancers.

A promising possibility that has not received sufficient research attention is that people with cancer-prone personalities are particularly susceptible to improvement from changes in their personalities. This would be consistent with the observations of LeShan, for the patients who came to him for psychotherapy obviously viewed themselves as psychologically troubled. It, of course, makes sense that if there was a significant psychological problem to begin with, it could have contributed to the etiology of the cancer and that its remediation could play a role in recovery from the cancer. In a study in which she examined seven people who had extremely remarkable recoveries from cancer (defined as occurring in less than 1% of the cases with a similar diagnosis), Lori Katz obtained self-reports about their cancer-prone personalities before and after they had cancer. She found that these exceptional patients reported having more cancer-prone personalities before the cancer and less cancer-prone personalities afterward than less exceptional patients who had recovered from cancers from which recovery was less unusual. She concluded that remarkable cures from cancer may be particularly likely in people for whom psychological factors were important in the etiology of their cancer and that recovery in such people can be facilitated by an improvement in personality. It remains to be seen if the findings can be reproduced in a prospective study.

The results from scientific studies are promising, although less than conclusive. However, there is suggestive evidence from individual cases that psychological factors are important, at least in some cases of cancer. For example, there are many authenticated cases of miraculous cures from cancer after visits to the shrine at Lourdes in France. Unfortunately, these cases, although well documented medically, contain little information on personality or other psychological influences. Individual cases from other sources, in contrast, are often anecdotally rich in personality information but lack medical documentation.

A most remarkable exception, a case that is amply documented on both the medical and psychological sides, is that of my wife, Alice Hopper Epstein. In her book, *Mind, Fantasy and Healing*, Alice tells how she recovered from terminal cancer by supplementing medical treatment with psychotherapy, which transformed her personality.

Alice had a rapidly advancing cancer that spread from her kidney to both lungs. A cancer specialist told us that Alice had no more than three months to live. That was in 1985. Twelve years later, Alice is completely free of any signs of cancer, and she is happier and healthier than ever before. Monthly X-rays are available to document the spread of the cancer, followed by its disappearance.

I am intimately familiar with the details of the case because I played a role in treating Alice. Not only was this the most dramatic experience of my life, but it taught me remarkable lessons about the nature of the mind and its power to influence the course of illness.

The news that Alice had cancer hit us like a thunder bolt. The diseased kidney was removed, but the cancer continued its rapid spread. Obtaining studies of metastasized kidney cancer from the National Cancer Institute, I learned that the odds of remission, let alone cure, at that time were less than 4 in 1,000. In one study of 250 patients, not a single person was alive at a two-year follow-up. The picture looked grim, indeed, particularly as there was no promising medical treatment.

Alice and I began to read whatever we could find about cancer. I was amazed to learn that some authorities, such as Carl and Stephanie Simonton and Kenneth Pelletier, seriously believed that psychological factors could play a role in a person's developing and recovering from cancer. At first, this viewpoint seemed to me to be on the fringes of scientific respectability. But as I read more about the immune system in animals and humans, I became convinced that there was something here worth looking into.

I really took heart when I read about the cancer-prone personality, for it could not have been a more accurate description of my wife. Although Alice was a highly intelligent person with excellent social skills, her constructive thinking was poor. She could love everyone but herself, and, as a result, she lived a life of quiet despair while projecting a picture of happiness and well-being. If psychological factors played a role in some cases of cancer, I thought, surely hers must be one of them.

Alice and I decided that her best hope lay in an all-out psychological approach aimed at reorganizing her personality. Alice's dedication to making this change was inspiring. She meditated, did visualization exercises, and was in psychotherapy seven days a week, counting her work with me as well as with her regular therapist. Part of her therapy consisted of using her rational mind to correct her constructive thinking. Another part, which we believe had a more profound influence, mobilized her imagination to influence her experiential mind. In Part IV, I say more about how Alice used fantasy to reorient her automatic thinking.

As the monthly X-rays showed, variations in the size of the tumors matched what was going on in Alice's life and in her psychotherapy. When she was engaged in her therapy, the tumors continuously shrank. When her psychological treatment was interrupted for a month while she prepared for our daughter's wedding, the tumors stayed as they were. When she resumed her psychological work, the tumors again began to shrink. The results convinced us that the progress was not a coincidence.

There were other signs of a mind–body connection as well. For many years Alice had had an almost permanent headache. After some weeks into psychotherapy, her chronic headache disappeared, never to return. She never used to perspire when she exerted herself. As a result, we could not play tennis long in hot weather because she would soon get overheated. One day, when we were playing tennis, Alice suddenly yelled in delight, "I'm sweating, I'm sweating!" As she began to reorganize her automatic thinking, her bodily reactions also began to change. The perspiration indicated that her endocrine system (the system that regulates hormones) was responding differently, and it is known that hormones affect the immune system.

As a result of therapy, Alice's automatic thinking, and with it her feelings, have changed. The underlying despair is gone, and she is now able to respect her own needs as much as she has always respected those of others. This deep personal transformation may well have saved her life. It certainly broadened my understanding of constructive thinking by leading me to appreciate a kind of wisdom that lies too deep to be accessed directly by the rational, conscious mind.

Why It Is an Example of Poor Constructive Thinking to Feel Guilty about Being Ill

Many physicians are reluctant to inform patients that psychological factors may contribute to causing and curing cancer. They are concerned that this knowledge may impose a burden of guilt on people who are suffering too much already. David Spiegel, explaining his resistance to the psychological approach, put it this way: "If failure to express emotion leads to the development of cancer, then a woman who gets cancer not only pays with her life for the illness but is supposed to feel guilty about having brought it upon herself by not having managed her feelings and relationships better. If her cancer spreads, she may be asked (as patients of mine have been): 'Why did you want your cancer to spread?' "

This issue not only is important in its own right but provides an excellent example of how destructive automatic thinking can distort conscious thinking that attempts to be rational. For those who worry that any suggestion that some cancers or other diseases may, in part, be psychologically caused (or cured) implies that a person has to feel guilty about having the disease, here are four reasons to reject this view.

First, there is a crucial distinction between blame and responsibility. Blameworthiness implies an intent to do something unacceptable, whereas responsibility implies the possibility of control. Certainly, no one intended to give himself or herself cancer. To assume responsibility, on the other hand, is to give oneself hope, for it means that one has at least a chance to influence events to come out as one wishes.

Second, one cannot be blamed for having a certain kind of personality, for one does not consciously will one's personality into or out of existence. One does not choose to have automatic destructive thoughts anymore than one chooses to get cancer. My wife certainly did not choose to have a cancer-prone personality; it developed as a result of experiences she had early in life. If she could have willed it away, she most certainly would have, but that is not the way personality changes. Personality is determined in great part by unconscious and habitual reactions that arise out of past experiences, over which a person often has had little control. Some of those reactions *can* be changed, but such change requires the kind of effort described in Alice's book as well as here.

Third, psychological dynamics are only one set of factors among many that can affect cancer. Because it is impossible to know whether or not psychological factors have played a significant role in any one case, it makes no sense to assume they are the cause and then to feel guilty about them.

Fourth, if psychological factors can, in fact, influence cancer, then that is all the more reason to refuse to accept guilt about having caused one's cancer. Such thinking accomplishes nothing positive and can only contribute to making the cancer worse. It is, therefore, a prime example of destructive thinking.

To see how the question of guilt can be reduced to absurdity, consider a less controversial "cause" of illness than psychological factors—namely, diet. Assume that for years someone ate a certain kind of food that she believed was good for her. After she was found to have cancer, scientists discovered that the food contained a potent carcinogen. Assume, further, that she is still eating the food. Should the new information be kept from her on the grounds that it might make her feel guilty for having caused her cancer, or should she be informed about it so that she can change to a healthier diet? I have never heard a physician say that cancer patients should not be advised to improve their diet because it might make them feel guilty about how they ate previously.

Likewise, the risk that a psychological interpretation of cancer may lead some people to feel guilty about having caused their illness does not justify withholding possibly useful information. Rather, the way to deal with this problem is to help people identify and reject the destructive automatic thoughts behind their unwarranted feelings of guilt.

The constructive way to think about defeating cancer is to create the best possible conditions for combating the disease. This means not only improving one's diet and utilizing the best medical treatment available but also achieving the best possible state of mental health. No matter what the medical outcome, self-improvement leading to an improved capacity to appreciate what life one has left is the best bargain available. Alice felt that her effort to become the person she wanted to be was a most worthwhile pursuit even if it did not prolong her life.

CONSTRUCTIVE THINKING, UNCERTAINTY, AND HEALTH

Even for a good constructive thinker, life comes with no guarantees; all you can do is improve the odds. If you eat wholesome foods, don't smoke cigarettes, and don't spend hours in the sun without protection, you will reduce, but not eliminate, your risk of cancer. After all, you have no control over your genes and relatively little over your exposure to air pollution, let alone other carcinogens. This uncertainty extends to treatment as well as prevention. A book called *Medical Choices, Medical Chances* explains how all medical decisions involve an element of "chance" as well as "choice." You can never be completely sure, in medicine or in life, because there are too many causal factors to keep track of, and these are constantly changing and interacting in different ways. These factors include your thoughts, feelings, and actions, over which you do have some control. As a good constructive thinker, you can make wise choices so as to reduce risks and maximize the probability that you will enjoy good health, but there are no guarantees.

PART III

Where Constructive Thinking Comes From and How It Changes

Chapter 12

Once a Constructive Thinker, Always a Constructive Thinker?

Remember John, the child in Chapter 3 who got the nursery school bully to build a tower of blocks with him? For a child of his age, John was an outstanding constructive thinker. People who hear that story sometimes ask how likely it is that John turned out to be a good constructive thinker as an adult. People want answers to such questions as: "Is a person born a good constructive thinker?" "Do children who are good constructive thinkers grow into adults who are good constructive thinkers?" "Do adults grow wiser or more foolish as they age?" "What is the likelihood that I can improve my constructive thinking?"

In this chapter I answer these and other questions about how people become and remain good or poor constructive thinkers, including whether or not constructive thinking has anything to do with gender. In the two following chapters I show how parents influence their children's constructive thinking, how some children manage to overcome an unpromising upbringing, and how emotionally significant experiences can make a child or an adult either a better or poorer constructive thinker. Keep in mind, though, that I am talking about what happens in the natural course of events. Most people are unaware that there even is such a thing as constructive thinking. These chapters are about what happens to the great majority of people who *don't* deliberately work at improving their constructive thinking. If you *do* work at it, you will have a much better prospect of improvement than most people.

HOW CONSTRUCTIVE THINKING MAINTAINS ITSELF

Did five-year-old John, so gifted with practical intelligence, carry his constructive-thinking skills into adulthood? Although we cannot be certain that he fulfilled his childhood promise, the chances are fairly good that he did. However, two kinds of situations can complicate the picture. One is that unexpected, extreme events sometimes produce drastic changes in constructive thinking. The other is that a child who thinks constructively when meeting certain life demands, such as getting along with playmates in nursery school, may have difficulty when faced with entirely new demands, such as learning to play the dating-mating game in adolescence. Countering these two reasons for change are several reasons for constructive thinking to remain stable.

Constructive thinking is grounded in the ways in which a person makes sense of the world, and such beliefs do not easily change. Indeed, one of the four basic human needs I discussed in Chapter 7 is to maintain a stable, consistent set of beliefs about oneself and the world. People experience overwhelming anxiety, even panic, when they find they can no longer make sense of their lives as they have been accustomed to doing. To maintain faith in their beliefs, not only do they interpret events so as to fit their expectations, but they even behave in ways that bring about the very outcomes they expect, and their beliefs become self-fulfilling prophecies.

Another reason good constructive thinking perpetuates itself is that such thinking is intrinsically rewarding. Optimists tend to have more favorable experiences than pessimists do. Because they expect the best, they are enthusiastic about trying new things, and their enthusiasm is often rewarded, thereby verifying their favorable expectations. Also, since people enjoy the company of happy, upbeat people, they tend to act favorably toward optimists and overlook their failings. President Reagan was known as the "Teflon president" because none of his bloopers, such as his remark that trees pollute the environment, stuck to him. He was even able to weather serious crises with relatively little damage, such as the charge that he traded arms for hostages and supported illegal aid to the Nicaraguan contras, which might have led to the impeachment of a less popular president.

Let us return to John, our model constructive thinker in nursery school. How does his automatic thinking maintain his positive view of himself and the world? John likes people ("People are good to me; they like me, and I enjoy their company") and is helpful to them ("It makes me feel good to help others"). He is confident ("I'm sure I can build a tall tower of blocks, and if someone knocks it over, I'll build it bigger next time") and a good emotional coper ("Things usually work out, so why worry? Besides, looking at the positive side makes me feel better").

When people start out with such upbeat, problem-solving ways of thinking about the events that arise in everyday life, there is no reason for their automatic thinking to deteriorate unless they suffer traumatic experiences or have their confidence shaken by unusually difficult challenges. It is likely, although by no means assured, that John will become an even better constructive thinker as he matures and gains experience in living.

Is a favorable explanatory style, or "positive thinking," an indication of good constructive thinking? Only up to a point. If you invariably take credit for the good outcomes and explain away the bad ones as someone or something else's fault, you will deny yourself the chance to learn from experience. It is more constructive to recognize particular shortcomings in yourself with a view toward remedying or compensating for them, not condemning yourself. At the same time, it is often constructive to give yourself the benefit of the doubt when there *is* a doubt, as long as this does not prevent you from taking necessary precautions. By making interpretations favorable to yourself, you are bolstering your self-esteem, and high self-esteem is associated with good constructive thinking.

HOW DESTRUCTIVE THINKING MAINTAINS ITSELF

If good constructive thinking persists because it works, then you would think that poor constructive thinking would not perpetuate itself. After all, if something doesn't work why not give it up?

Surprisingly, there is evidence that destructive thinking maintains itself just as stably as constructive thinking, perhaps even more so. That is what Martin Seligman found when he looked into the persistence of people's "explanatory styles"—how people interpret the outcome of events. People with favorable explanatory styles tend to attribute good outcomes to their own enduring character traits, such as competence, intelligence, and diligence, and bad outcomes to external factors such as luck and others' mistakes. If they fail a test, they are more likely to say that they had an off day or that it was a badly designed test than that they are basically incompetent. People with unfavorable explanatory styles do just the opposite. They blame their own shortcomings for failures but do not give themselves credit for their successes. For example, they are more likely to explain away a good test score than a bad one as resulting from "luck."

If people's explanatory styles remain stable over the years, then their self-esteem and, with it, their constructive thinking will probably remain stable as well. Seligman and a colleague compared letters people wrote in their youth with samples of their writing many years later. They found that those who tended to make *unfavorable* interpretations in their youth tended to make similar statements later in life. If a person in his or her twenties made statements such as "The reason I did such a poor job is that I'm not a very competent person," that person was likely to make similar admissions in his or her seventies.

However, if a young person made statements such as "The reason I succeeded is that I'm a very competent, well-organized person," that person did not necessarily say such positive things many years later—at least not with the same degree of consistency. In this one study, the negative thinking style turned out to be more consistent than the positive. You would think that people would keep the more beneficial ways of responding, the ones that make them feel good, and give up the ones that make them feel bad. Yet it turns out that people have compelling reasons for maintaining negative as well as positive ways of thinking.

A person may have a hard time letting go of *any* accustomed way of thinking, including even a negative one, simply because it represents the only way the person has of making sense of the world. Also, negative thinking is rewarding in its own way. It may not do much to increase a person's happiness, but it can help decrease disappointment. After all, expecting the worst to begin with takes the sting out of unfortunate events when they occur. This may sound like a defeatist strategy, but remember that it is a strategy chosen automatically by the experiential mind, not deliberately by the rational mind.

Another reason negative thinking is hard to eliminate is that what we learn under threat of punishment is more difficult to unlearn than what we learn by the promise of reward. This has a good evolutionary basis. It is more important for the survival of the species that individuals avoid danger than that they pursue pleasure.

Negative thinking often has its origins in highly stressful conditions, so it tends to become "fixated." Fixated reactions are rigid responses that do not change with experience. Once a fixated response is learned, it is extremely difficult to change it.

HOW CONSTRUCTIVE THINKING CHANGES WITH AGE

It is interesting to compare the changes in constructive thinking and intellectual intelligence over the life span. As you may recall, intellectual intelligence, or mental age, increases up to late adolescence and then gradually declines. This means that most people's abstract reasoning ability diminishes somewhat as they grow older. That is why mathematicians, whose work relies on abstract intelligence, usually have their best accomplishments behind them by the time they reach their late twenties. Fortunately, constructive thinking exhibits a very different pattern. Like good wine, the work of novelists, historians, physicians, and judges, the quality of whose contributions depend on accumulated wisdom, improves with age. As most other people mature, they too can profit from experience, which means an improvement in their constructive thinking and, therefore, in their practical, social, and emotional intelligence. Aristotle, in his *Nicomachaean Ethics*, explained the difference in mental abilities of older and younger adults as follows: "While young men become geometricians and mathematicians and wise in matters like these, it is thought that a young man of practical wisdom cannot be found. The cause is that such wisdom is concerned not only with universals but with particulars, which become familiar with experience, but a young man has no experience."

Can you look forward, then, to becoming a better constructive thinker as you grow older? The research that my associates and I have conducted on changes in constructive thinking with age does support the view that most people become better constructive thinkers as they grow older, at least up to the age level that our research has thus far examined. However, a considerable number of other people become poorer constructive thinkers, usually by becoming more negative or rigid in their thinking. Thus, your accumulating experience as you grow older does not guarantee that your constructive thinking will improve, but only provides you with an opportunity to make it happen, whether you do so consciously and deliberately or intuitively.

To aid us in our comparison of the developmental changes of intellectual intelligence and constructive thinking, I have prepared the accompanying figures (Figures 12.1–12.3) that examine their development from childhood to the later adult years. Each point that is plotted is an average of a large national sample for mental age and of between 100 to 300 cases for constructive thinking. In order to give you a better understanding of what lies behind the changes in global constructive thinking, I have plotted the course of development of five main components of constructive thinking as well as of the overall, or global, scale. You should keep in mind, as you examine the figures, that individuals differ from the average in both directions. What immediately strikes one in the figures is that the curves of global constructive thinking and mental age are nearly opposite to each other, as if one were an upside down reflection of the other. When intellectual intelligence is at its highest, constructive thinking is close to its lowest, and when intellectual intelligence gradually decreases over the adult years, global constructive thinking gradually increases, except for a slight decrease in the later years. It is encouraging to note that there is a compensation for the loss in intellectual intelligence by a gain in constructive thinking, and therefore in practical, social, and emotional intelligence.

Mental age rises rapidly and steadily during childhood up to the onset of adolescence, after which the increase slows down. Mental age reaches its peak in late adolescence, and then gradually declines through the adult years. In contrast, global constructive thinking changes relatively little between ages 10 and 12. With the onset of adolescence, it begins a sharp descent It reaches its lowest point in mid-adolescence, and then gradually increases throughout adulthood up to the latest years, when it exhibits a slight decline. It is noteworthy that adolescence is a time when people are almost simultaneously at the peak of their intellectual ability and at the nadir of their constructive thinking. Thus, they are smart and foolish at the same time, but in different ways. This creates the interesting situation in which the adolescent can defend his or her inappropriate behavior in an intellectually sophisticated manner, which can be exceedingly frustrating to adults who attempt to correct adolescents by appeals to reason.

Figure 12.1
Comparison of Mental Age and Global Constructive Thinking as a Function of Age

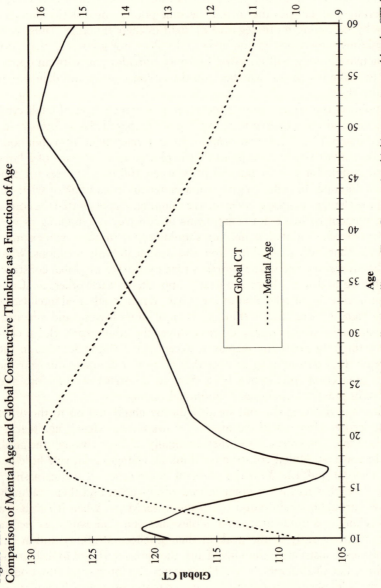

Notes: mental age was measured by the Wechsler-Bellevue Intelligence Test. Constructive thinking was measured by the CTI. The curve for mental age was adapted from D. Wechsler, *The Measurement of Adult Intelligence* (Baltimore: Williams & Wilkins, 1939).

Figure 12.2
Average Scores on the CTI Scales of Emotional Coping and Behavioral Coping at Different Age Levels

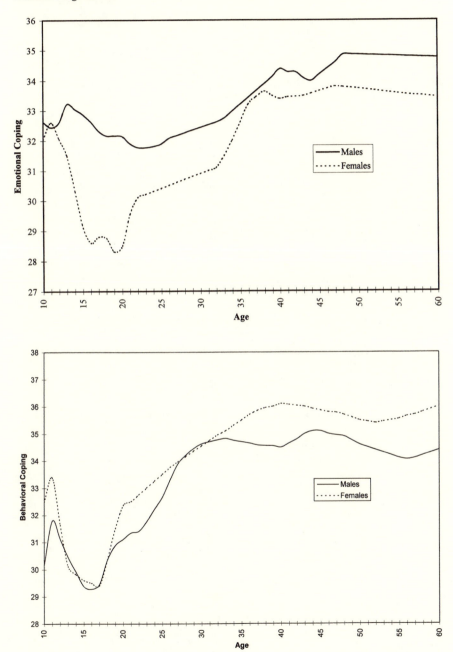

Figure 12.3
Average Scores on the CTI Scales of Categorical Thinking, Esoteric Thinking, and Naive Optimism at Different Age Levels

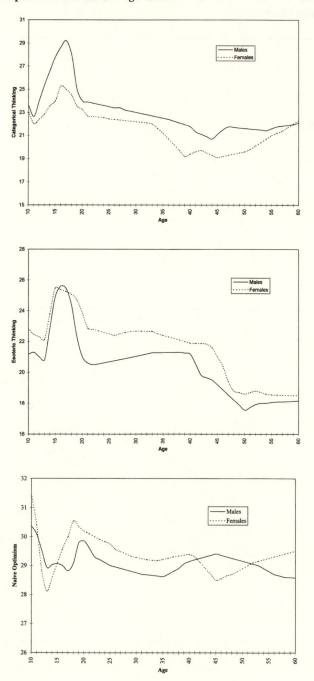

The reduced practical, social, and emotional intelligence in adolescents can be attributed to the destabilization of their identity. They are caught in a developmental stage in which they have lost the stability provided by their old view of themselves as dependent children and have not yet succeeded in establishing a new, more adult identity. In the language of CEST, their basic need for a stable, coherent theory of reality is being thwarted, and they, accordingly, lack a secure base from which to operate.

To obtain a more specific picture of what is occurring in the constructive thinking of people as they mature, it is helpful to examine the performance of adolescent boys and girls separately on the component scales of the CTI. It can be seen in the figure that the development of emotional coping is somewhat similar to that for global constructive thinking, but differs in two important respects. One is that it reaches its nadir in late rather than in middle adolescence, and the other is that the curves for the males and females begin to diverge at age 13, with the curve for boys showing a slight decline up to late adolescence, and the curve for girls showing a much more precipitous decline. (Only a single curve based on the combined groups was presented for global constructive thinking, as the sexes were very similar on that measure.) Beyond adolescence, both groups improve steadily over the years in their emotional coping, with the women continuing to remain slightly lower than the men.

How is one to account for the greater downward spiral in emotional coping in the girls than in the boys during adolescence? It is known from other studies that girls' self-esteem drops in junior high school and high school. This raises the question of how we are conditioning young girls to make adolescence such a difficult time for them emotionally. Girls often experience a period of uncertainty in puberty about what it means to be a success in life as a woman. Unlike boys, who are rewarded for being intelligent, competent, and assertive, girls are given a mixed message. They are told that it is good to be autonomous and accomplished but, at the same time, they are expected to please and accommodate parents, teachers, and boyfriends. Great emphasis is also placed on their appearance. The result is that adolescent girls experience a conflict between pleasing others and becoming autonomous, competent grownups. The research of Carol Dweck, a psychology professor at Columbia University, and her colleagues is illuminating in this respect. They discovered that a major factor in determining which children are most successful in solving problems is the extent to which they are *mastery-oriented* rather than *approval-oriented*. For the most part, our society has socialized boys to be mastery-oriented and girls to be approval-oriented. As a result, girls can succeed in the lower grades by behaving well and giving teachers what they want. As they move into the higher grades, they increasingly face the same performance demands boys do but are less psychologically prepared to meet them and are more confused about what is expected of them.

Turning to changes in behavioral coping over time, it can be seen that it reaches its lowest level for both males and females in middle adolescence, and then begins a sharp rise, which occurs shortly before the rise in emotional coping. It is noteworthy that the development of emotional coping, which does not begin its recovery until late adolescence, lags behind the maturation of behavioral coping. We can therefore expect the level of behavioral maturity in most adolescents to be more advanced than their emotional maturity.

Behavioral coping in the adult years, unlike emotional coping, does not consistently improve for both sexes with age. Rather, for men it is relatively stable from young adulthood through the later years, whereas for women it steadily improves until the women surpass the men. It then drops off slightly for the women, but still remains superior to the level of the men. For both groups, it increases slightly in the latest years.

Categorical thinking decreases during childhood up to the onset of adolescence, after which it increases sharply in early adolescence, reaches its peak in middle adolescence, and declines sharply in late adolescence. It then gradually declines, after which it increases slightly in the latest years. The very high level of categorical thinking during adolescence is an important aspect of the poor constructive thinking in that period. It suggests that adolescents are attempting to simplify their confusing world by thinking in black and white terms and, relatedly, by being prejudiced and intolerant of views that differ from those of their identification group. This is one of the reasons why adults have such difficulty in understanding and having productive conversations with adolescents. The two groups are simply operating on different wavelengths. The adolescents tend to judge people, including themselves, as all good or all bad, as brilliant or as idiots, and as admirably independent or hopelessly dependent. Moreover, one moment they are likely to see the world all one way and the next all the other way. They may judge people, including their parents, as completely for them or completely against them. On one occasion they wish to be treated as dependent children and on another they take offense at being treated as less than mature adults. When adults point out that issues are not so one-sided or otherwise extreme, it usually falls on deaf ears and they simply feel misunderstood. So what, you ask, is a poor parent to do? A constructive thinking one, recognizing the dichotomous thinking of the adolescent as an attempt to gain stability on the path toward establishing a new identity, rather than taking offense at it, understands it for what it is, recognizes that this, too, shall pass, and remains a firm rock of support and guidance. Although the contradictory demands of adolescents can seem quite humorous, the last thing constructive thinking parents should do is laugh at, rather than with, a sensitive adolescent, who frequently desires, above all else, to be taken seriously.

Preadolescent boys and girls are very similar in their categorical thinking. Both exhibit a decrease in categorical thinking up to adolescence. With the onset of adolescence, both exhibit an increase in categorical thinking, but the increase is much greater for boys. The greater categorical thinking of the latter is then maintained through the adult years. Adolescent and older males apparently have a greater need for certainty than females, whose thinking tends to be more open-minded and tolerant.

It can be seen in the figure for esoteric thinking that both sexes exhibit a similar developmental pattern from childhood through late adulthood for this open-minded and, in the extreme, unrealistic kind of thinking. There is a gradual decrease in esoteric thinking during the childhood period, followed by a very sharp increase in early adolescence that reaches its peak in mid-adolescence, then sharply decreases in late adolescence. There is then a leveling off up to middle age, after which another sharp decrease in esoteric thinking takes place. Esoteric thinking thereafter remains constantly low. In summary, children are moderate in their degree of esoteric thinking, adolescents are very high to the point of being unrealistic, young adults are moderate, and older adults are very low.

In all periods, with one exception, females report higher levels of esoteric thinking than males. The exception is in mid-adolescence, when both groups report very high, and about equal, levels of esoteric thinking. That the females at all other periods obtain higher scores than the males indicates that they tend to be either more unrealistic or more open-minded or both. It appears that each group tends to have its characteristic way of thinking, with the females being more unrealistic and open-minded than the males (as indicated by their esoteric-thinking scores) and the males tending to be more rigid and close-minded in their thinking than the females (as indicated by their categorical-thinking scores).

A caveat is in order, however, before applying these gender differences to individuals. It is important to consider that the results are based on group averages and that there is considerable overlap between the groups at all age levels. Many of the females are more categorical in their thinking than the average male, and many of the males are more esoteric in their thinking than the average female. In addition to gender differences, it is of particular interest that both groups exhibit, during middle adolescence, their highest degree of both esoteric thinking and categorical thinking. These are two opposites, with the former indicative of a looseness, or open-mindedness, and the latter with a rigidity, or closed-mindedness, in their thinking. Thus, here again we see evidence of a conflict between opposites and a resultant lack of stability in the thinking of adolescents.

It is not surprising that the youngest children report the greatest degree of naive optimism. Childhood is an age of relatively happy innocence. In a way, one might say that children are happy because they do not know better. As they learn more about the ways the world, have aversive experiences from which their parents cannot protect them, are forced increasingly to depend on their own resources, and have new demands to meet as they mature, they will lose their happy innocence. Naive optimism continues a steady decrease until early adolescence, after which it shows a variable pattern.

ACADEMIC VERSUS WORK EXPERIENCE

To demonstrate the different effects of school and work environments, our research team compared the CTI scores of college students who had been out in the workaday world with classmates with the same average IQ scores who had never been out of school. As you might expect, the students who had been out working were better constructive thinkers than those who had stayed in school continuously. In another study, we gave the CTI to college students between the ages of 18 and 22 and to their parents, who ranged in age from 35 to 70. The better constructive thinkers were not the bright-eyed youngsters at the peak of their abstract intelligence but their parents, whose IQs were declining!

People score significantly higher on global constructive thinking, behavioral coping, and emotional coping in the years after college, when they go out into the working world and assume adult responsibilities. Moreover, people over forty are slightly better constructive thinkers, on average, than younger adults. It is worth noting in particular that people score lower on naive optimism with age throughout the entire life span as they learn to be more realistic.

Remember, though, that our findings are based on *average* scores for people at different ages. As I noted before, experience in living cannot be counted on to improve every individual's constructive thinking. Some people become wiser with experience; others become more frustrated, embittered, and narrow-minded in their thinking.

People typically play the game of life as if they were learning to play tennis without instruction. Although some players pick up the right techniques that way, more develop bad habits that take a lot of work to unlearn. If anything, it is a hopeful sign that most people's constructive thinking improves or stays about the same even when they don't know what constructive thinking is, let alone try to cultivate it. Imagine, then, what you can accomplish if you do understand what is going on in your experiential mind and work at applying the principles of constructive thinking until you can do so automatically.

FOSTERING INSIGHT: AN EXERCISE

In our study of constructive thinking in men and women, Malhee Lee and I asked married couples to take the CTI from two perspectives: their own and their spouse's. That is, participants were instructed to answer as they believed their spouses would if their spouses were completely honest.

The men thought they were better constructure thinkers than they thought their wives were, whereas the women thought they were better constructive thinkers than they thought their husbands were. Moreover, each group rated the other group as less good in constructive thinking than the group rated itself. It seems that people are well aware of others' maladaptive automatic thinking but consider their own automatic thinking reasonable and adaptive.

If you wish to make use of this insight, you might make a point of asking someone you trust and feel comfortable with to help you identify your maladaptive automatic thinking as that person sees it. By now you know enough about constructive thinking to realize that you can benefit from an unbiased opinion, so try not to take offense. If possible, solicit feedback from more than one person on the same issue; any one person may have a biased, distorted viewpoint. But if, after speaking with several people, you see a consistent pattern emerge, there is good reason to take the criticism seriously.

Chapter 13

Parenting Good
Constructive Thinkers

By the time we go out into the world and experience life on our own, our parents have already exerted a strong influence on our constructive thinking. Largely from our parents we develop a model of what the world is like and how we expect people to behave in it. As we go through life, we automatically interpret events in keeping with these expectations. As a result, in the absence of unusual experiences that can change our expectations (as described in the next chapter), we continue to relate to people and to life in general in ways that were consciously and unconsciously influenced by our parents.

Understanding how parents influence their children's constructive thinking can give you insight into the origins of your own constructive and destructive thinking. It can also give you information that can be helpful to you in raising your children to be good constructive thinkers.

NATURE VERSUS NURTURE

Heredity does not play nearly as large a role in constructive thinking as it does in abstract intelligence, or IQ. This is to be expected, since it is part of the very nature of constructive thinking that it develops through experience. As you recall from the last chapter, college students who have been out in the workaday world have higher constructive thinking scores than those who have never been out of school.

Heredity does play some part in the development of constructive thinking through its influence on a child's temperament. According to Jerome Kagan, a developmental psychologist at Harvard University, about 10% of children are born with a tendency to be shy, anxious, and upset by new experiences, and an equal number are born with a tendency to be bold, sociable, and eager for new experiences. Most fall somewhere in between. Those who are most timorous and anxious by temperament are most likely to develop habits of thinking negatively and defensively and therefore to become poor constructive thinkers. The opposite is true of those who, by temperament, are more outgoing and adventurous.

However, heredity works not in a vacuum but in interaction with the environment, so all is not lost for the child who is born shy. Whether a child will thrive or develop poorly in a particular household depends on how the family reacts to her or him. An adventurous, extroverted child who would thrive in most households may feel out of place in a household in which quiet, orderly activities are valued. This child may continually be admonished to quiet down and control herself or himself. "What's wrong with you? Why are you always jumping around? Can't you behave like a normal person?" A temperament that would be advantageous in most environments can be a liability in one that exposes the child to criticism and perhaps even rejection. Conversely, a shy child can, with a sensitive upbringing, gain a feeling of security and competence, so that eventually she or he becomes sociable, confident, and secure.

Parents often say, "We treated both of our children exactly the same. How come they turned out so differently? One is a model student, and the other is always making trouble. It must be heredity." That is a common misconception, for the cause is actually heredity plus environment. The child with a high energy level may need help in settling down emotionally, while the one who is lethargic may need to be given incentives to react more assertively. The child who is sensitive to criticism may need a light touch and a lot of encouragement, while the one who is less sensitive may not need to be treated so cautiously. Once again, constructive thinking is flexible thinking. To create a constructive environment for a child, you need to be sensitive to the child's needs and temperament and to adapt your training procedures accordingly.

DO MOTHERS OR FATHERS HAVE A GREATER INFLUENCE ON CHILDREN'S CONSTRUCTIVE THINKING?

When Martin Seligman and his students tested the thinking styles of a group of ten-year-olds and their parents, they found that both boys and girls resembled their mothers more than their fathers in their thinking styles. Ann Levinger, Carolyn Holstein, and I found the same to be true in a study of constructive thinking in parents and young children. However, in early adolescence (ages 11 to 14), the girls began to switch their identification, so that their constructive thinking resembled their fathers' more than their mothers'. The boys were slower to make this change, but eventually they followed suit. Thus, when Malhee Lee and I (in an earlier study) gave the CTI to college students and their parents, we found that the constructive thinking of both men and women students was more like their fathers' than their mothers'.

It makes sense that young children would be more influenced by their mothers than their fathers, since most spend much more time with their mothers and are more dependent on them for meeting their daily needs. But why should they go to the opposite extreme as they grow toward adulthood and model their constructive thinking after their fathers'? They do not do it because their fathers are actually better constructive thinkers than their mothers, for the average CTI scores of the mothers and fathers in our research were nearly identical.

It seems that the teenage sons appropriately switched from their mothers to their fathers as models of constructive thinking because they were learning to identify with male role models. The daughters made the same switch even earlier, in the mistaken belief (which the sons in our study did not share) that their fathers were better constructive thinkers than their mothers. The daughters in our study were college students, almost all of whom were career-oriented. Identifying with their fathers in their career aspirations, they may have viewed the business world as predominantly a man's world where "male" thinking would lead to advancement. Because of their need to break with the traditional woman's role, they may have overestimated their fathers' constructive thinking in comparison with their mothers'.

In any study, of course, not everyone acts like the majority of people. As always, many individuals vary greatly from the norm. A fair number of sons and daughters do model their constructive thinking more after their mothers than their fathers.

Overall, our study revealed that parents who are good constructive thinkers tend to have children who are good constructive thinkers. However, the relationship between parents' and children's constructive thinking was not nearly as strong as we had expected. Children strayed farthest from the parental model in early adolescence, an age known for rebellious attitudes and behavior. Parents should be reassured to learn that this rejection of their way of thinking is usually temporary, since college students return to a way of thinking closer to that of their parents.

Among the more specific styles of thinking measured by the CTI, the one most closely shared by parents and children was esoteric thinking. A child whose mother or father believed in flying saucers, ghosts, or mental telepathy tended to subscribe to the same belief. Parents' naive optimism was shared by sons, but not by daughters. Categorical thinking was shared by fathers and sons in particular: fathers who were categorical thinkers tended to have sons who were categorical thinkers.

HOW PARENTS INFLUENCE THEIR CHILDREN'S THINKING

Have you ever wondered how a child picks up a parent's way of thinking, or how parents convey the message to a child that it is right to think in a certain way? In general, parents influence their children's thinking in three ways: direct training, indirect training, and modeling. All three play a part in every child's upbringing, and all can be used to transmit either constructive or destructive thinking.

Direct training The most direct way of training your children is to indicate clearly and purposefully what you expect of them, either by telling them outright or by rewarding and punishing them for their behavior. For example, you might say to your child, "Don't hit your little sister. That's no way to solve problems. Talk things over with her. If that doesn't work, come to me." Or you might punish the child with a time-out for hitting his or her little sister.

When you use direct training, it is important to do so properly, with patience and sensitivity. The last thing you want to do is lecture your child in a way that makes him or her feel misunderstood or demeaned. In that case, *what* you say may be intended to promote constructive thinking, but the *way* you say it—the implicit communication—is destructive.

Indirect training. Indirect training means *unintentionally* rewarding or punishing a child for behaving or thinking in a certain way. It is a common source of problems in child rearing, in that parents produce effects they did not intend. A widespread example of indirect training occurs when a parent pays extra attention to a child when the child fails or behaves improperly. A child who feels starved for attention thereby learns that the most effective way to get attention is to fail or misbehave. Parent and child alike may have no idea what is going on in this situation. All they know is that the child keeps failing or misbehaving and that the more they work on changing that pattern, the more it is sustained.

The idea that such indirect rewards and punishments can influence a child's development of constructive and destructive ways of thinking may seem unsettling. If you can have such a strong effect on your child without being aware of it, how can you do anything about it? The answer is that you have to work on becoming aware of this aspect of your child-rearing behavior just as you would any other behavior that is directed by your automatic thinking. The best assurance that your indirect training will motivate your child in a constructive direction is for you to become a good constructive thinker yourself. Then, your natural reactions to your child will tend to be constructive, and you will be a good role model, a topic to which we turn next.

Modeling. Modeling means teaching by example. Parents probably convey at least as much to their children in this way as they do by direct or indirect rewards and punishments. For example, during the bombing of London in World War II, there was great concern that the children would become disturbed by the destruction they saw all around them. As it turned out, what most affected the children was not the actual destruction they witnessed but their parents' reactions. If the parents were calm, the children were calm. If the parents were anxious or hysterical, the children became anxious and had night terrors.

Parents who say, "Do as I say, not as I do" are fighting a losing battle. Kids are not stupid; they know that actions speak louder than words. Parents who harshly spank their child for hitting another child are unintentionally training the child to solve problems by the use of force. Research has demonstrated that children who are subjected to severe physical punishment are more disposed than others to solve problems by physical violence.

Parents often try to train their children directly in constructive thinking. They tell them to plan ahead, not to worry when there is nothing they can do about a situation, not to make mountains out of molehills, and not to be shy because "no one is going to bite your head off." On the face of it, this is all good advice, but it usually is of little value because constructive thinking is more powerfully influenced by experience and observation of others than by instructions. Parents who tell their children that it is foolish to be shy but then show themselves to be uncomfortable when meeting others are letting the child know that at a deeper level they view people as threatening. If you want your child to be a good constructive thinker, you can hardly do better than to provide a model of good constructive thinking in your own thinking and behavior.

BASIC INGREDIENTS FOR PRODUCING GOOD CONSTRUCTIVE THINKERS

Tolstoi's great novel *Anna Karenina* begins with the famous comment: "Happy families are all alike; every unhappy family is unhappy in its own way." On the "happy" side, my recommendations boil down to a few basic principles, which have the ring of what your parents or grandparents might have called "good old-fashioned common sense." The difference is that we now have research to back up some of that common sense. We also know that some supposedly commonsense ideas, such as "Spare the rod and spoil the child," are not very sensible.

Bear in mind, too, that parents are far from all-powerful in their effects on their children. Parents must contend with the effects of inborn temperament and physical characteristics, social and economic conditions, the community and school environment, and the influence of teachers and other children. Even so, research has shown that certain child-rearing practices are more conducive than others to the development of constructive thinking.

Do give children acceptance and respect. One of my students, Todd Welsh, recently studied the effects of physical and emotional abuse on constructive thinking. With regard to "physical punishment," college students reported whether and how often their parents had spanked, slapped, kicked, bitten, pinched, or shaken them. With regard to "psychological punishment," they reported how often their parents had engaged in acts such as accusing them of being a bad person, deliberately embarrassing them, and making fun of them or teasing them.

Todd Welsh expected that physical punishment would have more dire consequences than psychological punishment. He found, however, that the opposite was the case. Students who said their parents had ridiculed and demeaned them were more emotionally disturbed and were poorer constructive thinkers—poorer emotional copers, in particular—than those who said they had been physically punished. Moreover, we found that physical punishment was damaging primarily because of its emotional effect; namely, it damaged the young person's self-esteem.

At the other end of the child-rearing spectrum were references to "respectful treatment" by parents:

- "Tried calmly to reason with me"
- "Listened carefully to my point of view"
- "Asserted his or her view without belittling mine"

Those whose parents had disciplined them in this respectful manner were better constructive thinkers in every respect and were more satisfied with their work, social adjustment, and intimate relationships than those who had been disciplined in a demeaning or coercive way. Clearly, the first principle of constructive child rearing is always to give your child basic acceptance and respect.

Unconditional respect does not rule out the assertion of parental authority so long as it is done with fairness and with due regard for the child as a worthy human being. You can be strict in your punishment, but you need to make clear that you are punishing the child for behaving badly, not for being a bad person. Both in word and in deed, you need to get across the message that "I love you very dearly, but I will not tolerate such behavior."

Do combine love with independence training. Essential as love is, it is not enough. Research has shown that a combination of love *and* parental guidance best prepares children to cope successfully with the world. For example, psychologists Carl Hindy and Conrad Schwarz found that people felt most secure about their love relationships in adulthood when their parents had given them both nurturance and reasonable discipline in child-hood. This "commonsense" finding is also borne out by our research. We found that those who developed into the best constructive thinkers, especially the best behavioral copers, had parents who made them feel loved and, at the same time, trained them to be independent. The poor constructive thinkers often had parents who gave them one but not the other or, worse yet, gave them neither. They had parents who were rejecting, over-protective, or both.

Discipline is the second essential ingredient of good child rearing. It entails both setting limits and making demands on the child that help bring out his or her best. By being reasonably disciplined, a child learns self-discipline, which is an important aspect of behavioral coping. Traditionally, mainly the mother supplies the secure love relationship, and the father supplies the discipline and training in independence. In my research, I have found that this is the most common child-rearing pattern for people who have developed into good constructive thinkers. However, it is by no means the only pattern that can produce the desired results. Children can benefit as well when both parents are loving and both encourage independence. The point is that a child needs both love and discipline, wherever they come from.

Parents sometimes hesitate to set limits for a child for fear the child may feel rejected and may, in turn, reject them. On the contrary, children often interpret excessive permissiveness as a form of abandonment, whereas they interpret reasonable discipline as an expression of caring. A child who is frightened and demoralized by the excesses of a peer group may react with relief when a parent says, "That behavior can really hurt you, and my love for you won't let me ignore it."

Do allow children to experience normal frustrations. How can you best prepare children to deal with adversity? According to psychoanalytic theory, which has had a widespread influence on child-rearing practices for the past two generations, children derive their strength of character primarily from secure relationships with their parents. From this viewpoint, a child who feels sufficiently secure will be able to cope with the vicissitudes of life.

It is true that a child who is generally emotionally secure will cope more effectively with challenging new situations than one who is not. Unfortunately, many parents misinterpret this to mean that they should protect their children from challenges. Because these children do not learn to cope with difficult situations, their emotional security depends on their remaining in a protected environment. Besides, children who have not tested their mettle usually do not feel secure anyway, since they are afraid they will prove inadequate when faced with demanding situations.

If children are protected from the knowledge that the world is not always fair and not always benign, they are apt to be overwhelmed when they learn these hard lessons from real-life experiences. In a study I did with George Catlin, people who said they had enjoyed a high level of acceptance and protection by their parents had their basic beliefs about life more severely shaken when they subsequently underwent a highly distressing experience (such as being physically assaulted or raped) than those who reported less protective relationships with their parents. The people in the first group experienced a "crisis of faith" when their unrealistic expectations about how meaningful, controllable, and predictable the world was were not met.

The study confirmed that people who have had to contend with a degree of adversity early in life often are the stronger for it. Children need to learn that they can handle difficult situations, and they learn it by being exposed to such situations. The experiences need not always be direct. Some can come from observing, reading, or hearing about challenging situations.

When my daughter, Lisa, was six years old, a child in her class called and left a message for Lisa to call back. When Lisa came home from visiting a friend, we gave her the message, and she promptly called. We heard her ask for the child by name, and then all we could hear was someone talking loudly at the other end of the line. Lisa's face turned ashen. She abruptly hung up the phone and dissolved in tears. Her sobbing was so intense that, for a while, she was unable to speak. Finally, she blurted out amid her sobs, "That woman said I'm a rotten kid, and I should never call her daughter again. I hardly know that kid. I was just calling back because you told me to. That lady is a grown-up, and she said I'm rotten, but I didn't do anything wrong."

Try as we might, neither her mother nor I could console Lisa. She had never before been treated that way by a grown-up, and apparently her view of how things work in the world was badly shaken by the experience. I later learned that the woman was a seriously disturbed person who kept her daughter under lock and key. In her loneliness, the poor child attempted to reach out to her classmates in the only way she could, by phoning them.

After a while, I went into Lisa's room. I explained to her that not only kids but grown-ups, too, are sometimes unfair and cruel. I told her that there was nothing for her to feel bad about: she had behaved properly. It was the grown woman, if anyone, who had reason to feel bad for what she had done. This explanation reached Lisa not at all. Then I said, "Remember Cinderella? She had a stepmother who treated her badly. Who do you think should feel bad for what she did, Cinderella or the wicked stepmother?" What I said worked, but not in the way I intended. Lisa began to laugh. She kept laughing and repeating, "I know who that lady is. She is Cinderella's stepmother!"

So, the good constructive thinking was there all the time. Lisa had learned it through a fairy tale—a kind of learning that had reached her in the depths of her emotional being. Because of her previous exposure to

"the wicked stepmother," her model of reality was all in place for absorbing the threatening new experience. It just needed to be activated. As this
anecdote illustrates, children derive vital experiential learning from reading
or hearing threatening stories in the form of fairy tales. It is not helpful to
feed children a completely bland intellectual diet that neither engages their
emotions nor challenges them. As Bruno Bettelheim has pointed out, fairy
tales have lasted over the generations because, among other things, they
have important lessons to teach about coping with adversity.

HOW PARENTS CONTRIBUTE TO DESTRUCTIVE THINKING IN THEIR CHILDREN: SOME COMMON PITFALLS

There are probably more ways of transmitting destructive thinking than
constructive thinking to children. Some of these are obviously harmful;
others are more subtle in their effects and may even come as a surprise to
you. But all of them are variations on a few themes—different ways of
violating the three positive principles: providing love, acceptance, and respect; facilitating self-discipline; encouraging the child to face challenges.

Don't act in a way that will be interpreted as rejection. Although outright
rejection is devastating for a child, it is, fortunately, relatively uncommon.
More commonly, children view parental behavior as rejecting because of
miscommunication or because their parents are insensitive to their needs.

Rejection, whether overt or covert, interferes with the development of
self-love as well as love for others, both of which grow out of the child's
experience of parental love. After all, if not even your parents can love you,
you must not be worth very much. Rejection can also result in learned
helplessness, a form of automatic destructive thinking that Martin Seligman
and others have found to be a source of widespread problems in living,
including a propensity toward depression.

Don't be an authoritarian parent. Authoritarian parents believe that
there is only one right way to do anything, and it happens to be their way.
Demanding that their children accept their view of things on faith, they
end up squelching their children's individuality and creativity. The authoritarian parent says, in effect, "Do as I say. You don't have to understand
why or how. The fact that I told you is enough." Hearing the message that
only the outcome matters, not the process, the child either complies me-
chanically or resists. What the child does not learn is how to think for
himself or herself, exercise judgment, and take initiative. In other words,
the child does not get practice in problem solving, the key to developing
constructive thinking. Through direct training and modeling, the children
of authoritarian parents tend to become authoritarian, inflexible, and categorical in their thinking, just like their parents, although some rebel and
go to the opposite extreme.

Don't overprotect your children. Most parents deeply love their children and wish to spare them difficulties in growing up. As a result, many parents, in particular those who strongly identify with their children, are over-protective. Although they have the best of intentions, they are not serving their children well.

Consider the example of a parent who does a child's homework in an effort to bolster the child's ego by having him or her get a good grade. This help is self-defeating, for the child who succeeds under these circumstances is unable to derive pride from the accomplishment and feels like a fraud. Instead of learning to cope with challenging situations, the child is learning that he or she is incapable of independent accomplishment and must rely on others to get by. In other words, overprotection tends to foster feelings of inadequacy and helplessness.

It does the child no favor to shield him or her from failure, for failure is an inevitable part of learning. You can be helpful to your children by teach-ing them that failure is not a tragedy but an opportunity to learn and to increase the likelihood of success the next time. As you recall from the section on experiencing adversity, there are few more vital lessons to learn on the path to becoming a good constructive thinker than to deal with failure constructively.

Don't give love with strings attached. Conditional love is love that has to be earned by behaving appropriately. It carries the message, "If you are a good child and do as I wish, I will love you, but don't expect me to love you just because you are you." Conditional love amounts to selective re-jection—a withholding of the basic acceptance and respect that a child needs. Children need the security of feeling loved for their own sake and not for what they do. As I explained earlier, there is a big difference be-tween saying (or implying), "I disapprove of what you did" and "What you did makes you a bad person whom I cannot love."

Conditional love produces insecurity about the child's love-worthiness. Often children who feel insecure about whether or not they are love-worthy develop an extreme need to please others. In their automatic thinking (of which they often are not consciously aware), they believe that the only way to get others to care for them is to sacrifice their needs and do as others wish. Even when they are loved, they derive little satisfaction from that love, as they resent the sacrifices they must make to earn it, and they dis-respect themselves for having to operate as they do. Moreover, so long as they keep denying their needs in order to please others, they do not have a chance to learn that this is an unnecessary sacrifice.

Don't treat children as if they have to be very special. Whereas it may not come as news to you that children suffer when their parents are re-jecting or authoritarian, you may be surprised to learn that it is also not the best thing for children to be made to feel that they have to be very special. Having children think that whatever they do is very important is a mixed blessing. On the positive side, it can promote high self-esteem, at least in the short run. On the negative side, it buys this advantage at a high cost in anxiety, for it burdens children with the constant need to excel and to be admired by others. Ultimately, unless they are very unusual, they will come to regard their moderate successes as failures, which can lead them to think less of themselves.

By now you may have noticed a common theme that runs through my discussions of overprotection, conditional love, and treating children as very special. Children brought up in any of these ways often grow up feeling a strong need to please others, whether it is to avoid alienating those on whose protection they depend, to assure themselves of being loved and accepted by others, or to confirm that they are, indeed, very special. In their concern to gain approval or avoid disapproval, they are outcome-oriented rather than problem-oriented, as good constructive thinkers are.

Children pick up this outcome orientation from parents who, instead of training children in independence and useful skills, take the tempting shortcuts of being permissive, authoritarian, or overprotective. Surely it is easier either to accept uncritically whatever the child does, to dictate every detail of what the child must do, or to do things for the child than to provide the guidance and training that enable the child to learn to do things independently. But the easy ways do not train the child to develop self-discipline.

Don't alienate children from their emotions. Some parents (particularly authoritarian parents) regard any display of emotion as a sign of weakness. In order to help their children "master" their emotions, they shame, admonish, or even punish their children for expressing emotions, such as fear, that they regard as signs of weakness. These parents do not realize that courage does not mean being unafraid when confronted with danger—one wouldn't last very long that way—but acting courageously in spite of fear. Other parents think emotions are a hindrance because they interfere with the exercise of reason. From what you know about the experiential mind and its close relationship with emotions, it should be evident that these parents overestimate the importance of reason and underestimate the part emotions play in coping with life's problems.

Emotional reactivity is a vital part of being human. Emotions can be trained, disciplined, and redirected, as you will see in Part IV, but they cannot simply be turned on and off like water in a faucet. They are like reflex reactions to pleasurable or painful stimuli. To suppress them would remove the most reliable guide—one's internal "weather vane"—for seeking pleasure and avoiding pain. Parents do not make their children more reasonable by requiring them to disown their emotions. On the contrary, they make them less reasonable, as they are at the mercy of the very emotions with which they have lost touch.

Dr. Nancy Eisenberg, a professor of psychology at the University of Arizona, and her colleagues have found that if mothers discourage their sons from expressing sadness and anxiety, although the boys report experiencing less distress than do other boys when viewing upsetting movies, when indirect measures are obtained of physiological arousal and facial expression, they reveal that these children actually experience more distress than other children. Such children have also been found to have more problems with their social adjustment than others. This and similar research makes it clear that parents do their children no favor when they teach them to suppress their negative emotions. All they accomplish is to drive the emotions underground, where they are experienced with increased intensity and are no longer under the control of the individual.

Another mistake parents make is to try to interpret their children's emotions for them. Wanting their children to have certain desirable feelings, they brainwash the children into thinking they have these feelings when, in fact, they have different ones. Five-year-old David was angry at his mother for not buying the toy he saw advertised on television. He pleaded with her, telling her how much he needed that toy, but to no avail. Finally, with tears in his eyes, he yelled at her, "I hate you. You never do anything I want." His mother replied, "I know you don't really mean that, David. You know how much Mommy loves you, and I know you love Mommy. You're just using the wrong word. What you *really* mean is you're frustrated because you can't have what you want."

Actually, David had it right in the first place. At that moment he did hate his mother, which, of course, does not mean that at other times he does not love her. Although his mother meant well, she was training him to be confused about his anger. What she could have said instead was, "I know you are angry at me, and that's OK. I know how you feel because I also get angry when I can't get things that I want very much. I don't think that's a good toy for you, so I'm sorry I can't get it for you."

Some years ago, one of my colleagues and his wife wanted to prepare their three-year-old daughter, Jennifer, for a new baby. So they bought her a doll they called "new baby." Day after day they played "new baby" with Jennifer, who was expected to show, by kissing and hugging the doll, how happy she was about the prospect of having a new little family member to play with. Their purpose was to teach Jennifer to love her new sister or brother instead of feeling jealous. To accomplish this, they launched what amounted to an intensive advertising campaign. If Jennifer intimated she was not so sure she wanted a new baby, she was told that babies were great fun and that she would soon learn to love her brother or sister.

When the real new baby arrived on the scene, Jennifer registered little enthusiasm, and she avoided going into the baby's room. One day, her mother coaxed Jennifer to go over to the baby's crib and give her a big hug and a kiss. On the way, Jennifer walked by "new baby," the doll, lying on the floor. Jennifer "accidentally" stepped on the doll and ground her heel into its face.

The moral of this story is that teaching children to deny or distort their emotions, rather than to accept and cope with them, is likely to backfire. When children lose touch with their emotions, suppressed feelings may be expressed indirectly—and destructively. Worse yet, children can become confused about who they are and what they want out of life. This is why people in therapy often say they are on a quest to discover "the real me."

Don't get down on yourself for not being a perfect parent. Now that I've told you all the things you should avoid doing to your children, I want to remind you about something you should avoid doing to yourself if you wish to be a good constructive thinker. Don't punish yourself with negative categorical thinking because you are not a perfect parent. No one is perfect as a parent, and most children survive quite well. If you see yourself engaging in one of the destructive forms of thinking and behavior I have just described, do work on improving it. Be as patient and tolerant with yourself as you would want to be with your child. By identifying the ways in which you behave destructively toward your children and then taking constructive action to influence the way your experiential mind operates (using the techniques outlined in Part IV), you will be breaking the cycle by which destructive thinking is transmitted from one generation to the next.

Chapter 14

How Life Experience Affects Constructive Thinking

Although parents have a great influence on whether or not their children become good constructive thinkers, they are hardly the only influence. For one thing, some individuals who have had difficult childhoods still grow up to be effective and resourceful people. Moreover, the basic beliefs that are an important part of constructive thinking—beliefs that the world is benign versus malevolent, that it is predictable versus capricious, that people are helpful versus threatening, and that the self is worthy versus unworthy—have their origins in emotionally significant experiences that can occur not only in childhood but throughout life. They may be extreme single events, such as being the victim of a violent crime, or, more often, recurring patterns of events, as might occur in an abusive relationship or in the course of growing up in an inner-city "war zone." Some experiences are so significant that they can change the patterns of automatic thinking that are learned in childhood, turning a person into either a better or poorer constructive thinker.

WHY PEOPLE MAINTAIN NEGATIVE VIEWS OF THEMSELVES

It is easy enough to see how people learn early in life to be poor constructive thinkers. But why do they *remain* poor constructive thinkers, even when they have ample reason to think better of themselves? I gained some insight into this when I did a study of how people overgeneralize from the outcomes of good and bad events. The people who participated in this study, in addition to taking the Constructive Thinking Inventory, answered "true," "false," or "undecided" to questions such as these:

- "If someone I know was accepted at an important job interview, he or she would feel very good and think that he or she would always be able to get a good job."
- "If someone I know was rejected at an important job interview, he or she would feel very low and think that he or she would never be able to get a good job."
- "If I was accepted at an important job interview, I would feel very good and think that I would always be able to get a good job."
- "If I was rejected at an important job interview, I would feel very low and think that I would never be able to get a good job."

The results came out loud and clear. Good and poor constructive thinkers did not differ in the way they answered the first three questions. That is, they did not differ as to how much they overgeneralized from either good or bad things that happened to other people or in the extent to which they overgeneralized following good things that happened to themselves. The only difference was in how they answered the fourth question. Poor constructive thinkers overgeneralized much more than good constructive thinkers following *bad* things that happened to *themselves.*

These findings tell us that poor constructive thinkers do not overgeneralize equally about everything. They overgeneralize most when it comes to bad things about themselves. Somehow they have developed low self-esteem, and they keep it going through negative overgeneralization about themselves.

Low self-esteem often comes from the parent–child relationship. People with high self-esteem carry within them a loving parent who is proud of their successes and tolerant of their failures. People with low self-esteem carry within them a disapproving parent who is harshly critical of their failures while offering only grudging approval when they succeed. As a result, they cannot appreciate their success.

Consider the case of Marilyn Monroe, who became far more successful than she could ever have imagined and had a great deal of love and admiration bestowed on her in her adult life. Yet she summed up her life when she said, "This sad, bitter child who grew up too fast is hardly ever out of my heart. With success all around me, I can still feel her frightened eyes looking out of mine." Marilyn Monroe had a miserable childhood in which she learned to think of herself as unlovable and of the world as rejecting. Once she had formed this outlook, all the success and attention that came to her could not penetrate her belief system to satisfy her insatiable need for love and acceptance. She once said that she reacted to applause as if she were an onlooker watching someone else being applauded.

But why doesn't a child shake off the disapproving parent whose strictures are not only damaging but often utterly unjustified? Why doesn't the child think, as a good constructive thinker would, "I am just a child, and I deserve to be loved like any other child. If my mother doesn't love me, it's not that I am a bad child; it's that she is a bad mother." This, of course, is a grown-up way of thinking. Besides, it is a counterproductive way to think, if you are a child who desperately needs to gain your mother's approval. If you are completely dependent on your mother's goodwill, it makes sense to judge yourself by the standards she has set for you. If your mother is bad, then there is nothing you can do about it. But if you are the bad one, then at least there is the hope that by changing your ways, you can eventually win your mother's love. That hope can be extremely difficult to let go of.

Do not underestimate the power of a child's desire to believe his or her mother is a good person—even when the child is being abused. Four-year-old James was beaten repeatedly by his mother. On one occasion, she broke his arm. When the boy was told that he would be separated from his mother, despite all assurances that he would be cared for by nice people who would not beat him, he still clung to his mother and pleaded with the authorities not to take her away. He said, "She is a good mommy. If you don't take her away, I'll be very, very good, so she won't have to beat me anymore."

Stories such as this suggest one reason people maintain negative self-images. As a result of their early childhood experiences, some people have learned to see themselves as bad in order to avoid being angry at those whose love they crave. By the time they reach adulthood, this way of thinking about themselves has become completely automatic, and they often have no idea of its origin.

THE RESILIENT MIND

Given that many children do grow up in homes or neighborhoods that are breeding grounds for negative attitudes and destructive thinking, will all of these children be scarred for life by their unpromising origins? We might well get that impression from the media, with their emphasis on the lasting effects of victimization, abuse, and trauma. Today the "child of an alcoholic" or "codependent" has become the symbol of the crippling effects that childhood experience is believed to have on an ever-widening circle of people. One book about children of alcoholics goes so far as to say that 96% of the population have come from "dysfunctional families." It's enough to make one wonder what a "functional" family really is, or whether life itself is to be regarded as one great trauma.

Fortunately, this defeatist outlook is being challenged by researchers and clinicians who take a more hopeful view of people's capacity for independent thinking and growth. Some of them have become interested in what they call "resilient children," children who were raised under conditions of severe deprivation or abuse yet managed to acquire unusual constructive-thinking skills that allowed them to transcend their environments and develop into successful, well-adjusted adults.

Originally, these children were referred to as "invulnerable children," but this designation was overly optimistic; no one is invulnerable. Even the children identified as resilient did not come through their ordeals unscathed but retained sensitivities associated with their early deprivation or abuse. For example, those who saved themselves by detaching themselves emotionally from a highly disturbed parent often remained insecure about establishing close relationships with others.

Steven Wolin, a psychiatrist, and Sybil Wolin, a child-development specialist, have written a book called *Resilience: How Survivors of Troubled Families Keep the Past in Its Place*. They define resilience as "the capacity to rise above adversity and forge lasting strengths in the struggle." For the resilient child, "the family is not only a destructive force but an opportunity. Survivors are challenged by the family's troubles to experiment and to respond actively and creatively." As we saw in the last chapter, the most devastating effect of parental abuse is the damage to a child's self-esteem. Resilient children, the Wolins found, manage to maintain their self-esteem despite their parents' negative influence.

How do they do it? Often they find a "polestar," an adult who takes a child under his or her wing, makes the child feel loved and appreciated, and serves as a mentor and an inspiration. Some resilient children seek out a polestar, while others are lucky enough to be discovered by one—for example, an interested relative or some other adult. The more I read about cases of unusual survival in both children and adults, the more impressed I am with the role such luck often plays. Still, one must have the capacity to take advantage of luck when it occurs.

According to the Wolins, one of the ways children emancipate themselves from the destructive thinking induced by a bad environment is by developing what amounts to good constructive-thinking skills:

Children—perhaps as young as five or six—develop a hunch that something is wrong with their troubled parents. Their first awareness may be sensory: the father's key rattling and missing the lock, the sound of feet dragging on the front walk. Over the course of development, these initial sensory impressions refine and diversify into empathy, introspection, clear thinking, and an ability to tolerate life with its complexities and ambiguities.

Simply in the course of everyday life, these children are learning to think independently. They are training their experiential minds to take in new evidence rather than to rely on the destructive interpretations of their parents.

However they do it, resilient children learn to make the best of their deprived environments. With or without a polestar, perhaps with the aid of luck and a questioning mind, they take what the environment has to offer and do not waste their energy fretting about what it cannot give them. In short, they become precocious constructive thinkers with a problem-oriented approach to living, an accepting attitude toward themselves and others, and an optimistic and hopeful attitude about the future.

Similar qualities, except for the need to find a polestar, have been observed in adolescents and adults who survive in extremely difficult conditions. Not only do these individuals not break down, but they often acquire unusual coping skills and wisdom in their crises of survival. In this way, some have surmounted such ordeals as being sent to a Nazi concentration camp after seeing their families murdered or having to serve in combat under brutalizing conditions. Typically, these survivors have displayed the following qualities:

1. __ Self-accepting
2. __ Accepting of others
3. __ Confident
4. __ Flexible and adaptable
5. __ Independent, able to act on one's own and trust one's decisions
6. __ Optimistic, maintains positive attitude toward life
7. __ Resilient, bounces back quickly following frustration, maintains hope and avoids depressive, self-defeating thoughts
8. __ Realistic, takes reasonable but not unreasonable risks, knows whom and when to trust
9. __ Reaches out to others, accepts help when appropriate, and does not try to do everything oneself
10. __ Maintains a sense of purpose and a broad perspective

These traits are useful not only for coping with extreme adversity but also for successful living under normal circumstances. Not surprisingly, the list describes the attributes of a good constructive thinker. How would you come out on this list? Rate yourself by entering a number from 1 to 7 in the space to the left of each item, according to the following scale:

1 = much less than most people
2 = somewhat less than most people
3 = slightly less than most people
4 = about average
5 = slightly more than most people
6 = somewhat more than most people
7 = much more than most people

To find out how much you share the attributes of supersurvivors, add up the numbers you have assigned yourself. Interpret your score as follows:

10–19 = very low
20–29 = low
30–49 = average
50–59 = high
60–70 = very high

So now you have an indication of how suited you are to survive under extremely adverse conditions, plus an additional measure (along with your CTI score from Chapter 2) of how good a constructive thinker you are. But it is only an indication, not a definitive judgment. If your score was not as high as you would want it to be, remember that this was just a brief test that revealed only what you thought about yourself at a particular moment. If you conclude that you really could stand to improve your constructive thinking, the next four chapters show you how you can work systematically to do just that.

As you set out on the path to improving your constructive thinking, you have ample reason for optimism. As the evidence in this chapter shows, people change by learning from experience. Even without deliberately trying to improve their constructive thinking, people overcome difficult early environments more commonly than was once believed possible. Several studies that followed people from birth to maturity have confirmed that most children who were exposed to difficult childhood environments—such as severe parental conflict, alcoholism, divorce, and death—ultimately become well adjusted adults. In one of these studies, Alexander Thomas and Stella Chess compared 133 children from disturbed backgrounds to a group of children with normal childhoods. They found that only six of the 133 children from disadvantaged backgrounds were seriously emotionally disturbed as young adults. The vast majority were no less happy and successful than those in the comparison group. Steven and Sybil Wolin's research has similar findings. The obstacles we meet from childhood on, even severe ones, can serve not only as a source of distress and maladjustment but also as a challenge and a training ground for developing unusual skills in constructive thinking.

I will give the last word on the subject of resilience to television star Roseanne Barr, who offers this capsule summary of her life:

I'm thirty-seven years old. I've got four kids. I'm Jewish and I was raised in Salt Lake City, Utah. I was raised a Mormon and my dad sold crucifixes door-to-door to Mexicans. When I was seven, I fell down and bit off my whole lip and had to have that sewn back on. When I was sixteen, I got hit by a car and got my head impaled on the hood ornament. I got pregnant the first time I ever had sex. My parents made me give her up for adoption. I found her eighteen years later after her face was splashed across the front page of the *National Enquirer*. Spent eight months in a state mental institution. Hitchhiked across country three times all by myself—with hepatitis. Lived in a car, a cabin, and a cave. Married a guy just because he had a bathtub. Had three more kids. He treated me like [expletive] for sixteen years, and when I finally had the guts to dump that SOB, I have to pay him half the money I make for the rest of my goddamn life.

You want to mess with me? Don't even think about it. I've been through it all, and I'm as tough as they come.

HOW EMOTIONALLY SIGNIFICANT EVENTS INFLUENCE CONSTRUCTIVE THINKING THROUGHOUT LIFE

What kind of experience would be powerful enough to redirect your ways of coping with your environment and your basic beliefs about yourself and the world? Assuming you had a negative self-image, you might, on the positive side, fall in love with someone who cared about you deeply. By experiencing such a gratifying relationship, you would probably become more optimistic and trusting in others, and your self-esteem would increase. On the negative side, your spouse might leave you or die in an accident, leaving you to raise three young children by yourself. Depending on how you interpreted that event, you could become more pessimistic and feel more helpless.

To see just how great an effect events like these have on people's thinking, George Catlin (a graduate student at the time, and now a Ph.D. psychologist) and I asked more than 300 college students to report whether, and at what age, they had experienced certain emotionally significant events. At the same time, we gave them a specially constructed test of their basic beliefs. This test asked them to respond to statements such as these:

- "By and large, I feel that my personal world is a reasonably safe and secure place."
- "My life is lacking in purpose and meaning."
- "I feel that I have little control over the important events in my life."
- "I feel I get a raw deal out of life."
- "I like people and believe in giving them the benefit of the doubt."
- "I nearly always have a highly positive opinion of myself."
- "I am often lacking in self-confidence."
- "There are times when I have doubts about my capacity for maintaining a close love relationship."

In this way, we learned whether they believed the world is benign, meaningful, controllable, and just; whether they believed people are trustworthy;

and whether they believed themselves to be worthy, competent, and lovable.

We found that extreme events, favorable and unfavorable alike, had strong immediate effects on people's basic beliefs. These effects diminished over time but never completely disappeared. Sexual abuse, being the victim of a violent crime, and undergoing a severe rejection all had a lasting effect on a person's outlook. People who experienced these events were, on the average, more negative thinkers and had lower self-esteem than people who had not had such experiences. The same was true in the opposite direction for people who experienced very favorable events, such as a great success or an unusually rewarding love relationship. The greater the number of extremely bad experiences a person had, the stronger the negative effect on the person's self-esteem and outlook on the world. The greater the number of extremely good experiences, the stronger the positive effect.

Can an initially unfavorable experience ultimately have a *favorable* impact on a person's constructive thinking? What we have learned about resilient children suggests that this is, indeed, the case. Psychologists Carl Rogers and Abraham Maslow speak of a "growth principle," by which initially destructive experiences become constructive ones as a person rises to the challenge of surmounting them. I observed the operation of this principle in a study I conducted with a student, Marguerite Ofria. We had people report the single most devastating event in their life and how, if at all, they got over it. We were surprised at how many people said that what had originally been a devastating event ultimately turned into a positive growth experience. Even the death of a parent led some children to develop greater self-reliance and initiative. Not everyone, of course, reacted like this. Some became disillusioned and cynical. The difference, we found, resulted from what their attitudes toward others had been before the incident. Those who had the positive growth experiences said they were initially more trusting of others than those who did not. Those in the other group reported that they were originally suspicious of, and distant from, others and that the adverse experience made them even more so. As a result, they shut themselves off from the possibility of having healing relationships or otherwise being favorably influenced by others.

TRAUMATIC STRESS: THE SEVEREST TEST OF CONSTRUCTIVE THINKING

What are the limits of human resilience? This question has come to haunt our consciousness and our conscience since the Vietnam War, as the aftereffects of that tragic conflict have drawn our attention to the term *posttraumatic stress disorder* (PTSD). Posttraumatic stress disorder, which was recognized by professionals as far back as World War I, may occur not only in the aftermath of war but also following a wide range of traumatic events, such as rape and other violent crime, physical and sexual abuse, automobile and plane crashes, the loss of one's home through a natural disaster, or financial collapse.

That does not mean, of course, that it happens to everyone who suffers these losses. According to a recent book by Lisa McCann and Lori Pearlman, the effect of a potentially traumatic event depends on how vulnerable a person is to that particular kind of trauma. A person who has sensitivities about self-esteem is particularly susceptible to being traumatized by events the person can interpret as demeaning. A person with sensitivities about intimate relationships is particularly susceptible to being traumatized by rejection by a loved one.

A person who has PTSD regularly reexperiences the traumatic event in the form of nightmares, frightening memories intruding into daytime consciousness, or flashbacks in which the person relives the trauma. These sensations are always accompanied by intense anxiety. In a self-protective reaction to the overstimulation brought on by recurrent memories of the trauma, the person periodically becomes numb and unresponsive.

Additional basic symptoms of PTSD include sleep disturbance, sensitivity to reminders of the trauma, feelings of detachment and sometimes an inability to form close relationships, loss of interest in normal activities (such as holding a job), guilt feelings over having survived when others were killed or seriously injured ("survivor guilt"), unreasonable risk taking, and inappropriately violent or hostile behavior. Which of these symptoms will be present depends on the nature of the trauma. Finally, as you might expect, people with PTSD typically engage in various forms of destructive thinking, such as negative views of oneself and the world, poor emotional coping, poor behavioral coping, and categorical thinking ("Nothing that comes from the government is trustworthy").

How do previously normal, well-functioning individuals get to think in this way? It is by having their basic beliefs shattered by an experience so emotionally significant that it invalidates the way they previously made sense of the world. The recurrent intrusions of the traumatic memory represent the mind's attempt to make sense of what its old belief system could not accept. It is as if the mind cannot let go of the experience until it can assign it a place in its system of meaning.

The effects of posttraumatic stress on the basic beliefs of Vietnam veterans were the subject of a doctoral dissertation by a student of mine, Kenneth Fletcher. He found that soldiers' beliefs about themselves, other people, and the world became less favorable during the war and continued to decline for some months following discharge, regardless of whether or not the soldiers developed PTSD. For those who did not develop PTSD, this downward course reversed itself, and the veterans began to recover their earlier, more favorable attitudes toward themselves, the world in general, and other people. Years later, their basic beliefs had rebounded considerably, although not quite to the level of their youthful innocence. They had become sadder, but wiser, people who could accept both the good and the evil in the world.

For those veterans with PTSD, on the other hand, the decline continued after the war without ever reversing itself. The only way these soldiers' experiences differed from the experiences of those who did not have PTSD was that they had been exposed to more severe combat stresses. As a result, their belief systems were not simply temporarily altered, but radically transformed. They developed a new belief system built around their disillusionment with a hostile and destructive world, their mistrust of other people, and their disrespect for themselves. Moreover, they believed it was dangerous to relate to others because they had learned how much it hurt to lose people they cared for.

Such beliefs, once firmly entrenched, became the foundation of a new, thoroughly negative belief system that produces self-fulfilling expectations and colors the interpretation of new experiences. Having accepted a new model of the world, these veterans were driven to prove its validity, just as they had previously tried to maintain the validity of their more benign belief system, and so they often brought about the very conditions about which they complained.

Observing the symptoms of PTSD and the course of the disorder over time helps us to understand how people's basic belief systems, formed and maintained by automatic interpretations of emotionally significant experiences in the experiential mind, determine whether we live in a heaven or a hell on earth. Once we understand this process, we can begin to intervene to make it work to our benefit. By using special techniques to teach the experiential mind that the present is not the same as the past, we can free our experiential minds—and thus free ourselves—from the destructive experiences of the past.

PART IV

Improving Your Constructive Thinking

Chapter 15

Getting to Know Your Experiential Self

All of us have at times found ourselves unable to get maladaptive thoughts out of our heads. "Why am I so sensitive; why do I let that person's foolishness get to me? It's over and done with, so why don't I just forget it?"

Many people chastise themselves when they find their willpower is not up to the task of changing such automatic thoughts. This simply adds insult to injury or, more precisely, adds more destructive thinking to some destructive thinking. It is important to remember that it is impossible to change your automatic thinking by willpower alone. If it *were* possible, you would probably have gotten rid of your destructive thinking long ago. In fact, research by Dr. Daniel M. Wegner, a psychologist at the University of Virginia, indicates that the harder you try to not have certain unwanted thoughts, the more you will have the thoughts the moment you relax your attention. You need to make changes in your experiential mind, not your rational mind, because your experiential mind is responsible for such destructive thinking. You can no more order your experiential mind around than you can lecture your dog or cat on how to behave.

To change your experiential mind, you need to understand how it operates, to approach the task with an appropriate attitude, and, most important, to practice changing your automatic thinking. Because your experiential mind learns from experience, understanding is not enough. That is why this chapter and the ones that follow give you exercises for gaining experience in implementing your understanding.

In order to understand how your experiential mind works, you first need to diagnose your automatic thinking. You have already diagnosed it in one way by taking the CTI in Chapter 4. The purpose of that test, however, was to show you how well your automatic thinking equipped you for various kinds of success in living. When it comes to *improving* your constructive thinking, you need a more detailed diagnosis that reveals the actual operation of your automatic thinking. This chapter gives you diagnostic procedures that tell you what you specifically must change if you wish to improve your constructive thinking.

AN ATTITUDE OF ACCEPTANCE

To improve your automatic thinking, you need to adopt a problem-solving orientation and an attitude of acceptance. The more you judge yourself to be bad for having certain thoughts, the less open you will be to identifying your automatic thoughts. You should start by observing your automatic thoughts without evaluation in a spirit of curiosity. Don't scare your automatic thoughts away by threatening them with judgment. Simply be a good observer.

Despite your best intentions, you will no doubt find yourself slipping and making judgments. What do you do then? You put your judgments aside and continue to observe your automatic thoughts without judgment.

UNDERSTANDING YOUR CHAIN OF REACTIONS

The following sequence of reactions takes place between an event and a behavioral response:

1. You interpret, or "construe," the event.
2. You react to the construal with an emotional response.
3. You may then have further thoughts, or "secondary mental responses."
4. The secondary mental responses may produce a change in your emotion.
5. Finally, you will often (but not always) make a behavioral response.

Here is a simple example, with an accompanying diagram (Figure 15.1), that compares a constructive and destructive sequence of reactions to the same initial event. John says "Good morning" to Mary. Mary walks by without replying. John construes her behavior as a snub. He reacts to the construal by becoming angry. Continuing in this vein, he decides that Mary is a snobbish person and that he will treat her in kind by snubbing her. Thinking this way increases his anger. The result is that he and Mary become antagonistic.

John could have initially viewed the situation differently by considering that Mary might be too preoccupied to see or hear him. Or else, after becoming angry and thinking about snubbing Mary next time, he could have had a corrective "second thought," such as that his first thought was

Figure 15.1
Constructive and Destructive Reactions to the Same Event

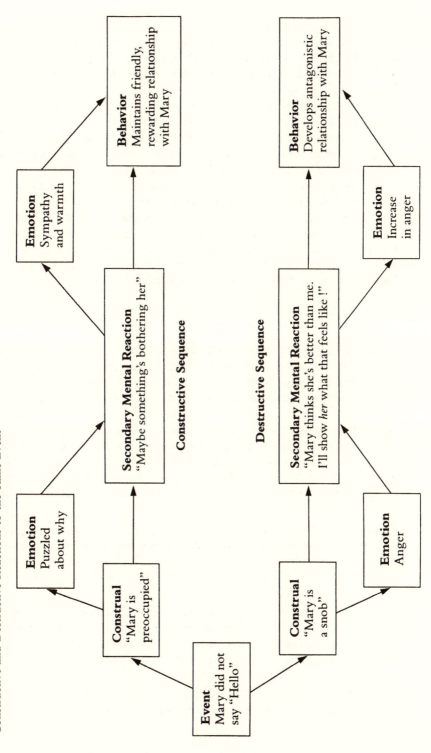

destructive. He could then have revised his initial construal and decided that Mary was just distracted. His anger would then have subsided, and he would greet Mary next time with a warm hello, to which she would probably respond in kind. As a result, John and Mary would remain friendly.

Many self-help programs miss the point when they emphasize coping strategies while disregarding construals. Once people have construed events in nonconstructive ways, their coping reactions can do just so much in damage control. Damage control is helpful, but it is even better to avoid the damage in the first place. That is why construals are usually the most important part of constructive and destructive thinking; yet people are usually much more aware of how they cope with events after they have interpreted them than of how they interpret (construe) them in the first place. In fact, most people are often completely unaware that they are constantly interpreting events and can choose to interpret them differently. By assuming that they respond directly to objective events, they are at a loss as to how to go about changing their feelings and behavior.

BECOMING AWARE OF YOUR CONSTRUALS

The way we construe events influences almost everything we think, feel, and do. As soon as we are born, we begin to interpret events automatically and to build a model of the world, or "theory of reality." Once we make certain interpretations, they become part of our personal theory of reality. In the beginning, each emotionally significant event we experience has a relatively good opportunity to influence the theory. However, as our personal theory of reality is filled in by a growing body of experience, it increasingly influences new experiences more than they influence it. That is why what we experience in childhood does so much to shape our outlook on life. Carlos Castaneda elegantly described this phenomenon as follows:

Sorcerers say that we are inside a bubble. It is a bubble in which we are placed at the moment of our birth. At first the bubble is open but then it begins to close until it has sealed us in. That bubble is our perception. We live inside that bubble all of our lives. And what we witness on its round walls is our own reflection.

The most useful way to become aware of your automatic construals is by becoming aware of the thoughts and images that precede your feelings. When any event occurs that might affect you emotionally, pay careful attention to two aspects of your automatic reactions:

• *Self-talk*: the stream of verbal commentary that goes on in your head and that becomes more evident when your emotions are strong

- *Imagery*: visual images, word pictures, and metaphors of varying degrees of clarity (including vague impressions)

People differ in the degree to which their thoughts consist of words as opposed to images. Although you will probably be more readily aware of self-talk than of imagery, try to be alert to both.

When you have a strong emotion, the construals that produced the emotion will usually be evident because your self-talk tends to be loud and clear. You may even curse aloud or make audible statements to yourself, such as "What an idiot I am!" or "How could he do that to me? I'd really like to give him a piece of my mind!" When you make such statements, observe how they cause your emotion to intensify.

It is especially revealing to see how sad statements exacerbate sad emotions. You can observe this most easily in children. A young child may be completely composed until she tells her mother about how her sibling took away her ice cream cone. Hearing her own sad story causes her to dissolve in a flood of tears. The same process occurs as well when a person silently thinks similar thoughts.

Particularly for weak emotions, there may be no detectable self-talk or discernible imagery. In such cases, you may need to do some mental experimentation to detect your implicit construals. Try making different statements to yourself until you get one that "clicks," that *feels* exactly right for the emotion you experienced. Another helpful technique is to see what self-talk you would have to engage in to intensify the feeling. With practice, you will learn both to catch the fleeting statements you make to yourself and to improve your ability to infer meanings when you cannot find explicit statements.

AN EXERCISE FOR DETECTING YOUR AUTOMATIC CONSTRUALS

The purpose of this exercise is to give you practice in detecting the automatic construals behind various emotions. Each of the three following vignettes describes something that might happen to you. For each event, place a check after the emotions you think you would experience. Next, write in the automatic thoughts you would most likely have *that can account for the specific emotion(s) you checked.*

Base your answers on how you have reacted to similar situations in the past. If you have not had a similar experience, imagine the situation as vividly as you can and estimate how you would probably react.

If you think your main emotional reaction would be different from any of those listed, write it down in the space for "Other emotion." Then place a check next to it and fill in your automatic thoughts just as if that emotion had been listed. For additional practice, write in the automatic thoughts that you think would produce the emotions you did not check.

It is important that the automatic thoughts you report clearly account for the emotions you checked. Be sure to select, from all the automatic thoughts you might have, *only those that account for the emotion you reported*. Remember, the point of this exercise is to give you practice in sorting out the specific automatic thoughts that are the sources of different emotions.

The first vignette is followed by an example of how someone might fill in the blanks. When you fill in your own answers, be sure to report what *you* would actually think *that can account for the emotion in question*.

Situation 1

You are at a restaurant with a group of people you know only casually. You agree to collect the money from the others and pay the bill. You find you have been shortchanged by five dollars, yet everyone claims he or she has put in the right amount.

Sample Response

Angry at others: ____ Automatic thoughts: *Those damn fools! Either they can't count right or they are downright dishonest.*

_____

Angry at yourself: √ Automatic thoughts: *What an idiot I am! Won't I ever learn? I can't blame them for taking advantage of someone as dumb as me.*

_____

Amused or unconcerned:____Automatic thoughts: *You win some, and you lose some. Everybody makes mistakes. What's a few bucks, anyway?*

_____

Other emotion (write in): _____ Automatic thoughts:_____

_____

_____

Now fill in how you would probably respond to Situation 1.

Your Response

Angry at others: ____ Automatic thoughts: _____

_____

_____

Angry at yourself: ____ Automatic thoughts: _____

_____

_____

Amused or unconcerned: ____ Automatic thoughts:_____

_____

_____

Other emotion (write in): ____ Automatic thoughts: _____

_____

_____

_____

_____

Situation 2

You have been waiting in line at a supermarket for a long time when someone with a full cart of groceries cuts in to join a friend at the front of the line.

Angry: ____ Automatic thoughts: _____

_____

_____

Amused or unconcerned: ____ Automatic thoughts: _____

_____

_____

Other emotion (write in): ____ Automatic thoughts: _____

_____

_____

Situation 3

You are working for an organization that is laying off some people and promoting others in order to streamline its operation. You have just learned from a fellow employee that management has been asking questions about your performance.

Frightened: _____ Automatic thoughts: _____

_____

_____

Happy: _____ Automatic thoughts: _____

_____

_____

Sad: _____ Automatic thoughts: _____

_____

_____

Other emotion (write in): _____ Automatic thoughts: _____

_____

_____

_____

Now go back over the exercise to make sure that the automatic thoughts you described would produce the specific emotions you reported. Examine your responses. Note how the ways you think determine the emotions you feel. It will be evident that it is possible to change the emotions you feel by changing the thoughts you automatically think. This is something you will be working on later. For now, it is enough to become aware of the connection between your automatic construals and your emotions.

BECOMING AWARE OF YOUR SECONDARY MENTAL AND BEHAVIORAL RESPONSES

Once you construe a potentially stressful event a certain way, you then have to cope with the consequences of your construal. Take the example of an employee whose first reaction to a supervisor's criticism is to construe it as an attack. Having made this interpretation, he may have any of a variety of second thoughts (secondary mental responses), such as he should get back at the employer, or improve his performance so the employer will not be angry with him, or reconsider whether he was really attacked. These thoughts will be followed by behavioral responses, such as acting aggressively toward the supervisor, working on improving one's performance, or doing something else.

The employee's construals, secondary mental responses, and behavioral responses all reveal something about his constructive thinking. To be a good constructive thinker, you have to think and behave constructively in all of these ways.

Let us examine the employee's responses more closely. Once he construed the criticism as an attack, his automatic thoughts might continue along these lines: "I can't stand that supervisor. He is always picking on me. He makes me feel awful. I don't have to take that from anyone. I'll get back at him at every opportunity I can get away with." Both the secondary mental responses and the behavioral responses are clearly destructive. The secondary mental responses make the employee feel terrible about the supervisor's criticism. The behavioral responses are sure not only to antagonize the supervisor, which is to the employee's disadvantage, but also to prevent the employee from improving his job performance, which is also to his disadvantage. The employee may have a high IQ, but his constructive thinking is so poor that what he does is no smarter than cutting off his nose to spite the supervisor's face.

You can become more aware of your secondary mental responses and their influence on your feelings and behavior by tuning in to your stream of consciousness and observing the procession of thoughts. Imagine yourself standing at the door of a restaurant, waiting for an acquaintance who is late. You might well be annoyed, a feeling triggered by a construal such as "She didn't care enough about our lunch date to get here on time." As your secondary mental responses enter the picture, this negative interpretation might escalate to "What a careless person—I'll bet she forgot all about it." This would intensify your feelings of anger. Then again, your thoughts might run in a different direction, such as "What if she had an accident on the way? What if she was mugged?" That interpretation would trigger a feeling of concern: "I hope she's OK." This feeling, if you dwelt on the interpretations that produced it, could escalate into intense anxiety.

Your behavior, too, would vary according to the way you thought about the situation. In the one case, you might stomp off in a huff; in the other, you might pace nervously back and forth, when, in fact, there would be nothing you could do to help the person or even to ascertain her whereabouts.

A more constructive way to react would be to do what you could to clarify the situation and, if nothing could be done, to avoid jumping to conclusions. In that case, any feelings of annoyance or concern you might have would not be elevated to strong feelings of anger or anxiety, and you would remain relatively calm. This hypothetical example shows how you can use your emotions to detect your underlying thoughts, whether they are immediate construals or delayed responses. The implication, which will be implemented in later chapters, is that you can change your emotions by changing your thoughts.

Having encouraged you to attend to your secondary mental responses, I must reiterate that this amounts to mere damage control if your construals are destructive. It is easier to catch and to correct faulty secondary mental responses than to identify and correct maladaptive construals. Yet, correcting the construals is worth the effort, for it is the most important thing you can do to improve your constructive thinking.

BECOMING AWARE OF YOUR SENSITIVITIES AND COMPULSIONS

As you may recall, sensitivities and compulsions are hot spots of destructive thinking. Identify your sensitivities by noting the kinds of situations that you are touchy about, that get you more upset than most people in the same situation. Some common areas of sensitivity are failure, being made fun of, being unappreciated, being treated with disrespect, observing others having more than you have, and being dependent on someone. If you are not aware of your sensitivities, ask people you know to point them out to you. To guard against the possibility that their judgments will be influenced by their own sensitivities, look for agreement among several people.

Attend to your compulsions in the same way. In what situations do you feel driven to act in a certain way, feel uncomfortable when you don't act that way, and on later reflection, decide that your action was counterproductive? List your most extreme traits. Then determine whether each trait is reasonably flexible, or whether it is a rigid, driven way of behaving that makes trouble for you. Your friends can be especially helpful in making this discrimination. They may recognize that you "always" have to act in a certain way, such as being in charge.

Keep in mind, too, that sensitivities and compulsions are likely to occur in areas where you are especially concerned about meeting your four basic needs (the needs for pleasure, for understanding what is happening, for establishing and maintaining satisfying relationships, and for self-esteem). You may be so sensitive about your need for pleasure that you are unwilling to accept discomfort even when it is constructive to do so—such as being unwilling to miss some sleep in order to complete an important assignment. You may be so sensitive to your need for understanding events that you become anxious when things are uncertain, and you therefore come to conclusions too rapidly. You may be so sensitive to relationships that you are constantly on guard against being rejected and are thus compelled to reject people before they reject you. Or you may be so sensitive in the area of self-esteem that, experiencing any slight failure as devastating, you avoid challenges of any kind.

Patricia was a client of mine who used her sensitivities as a gateway to understanding her basic needs. She became involved in community protests over the closing of a women's shelter. Having previously turned to the shelter herself at a difficult moment in her life, Patricia was angry when the city government announced that budget cuts necessitated its closing. With no prior experience in political action, Patricia helped organize public protests. Speaking at these rallies stood out among her daily activities as a stressful experience. This is how she described her construals and feelings about these events:

I construed public-speaking situations as representing the threat of failure by my own standards as well as disapproval and rejection by others. I worried that I would forget everything I wanted to say or not say it well enough. I was afraid that others would put me down and reject me, either because of my awkwardness as a speaker or because I was revealing that I had been a client of the shelter. My main automatic thought was "What will people think if I come off sounding stupid?" These construals created a great deal of stress for me.

Patricia's distress about speaking in public made her aware of her sensitivity to threats to her self-esteem and to her need for acceptance by others. In Chapter 17, I describe how she substituted more constructive construals to reduce the stress and increase the satisfaction she experienced when she spoke publicly.

Chapter 16

Evaluating Your Automatic Thinking

You are now ready to move from awareness in the absence of evaluation of your automatic thinking to judging its constructiveness. As you observe your automatic thoughts—which include construals, secondary mental responses, and behavioral decisions—you will be deciding whether they are constructive or destructive. This chapter helps you make those judgments by providing descriptions of various forms of maladaptive automatic thinking, followed by an exercise in which you will observe and evaluate your automatic responses. Just remember that it is only the specific thoughts you are evaluating, not yourself as a person.

APPRAISAL OF CONSTRUALS

When evaluating a construal, it may seem to you that the only important consideration is whether the construal is accurate or inaccurate. This would certainly be true if all events were completely unambiguous. However, many, and very likely most, events in everyday life can reasonably be interpreted in different ways. It is to your advantage, then, to make the most constructive interpretation possible, which, as you have already learned, is not simply the most positive interpretation. Consider how a certain interpretation makes you feel and what its short-term and long-term consequences are. Will interpreting events in that way make life better or worse for you? There are no absolute formulas for deciding what is constructive and destructive. What works for someone else may not work for you, and what works for you in one situation may not work in another. You must use your judgment. Still, as benchmarks for your appraisal, it is helpful to be aware of the following common maladaptive construals, which you can try to avoid.

Overestimation of significance. No sooner had Mary walked into the house after a hard day in the office than her husband asked when dinner would be ready. She flew into a rage but then made dinner anyway. As she prepared the meal, she thought about how insensitive her husband was and whether or not she might be better off without him. By the time dinner was ready, she had a splitting headache and did not feel like eating.

Jane, when asked the same question by her husband, replied tongue in cheek, "It will be ready when you make it." They both had a good laugh and decided to go out for dinner.

Overestimation of the significance of negative events—or, as Albert Ellis calls it, "catastrophizing"—is a major source of stress because it results in emotional overreactions. The fact that you react to an event emotionally is a measure of its significance for your experiential mind. Your rational mind may well know that being treated with disrespect by a shopkeeper is of trivial significance. Yet, if you get upset over it and can't let it go, you can be sure that your experiential mind has taken it seriously. Because it is such an emotional trigger, there is no other construal or secondary mental re-action that contributes as much to stress and therefore to bodily wear and tear as overestimation of significance.

In the research my associates and I conducted on stress in everyday life, in which we had 118 people keep records of their most stressful experience each day for a period of thirty days, the aspect of their construals that was most strongly associated with the amount of stress they experienced was the significance they attributed to events. If they interpreted events as very important, they experienced a great deal of stress, whereas if they took them in stride and avoided "sweating the little stuff," they led a much calmer life. It is interesting to know that when people interpreted the same events in retrospect, they judged their significance as much less than they originally had. Thus, they caused themselves a lot of needless anguish by their initial overestimates of significance.

Overgeneralization. On their first meeting, Michael behaved in a way that Becky considered inconsiderate and insensitive. She assumed Michael was always that way and refused to see him again. Actually, Michael was normally a considerate and thoughtful person. He behaved as he did on that one occasion under the stress of circumstances that Becky did not know about. Had she given him another chance, she might have had a rewarding relationship with him. Becky erred by overgeneralizing from a single event.

Overgeneralization can result in distorted judgments not only about others but also about yourself. Think back to a few times when you failed at a task or behaved in a way of which you later disapproved. Did you react by thinking, "Why can't I ever do anything right?" If you did, you were overgeneralizing, because you were ignoring all the times you had performed or behaved well. To avoid being "down" on yourself or someone else, try asking yourself whether or not you have an adequate sample of observations to justify whatever generalization you are making and see if you can think of any observations that are inconsistent with the generalization.

Categorical thinking. Not long ago a student came to my office in tears. Amid her sobs she blurted out that she had failed a test and spoiled her chances of getting into a good graduate school. This student's grade point average was close to a straight A. When I asked her how badly she had done, she said she had received a B. For her, there were only two categories: A, which meant success, and anything else, which meant failure. Clearly, her categorical thinking was causing her a lot of misery.

As you may recall from taking the CTI, categorical thinking refers to all-or-none or black-and-white thinking. Categorical thinking has its uses, as it is a quick and convenient way of organizing information that permits you to make decisions rapidly and efficiently. Indeed, we could not operate effectively without being able to sort our views into categories. Unfortunately, it is all too easy to categorize too broadly and inflexibly.

Labeling. Labeling has much in common with categorical thinking, but it is such an important source of destructive thinking that it is worth talking about separately. Once you label people a certain way, the judgment you have made tends to be treated as if it were etched in stone. Having decided that someone is a "loser" or a "jerk," you may apply this label so quickly and automatically that you ignore any information that is inconsistent with it. Moreover, you are judging the whole person rather than the specific behavior of which you disapprove; thus, overgeneralization is also often involved in labeling. Like categorical thinking, labeling is necessary but easily misused. When you find yourself applying labels to a person rather than to a particular kind of behavior, be aware that you are probably using labeling in a counterproductive way. Although doing so may make you feel good at the moment, it is more likely to make problems in living than to solve them.

Interpreting challenges as threats. Two newly appointed midlevel executives were invited to give a speech at a national convention. One of them thought, "Isn't this terrific. What an opportunity! They really must think highly of me. If I do a good job, it will help advance my career. If I do a poor job, I'll learn from the experience and do better next time. Besides, most people are sympathetic, and they've got more important things to think about than my lousy talk."

The other executive had very different thoughts: "It's an honor, all right, but who needs it? It's not worth the anxiety I'll suffer. Besides, I'll probably do a lousy job, and then I'll feel terrible. How will I face people if I do poorly? I wish I hadn't been invited, but since I have been, I'd better grit my teeth and go ahead with it because it won't look good if I back out."

The implications of these two ways of thinking are obvious. To the extent that you construe situations as challenges rather than as threats, not only will you experience a lot less stress but you will perform better, as your mind will be on the task, not on yourself. Besides, positive as well as negative expectations have a way of coming true. So when you observe yourself viewing a situation as a threat, consider what it would do for you to regard the same situation as a challenge. Then evaluate how constructive or destructive each reaction is. In our research on daily stress, the one construal that was most strongly associated with constructive thinking, as measured by the CTI, was viewing situations as challenges rather than as threats.

Personalization. Jerry, a new counselor at a drug rehabilitation center, gave his first case presentation at the weekly conference of the clinic in which he worked. He thought he was doing well until, in the middle of his recommendation on how the case should be treated, the chief of the clinic walked out. Jerry's confidence was severely shaken. He continued in a subdued and halting voice and had trouble maintaining his train of thought. All he could think of was that he had blown it. After the conference, the clinic director came over to him and apologized for having had a desperate need to go to the bathroom at such an inopportune time.

The pitfall Jerry succumbed to was personalization, which means assuming, in the absence of adequate evidence, that you are the focus of other people's attention and behavior. To the extent that you make unwarranted personal interpretations, you will experience increased stress in living, as inconsequential events will take on undue significance. When you are in ambiguous situations, ask yourself whether it is more constructive to assume that people's behavior is or is not centered on you.

The tyranny of the "should." Some people accept reality for what it is and deal with it as best they can. Others demand that reality should be different from what it is and make themselves miserable because it is not. Psychoanalyst Karen Horney coined the phrase *the tyranny of the "should"* because she commonly observed such reactions among her patients. No matter what they accomplished, those who thought this way were not satisfied because they felt they "should" have been able to do better. Despite the misery they experienced, they were reluctant to give up their "shoulds" because they took pride in the standards they were trying to uphold.

It is necessary, of course, to have standards for how things should be in order to be motivated to improve them. However, it is easy to carry this too far. When you make "should" judgments, observe carefully whether they motivate you to take effective action or whether they only serve to make you unhappy.

Negative thinking. As I have emphasized before, a great deal of evidence indicates that people with a positive bias are happier, healthier, and more successful—provided that their optimism remains within reasonable limits. To see whether negative thinking is a problem you would benefit from working on, observe how frequently you have a positive, as compared to a negative, bias in interpreting events. In each instance, note how the positive or negative bias affects your feelings, your performance, and people's reactions to you.

Naive optimism. As I showed earlier, although constructive thinkers tend to be positive thinkers, they are not naive optimists who take unreasonable risks and fail to take reasonable precautions.

Assuming the validity of feelings. As I noted in Chapter 6, we assume that the more strongly we feel something, the more it must be true. Yet judgments based on feelings can be completely inaccurate. The intensity of your feelings may indicate more about your personal sensitivities than about what objectively happened. Feelings color memory, perception, and reasoning. As a result, when people react to a situation with strong emotions, they are usually able to support the validity of their feelings to their own satisfaction by selectively noticing and recalling supporting information. As you observe the stream of your daily reactions, see if you can catch thoughts or statements like this: "Of course I'm angry! I wouldn't be so angry if you had not behaved so badly" or "I wouldn't love him so much if he weren't a really good person down underneath."

Assuming intentionality. A mother rises to the defense of her children in an argument they are having with their father. Feeling threatened, he thinks, "She is trying to undermine my authority. She has no respect for my opinion." In reality, she has a great deal of respect for his opinion and is usually careful to avoid getting between him and the children, but this time she interfered because the argument touched on an especially sensitive subject for her.

When a person's actions make us feel embarrassed, inadequate, or wonderful, we tend to think the person meant to make us feel that way. Yet people often elicit reactions in others that they do not intend. As Aaron Beck puts it, to do "mind reading" in figuring out people's intentions can create a lot of personal misery and conflict between people. Observe your tendency to mistakenly interpret the intentions of others or otherwise engage in "mind reading." Ask yourself if there is solid evidence for your interpretation. See if you can find another way of explaining the other person's behavior. Sometimes there is just not enough information to explain someone's behavior, and in that case you are far better off not trying to explain it than jumping to conclusions.

Targeting. People have a natural tendency to find an individual or group to attack when they feel frustrated. This is because the experiential mind, being action-oriented, automatically seeks targets to react to. Observe whatever tendency you may have to look for someone to blame and recognize that, however satisfying and natural it may seem, in the long run it is often counterproductive. Not only is it likely to damage your relationships, but it can prevent you from taking responsibility for your own behavior and therefore from learning from experience.

Jumping to conclusions. The more emotional you are (which means that you are reacting mainly with your experiential mind), the more you will be likely to jump to conclusions so you can act on those conclusions. That is why when a terrible crime is committed, people tend to lose patience with time-consuming methods of justice and want to take matters into their own hands. Jumping to conclusions is a prevalent source of destructive thinking, not only in extreme conditions but in ordinary situations as well.

Inappropriate rules of interpretation. In order to make sense of the world, we all need implicit rules for interpreting events. But if they are inaccurate or too rigid, they can lead us astray. For example, if a person smiles at us, it generally conveys approval. But people can smile for many reasons, such as trying to make you believe they approve of you when they do not. Misunderstandings can also arise from cultural differences (such as when a person applies rules learned in one culture to another culture) or from personal sensitivities. For a person who is sensitive to disapproval, criticism is never constructive evaluation; it is always an attack. For a person who is sensitive to sexual exploitation, a friendly kiss may not be just a kiss; it may be an attempt at seduction. By taking into account the context in which an event occurs, rather than relying on broad, rigid rules, you can reduce misinterpretations.

Untestable hypotheses. An untestable hypothesis is an interpretation or belief that cannot be shown to be true or false. As Albert Ellis pointed out, you have two reasonable choices as to how to treat such hypotheses. You can either discard them as useless or retain them if they make you feel good. An untestable hypothesis that makes you feel bad—for example, that you are a worthless, unlovable person who will never amount to anything—is a prime example of destructive thinking. To evaluate whether your untestable hypotheses are constructive or destructive, think of what they do for you—how they make you feel and what they otherwise accomplish—in the long run as well as in the short run.

EVALUATING SECONDARY MENTAL RESPONSES

Once you have construed an event, your further reactions will be to the construal, not to the event itself. As explained in the previous chapter, the thoughts that follow your construals are called secondary mental responses. Like the construals themselves, these mental responses influence your feelings and behavior, and you should therefore learn to evaluate them as well.

Consider the following story. Stan was upset because Cindy said she was unable to get together with him as planned, since she had to bring home a lot of work from the office. At first, he did not know what to make of her behavior. Was she really that busy? Was she being inconsiderate by putting her interests before his? Was she giving him the brush-off because she had found someone else? That last thought struck a sensitivity. He kept dwelling on it and reviewing all of her past behavior that might give him a clue as to what was going on now. He remembered that two weeks ago she had been cool to him and seemingly uninterested in anything he said. He also recalled that when he first met her, she wasn't so sure she wanted to go out with him as she was interested in someone else. Maybe she still had not given up the other man. He rejected that thought because this other man had since married, and Cindy was too practical and too interested in getting married to get involved with a married man.

The thought occurred to Stan that maybe Cindy had met someone new. A surge of jealousy swept over him. He was reminded of another woman he had lost to someone else, and this made him feel defeated and helpless. He had done everything he could to retain the affection of that woman, but his best just wasn't good enough. "Let's face it," he thought, "where women are concerned, I just don't have it. I'm a loser." It became evident to him that no woman whom he loved could ever love him. He was destined to be a bachelor and would never have the family life he dreamed about. He would just have to make the best of a lonely existence and derive whatever satisfaction he could from his work.

Stan had a restless night and was sad throughout the next day. That evening the phone rang. It was Cindy, sounding very chipper: "Stan, I got my work done faster than I thought possible. Could you come over for dinner? I'd love to see you."

Stan had caused himself a lot of misery, not only with his initial destructive construal that Cindy's cancellation of their date meant that she was rejecting him but with his secondary mental responses. His construal was destructive because there were alternative interpretations that were at least as plausible and would have been much less distressing, such as assuming that Cindy was telling the truth. His secondary mental responses were no better because he marshaled all the evidence he could to prove to himself not only that he would lose Cindy but that he would be lonely all his life. None of these thoughts were supported by evidence, and most of them were untestable. Stan is no fool. He has a high IQ. But his experiential mind surely was not acting in an intelligent manner, for it made him die a thousand deaths unnecessarily.

A more constructive approach would have been for Stan to reassess his construal, recognize that it lacked supporting evidence, and decide, for his own peace of mind, that he should give Cindy the benefit of the doubt. Or having made the destructive construal he did, he could have done some damage control by learning from the experience. He could have learned about his sensitivity to rejection and how it interfered with his interpretation of events. He could then have told himself to be alert to this sensitivity in the future, so that he could correct it before he got swept along in his destructive way of thinking.

Are there any general rules for evaluating secondary mental responses? The fifteen maladaptive forms of construal described in the previous section apply equally well to evaluating secondary mental reactions. In addition, some mental responses occur only at the stage of secondary mental responses. Here are three that are often destructive.

Berating yourself. Berating yourself means finding fault with yourself as a person, for example, telling yourself you are no good, a loser, a fool, or worthless. Such thinking usually involves overgeneralization, categorical thinking, and untestable hypotheses. It is destructive because, unlike evaluating your performance on a specific task, it interferes with performance and lowers self-esteem.

Denial. Denial means refusing to accept what you do not wish to believe, including the seriousness of threatening or distressing events. It includes escaping into fantasy and wishful thinking. Research has shown that denial can be adaptive in the short run, but it is usually maladaptive in the long run.

Unrealistic thinking. Unrealistic thinking is thinking that is inaccurate. Typically, a person's thinking becomes unrealistic when it is driven by sensitivities rather than an objective evaluation of the situation.

Be aware, however, that not all unrealistic thinking is maladaptive. As I have already shown, good constructive thinkers are not completely realistic but have a positive bias that seems in itself to increase their chances of success. It is usually more constructive to give people the benefit of the doubt and to be slightly optimistic than to attempt to be rigorously accurate.

EVALUATING BEHAVIORAL REACTIONS

It is also helpful to evaluate your behavioral reactions as constructive or destructive. Again, you need to allow for circumstances. A response that is effective for coping with stress under some conditions can be destructive under others, and vice versa. For example, although withdrawal is usually a poor way to cope with stress, at times, in order to keep from being overwhelmed by distressing feelings, it may be the most adaptive reaction.

Here are some broad categories of behavioral responses that are often destructive.

Attack. To attack is to take action to injure someone, physically or psychologically. It includes physically assaulting people, telling them off, embarrassing them, or otherwise treating them in ways intended to make them feel bad. Sometimes attack is a useful way of protecting yourself. Usually, asserting yourself—making your needs known and standing up for your rights without belittling, demeaning, or assaulting someone else—is more constructive than attack.

Like other forms of destructive thinking and behavior, attacking someone may make you feel good in the short run, but you frequently have to pay a price for it in the long run. Most of us have felt the immediate satisfaction that comes from firing off an angry letter, only to wish later that we hadn't sent it. "I'm good; you're no good"—the thought that often lies behind anger and attack—is often a self-defeating way of raising self-esteem. You pay for it in two ways: it keeps you from learning from other people, and it motivates them to attack you back. In my research on coping with daily stress, people who often attacked others were, not surprisingly, poorer constructive thinkers than those who asserted themselves.

Undercontrolled emotional expression. The notion of expressing your feelings without restraint was so highly valued by many people in the 1960s that it was given a colloquial name: "letting it all hang out." Such emotional expression, although it often produces temporary relief, exacts a great price in the long run because it does not solve the underlying problem and often alienates people. It also short-circuits the development of more mature ways of coping with problems in living.

It is a common misconception that it is important for your health to express your emotions without inhibition. Presumably, if you don't express your feelings, you will bottle up a lot of stress and become ill. Yet, in my research, I found that good constructive thinkers showed more, not less, emotional control than poor constructive thinkers. George Vaillant, a psychiatrist who followed up a group of Harvard students from their undergraduate days to middle age, found to his surprise that those who showed the greatest emotional control as students turned out to be the happiest, healthiest, and most successful people later on.

People who express their emotions in an undercontrolled way are poor constructive thinkers who interpret situations in ways that upset them; they then feel compelled to express their feelings without considering the consequences of doing so. The most effective way to deal with problems is to avoid becoming unnecessarily emotionally distressed, and you can do that by thinking constructively in the first place. Then there is nothing you feel under pressure to release, and it is easy to exercise reasonable emotional control.

Overcontrolled emotional expression. At the other extreme, you might risk inhibiting the expression of your feelings to the point where you lose all spontaneity and cannot resolve the situations that give rise to unpleasant emotions. Good constructive thinkers are neither emotionally undercontrolled nor overcontrolled. It is useful to express emotions, within reason, because it lets people know where you stand on issues and lets you work out problems rather than deny them. People feel more comfortable with those who express their emotions than with those who keep their feelings hidden.

Self-punishment. Self-punishment is always destructive if you use it to punish yourself for being a bad, blameworthy person. On the other hand, it can be of some value as a training procedure, if you keep it focused on specific destructive actions that you want to control. In general, self-punishment is a more risky procedure than self-reward, since learning under punishment tends to be rigid and not easily unlearned.

Dependency. Enlisting the aid of others, including seeking advice, can be highly adaptive. However, relying too much on others may reduce your self-esteem, prevent you from developing your own resources, and make you vulnerable to abandonment.

Excessive independence. Independence normally is a highly desirable attribute. However, like emotional control, it can be carried too far. At times, seeking the help of others is more sensible than trying to do everything yourself. Besides, people like to feel that they can contribute to others and that true friends will not refuse either to accept or to give help. To give to others while refusing to accept their help is a form of subtle one-upmanship. It carries the implicit message that you are a nicer or stronger person than they are and therefore that you are superior.

Withdrawal. Withdrawal means disengaging yourself from active participation. At times such a reaction is adaptive, such as when further striving would bring you nothing but added frustration. People, like animals, need time to lick their wounds and disengage from the fray. However, more often than not, withdrawal is maladaptive because there are active steps you can take to improve a situation, such as to assert yourself.

SUMMARY LIST OF DESTRUCTIVE AUTOMATIC THOUGHTS

One of the things you will be asked to do in the exercise that follows is to identify your destructive thoughts and explain what is maladaptive about them. You can consult this list when you do the exercise.

Common Destructive Construals (this list also applies to secondary mental responses)

1. *Overestimation of significance*: Overevaluating the importance of events, as indicated by emotional overreactivity (making mountains out of molehills)

2. *Overgeneralization*: Assuming that what happened in one or a few situations will happen in almost all situations

3. *Categorical thinking*: All-or-none, black-and-white, or polarized thinking

4. *Labeling*: Applying labels to people or events and then treating the labels as if they accurately described the whole person or event

5. *Interpreting challenges as threats*: Viewing challenging situations in terms of their possible negative consequences rather than positive ones; emphasizing what can be lost rather than what can be gained in a situation

6. *Personalization*: Taking things personally; assuming without justification that you are the focus of other people's attention and behavior

7. *Tyranny of the "should"*: Becoming distressed because things are not the way you think they should be

8. *Negative thinking*: Interpreting events with a negative bias

9. *Naive optimism*: An extreme, unrealistic form of positive bias

10. *Assuming the validity of feelings*: Assuming that if you have strong feelings about something, it must be true

11. *Assuming intentionality*: Assuming that when people do something that affects you in a certain way, they intended it to have that effect

12. *Targeting*: Finding someone or something to blame for your distress

13. *Jumping to conclusions*: Making hasty judgments on the basis of insufficient evidence

14. *Inappropriate rules of interpretation*: Rigid or inaccurate automatic rules for interpreting events

15. *Untestable hypotheses*: Beliefs that cannot be shown to be either true or false

Common Destructive Secondary Mental Responses

These include the fifteen common destructive construals plus the following additional responses:

1. *Berating yourself*: Finding fault with yourself as a person; telling yourself how stupid, inadequate, or worthless you are

2. *Denial*: Refusing to accept as true what you do not wish to believe

3. *Unrealistic thinking*: Thinking that would be recognized as inaccurate by a consensus of informed people

Common Destructive Behavioral Responses

1. *Attack*: Hurting others physically or psychologically

2. *Undercontrolled emotional expression*: Expressing your emotions freely without regard to the consequences ("letting it all hang out")

3. *Overcontrolled emotional expression*: Excessive emotional control that interferes with spontaneity and satisfactory relationships with others and that leads to avoidance rather than resolution of problems

4. *Self-punishment*: Depriving yourself of something desirable or making yourself

do something unpleasant as punishment for being a bad person (as contrasted with training yourself not to engage in specific destructive behaviors)

5. *Dependency*: Enlisting the aid of others, including seeking advice, in situations where you should be able to rely on your own ability and effort

6. *Excessive independence*: Insisting on doing things yourself that could more reasonably and conveniently be done with the help of others

7. *Withdrawal*: Disengaging your interest and involvement from a situation when active participation or self-assertion would be appropriate

AN EXERCISE FOR EVALUATING YOUR DESTRUCTIVE THINKING AND SELECTING CONSTRUCTIVE ALTERNATIVES

This exercise is a continuation of the one you did in the last chapter, where you identified your emotional reactions and the automatic thoughts behind them. In the previous chapter I asked you to set aside any judgment about your reactions. Now it is time to judge how constructive or destructive your automatic thoughts are and to replace destructive automatic thoughts with more constructive ones.

The exercise gives you practice in evaluating your automatic thinking and in replacing destructive automatic thinking with constructive alternatives. It also helps you identify some of your characteristic ways of destructive thinking.

For each of the four vignettes, follow these instructions:

1. *Write in what your most likely construals, secondary mental responses, and behavioral responses would be.* Base your responses on how you have actually reacted to similar situations in the past, not on what you think would be the best responses.

2. *Rate your construals, secondary mental responses, and behavioral responses as to how constructive you regard them to be.* In rating a given response, consider how it would make you feel and whether it would most likely make life better or worse for you in the long run. Write your ratings in the spaces marked CR (construal rating), SMR (secondary mental response), and BR (behavioral response). Use the following scale:

   1 = very destructive
   2 = moderately destructive
   3 = slightly destructive
   4 = neither destructive nor constructive
   5 = slightly constructive
   6 = moderately constructive
   7 = highly constructive

3. *Indicate in what way(s) you regard each response that received a rating of less than 4 as maladaptive.* Do this by entering in parentheses one or more labels from the summary list that appears just before this exercise. Use the labels that are appropriate for the type of response you are rating: construal (CR), secondary mental response (SMR), or behavioral response (BR). If you cannot find an appropriate label among those listed, make up your own and add it to the table. Use the same label in your future ratings.

4. *Think of more constructive alternatives.* If you are not completely satisfied with one of your responses, write in the most constructive practical alternative you can think of and rate it. Additional spaces are provided for this purpose.

Here is an example I have worked out for you, based on the story about Stan's poor constructive thinking after Cindy told him she was too busy to get together with him as planned.

Sample

Your most likely responses:

Construal: *"Cindy doesn't love me." (negative thinking, jumping to conclusions)*   CR _2_

Secondary mental response: *"No one will ever love me." (overgeneralization, untestable hypothesis)*   SMR _1_

Behavioral response: *Do nothing.*   BR _7_

Constructive alternatives:

Construal: *"I will accept her word that she is busy, as there is no good reason to doubt it."*   CR _7_

Secondary mental response: *"No point in worrying about it. Time will tell."*   SMR _7_

Behavioral response: *Do nothing.*   CR _7_

Now, here are the vignettes for the actual exercise:

Situation 1

Someone you care for very much (a lover or a spouse) has just told you that he or she is interested in someone else and wants to end his or her relationship with you.

Your most likely responses:

Construal: _____

_____ CR __

Secondary mental response: _____

_____ SMR __

Behavioral response: _____

_____ BR __

Constructive alternatives:

Construal: _____

_____ CR __

Secondary mental response: _____

_____ SMR __

Behavioral response: _____

_____ BR __

Situation 2

You are about to give a speech to a large group of people, and you can't find your notes.

Your most likely responses:

Construal: _____

_____ CR __

Secondary mental response: _____

_____ SMR __

Behavioral response: _____

_____ BR __

Constructive alternatives:

Construal: _____

_____ CR __

Secondary mental response: _____

_____ SMR __

Behavioral response: _____

_____ BR __

Situation 3

At a routine physical examination, the physician detects a growth and takes a biopsy to see if it is cancerous.

Your most likely responses:

Construal: _____

_____ CR __

Secondary mental response: _____

_____ SMR __

Behavioral response: _____

_____ BR __

Constructive alternatives:

Construal: _____

_____ CR __

Secondary mental response: _____

_____ SMR __

Behavioral response: _____

_____ BR __

Situation 4

Your spouse (or if you do not have a spouse, someone else you care for) was supposed to meet you at a restaurant at seven o'clock in the evening. It is now eight o'clock, and he or she is not there.

Your most likely responses:

Construal: _____

_____ CR __

Secondary mental response: _____

_____ SMR __

Behavioral response: _____

_____ BR __

Constructive alternatives:

Construal: _____

_____ CR__

Secondary mental response: _____

_____ SMR __

Behavioral response: _____

_____ BR__

After completing the exercise, examine your responses for repetitive patterns. Ask yourself the following questions:

1. Do your destructive responses most commonly take the form of construals, secondary mental responses, or behavioral responses?
2. What particular kinds of destructive responses do you most commonly make? For example, among your construals, do your poor responses consist mainly of overgeneralization? Categorical thinking? Some other type of maladaptive construal?

If you detect a repetitive pattern, it will give you something you can work on to improve your constructive thinking. You can also work on developing a wider range of constructive alternatives by building upon the constructive responses you have listed here. These are the kinds of reactions you want to eventually turn into automatic responses.

Many people have found this exercise a valuable starting point on the road to improving their constructive thinking. If you routinely practice this same exercise with daily events as they arise in your life, your preferred alternative constructive reactions will ultimately become automatic, and you will improve your constructive thinking.

Chapter 17

Training Your
Experiential Mind

You have learned that the main reason smart people think dumb is that their automatic thinking is maladaptive. To become a better constructive thinker, you must therefore change your automatic thinking.

There are three basic approaches you can use for improving your constructive thinking and, therefore, your emotional intelligence:

1. You can use your rational mind to train your experiential mind.

2. You can provide your experiential mind with corrective experiences.

3. You can learn from your experiential mind.

In this chapter, I discuss the first two of these approaches, leaving the third for the next chapter.

BASIC PRINCIPLES FOR IMPROVING YOUR CONSTRUCTIVE THINKING

Before going on to specific procedures, it will be helpful to provide some general principles. Remember that changes in the experiential mind do not come easily, and intellectual understanding, no matter how great, is never enough. It will take considerable practice before your new, more constructive ways of thinking replace the old ways you have practiced all your life. You should also know that the duration of your reactions to distressing events will decrease much more quickly than the intensity of your initial distress. With progress, what used to bother you for several days will no longer bother you after a single night's sleep. If you look only at your initial reactions, you are likely to be disappointed. Look instead at how long it takes you to recover, and you will be in for some pleasant surprises.

Keep in mind the importance of being a good therapist to yourself. A good therapist does not chastise a patient for thinking maladaptively. Rather, the therapist treats the patient with understanding and respect. So if you're going to be your own therapist, be a good one: be accepting and tolerant of yourself and regard your setbacks as opportunities for learning rather than chastise yourself for having them.

USING YOUR RATIONAL MIND TO TRAIN YOUR EXPERIENTIAL MIND

You have already learned a great deal about using your rational mind to correct your experiential mind. You have learned to identify your automatic thoughts and to evaluate them as constructive or destructive. You know the most common ways in which people think destructively, and you have begun to practice replacing destructive thoughts with constructive thoughts. You have also diagnosed your destructive ways of thinking—first, in broad outline, by taking the CTI; then, more minutely, by becoming aware of the basic processes associated with maladaptive automatic thinking. So you know what to be on the lookout for. All that remains is to put this knowledge into practice.

The Basic Procedure

How do you change intellectual information into experiential habit? You do it by identifying the ways in which your automatic thinking is constructive or destructive and by substituting constructive thoughts for destructive thoughts. In other words, you do the same thing you did in the exercise in Chapter 16, only now you do it with real-life, instead of make-believe, events.

You may think it will be a terrible chore to monitor your automatic thinking continuously. At first, until you are accustomed to the procedure, it will take some effort and seem unnatural. With practice, it will become second nature. You will find it interesting to identify the different ways you and others think destructively. The process, rather than being a burden, will open up an exciting new avenue for understanding human behavior.

As I noted earlier, there are three approaches you can take to reading this book. You will obtain worthwhile results from any of them, but it is understandable that you will gain the most from the more demanding procedures. The most casual approach is to simply read this book, becoming aware of the principles of constructive thinking and applying them to whatever extent you can in everyday life. The second and third, more systematic approaches, which I refer to, respectively, as informal and formal procedures, require more sustained effort and discipline.

The informal procedure. Set aside a regular time at the end of the day when you can review the day's events without distraction. Many people choose the time when they are in bed for the night. Select the situation that was most distressing to you during the day and review what happened and how you reacted: how you automatically construed the situation and what your secondary mental and behavioral reactions were. Evaluate how satisfied you are with each of these reactions as you did in Chapter 16. Identify what was wrong with your reactions by using the labels in the list of maladaptive reactions. Be especially alert to the kinds of automatic thoughts that are most in need of improvement according to your CTI scores and the more detailed diagnosis of your destructive thinking in Chapter 16. Note whether your destructive thinking resulted predominantly from poor emotional coping, poor behavioral coping, categorical thinking, or superstitious thinking. Did you overreact, overgeneralize, or tyrannize yourself with "shoulds"? This information will give you an idea of the kinds of thoughts that would be desirable to replace.

Let us go through an example together. Assume that in reviewing the events of the day you select one in which you felt discouraged because your progress at some task was too slow. Examining your automatic thinking, you decide that your negative feelings were produced by construing yourself as a failure. Your secondary mental responses intensified your feelings of distress because you told yourself that you are an absolute idiot and that, try as you might, you will never be proficient at the task. Your behavioral impulse was to pack it all in. The result was that you were demoralized and accomplished less than you otherwise might have.

You now identify your maladaptive responses and consider, more specifically, how they are self-defeating. Your construal is an example of labeling, overgeneralization, and the tyranny of the "should." Your progress on this one task may be slow, but that does not make you a failure as a person. Your unhappiness was produced by your belief that you "should" be able to progress more rapidly. You are doing the best you can, and expecting more of yourself simply adds to your misery and is therefore an example of destructive thinking. Your secondary mental responses include negative thinking, berating yourself, and untestable hypothesizing. How can you possibly know you will never be proficient at the task? Your behavioral response is counterproductive because you *will* be able to master the task, although not as rapidly as you would like, and thinking about giving up simply interferes with your performance.

Your final task is to come up with constructive alternatives. These might be as follows: "It's too bad that it is taking me so long, but I'm doing my best, and I will eventually get there. Maybe I'm not as good at this kind of thing as I would like, but I will improve with practice."

In addition to setting aside a specific time for evaluating the most stressful event of the day, it is also helpful to label maladaptive thoughts immediately after they occur and to think of more constructive alternatives.

The formal procedure. Using this procedure, you write down your responses, evaluations, and constructive alternatives rather than just think about them. The only way this procedure differs from the exercise you did in Chapter 16 is that now you will be using actual events from your everyday life. Set aside a time at the end of the day to review the day's events. Select the one event that was most distressing to you and record it on a copy of the form on the next page. (Please feel free to photocopy as many forms as you need.) Summarize the event in an objective way in the space provided by noting what actually happened from the viewpoint of an objective observer. Then indicate your reactions to the event by recording your construals, secondary mental responses, and behavioral responses in the appropriate spaces. Next rate the constructiveness of each reaction on the same 7-point scale you used in Chapter 16 where 1 = very destructive, 4 = neither destructive nor constructive, and 7 = highly constructive. Record your constructiveness ratings in the column under "Rating." If the rating is less than 4 in any category, enter, in parentheses immediately after the relevant part of the description, the label(s) from the list in Chapter 16 that describe in what ways the response was maladaptive, such as that it involves overgeneralization, overestimation of significance, or tyranny of the "should."

Under "Constructive alternatives" enter an improved way of reacting for every response that you rated less than 7 and rate how constructive you consider the improved way to be. Select for your improved responses practical alternatives that you can actually imagine yourself performing.

Event number _____ Date _____ Description of event: _____

_____

_____

_____

_____

Construal: _____ **Rating**

_____   _____

Secondary mental response: _____

_____   _____

Behavioral response: _____

_____   _____

Constructive alternatives:

Construal: _____

_____   _____

Secondary mental response: _____

_____   _____

Behavioral response: _____

_____   _____

It will take a number of records before a distinct pattern emerges. It is usually necessary to record at least ten events. Thirty would be better. By doing more recording, you will not only be able to establish more reliable patterns of your destructive thinking but also to get more practice in substituting constructive alternatives.

As with the informal procedure, it is helpful to supplement the formal procedure by labeling in your mind your maladaptive reactions shortly after they occur and substituting constructive thoughts for destructive thoughts.

What you can expect. At first, you will think of appropriate constructive alternatives only after you have made destructive responses. With practice, you will become increasingly aware of the circumstances in which you tend to make certain destructive responses. You will then be able to make the substitutions more quickly, until finally you will make the constructive response without having first made the destructive one. This is the goal you are aiming for: to respond automatically with constructive construals, secondary mental responses, and behavioral decisions.

After you have written down the observations of your automatic thinking for a sufficiently large number of events, it will become second nature for you to continue the process mentally, whether or not you continue writing down further incidents. Responses to follow-up questionnaires I have sent to students who took my course on coping with stress indicate that once a person has gone through the formal procedure, the process tends to become automatic. Many students have volunteered that this way of thinking has considerably improved the quality of their lives. They experience less stress, feel in greater control of their lives, and have a better understanding of others as well as of themselves.

Auxiliary Techniques

The basic procedure for using your rational mind to improve your constructive thinking is a form of cognitive therapy, which uses rational methods to correct maladaptive automatic thoughts. Cognitive therapists and others employ a number of additional techniques for using the rational mind to influence the experiential mind, including the following ones.

You don't need to use all of these techniques. Try some of them out and see which work best for you. You may find, for example, that reframing is much more useful to you than meditation, or vice versa. Many people find it helpful to employ different approaches at different times or to use different techniques for dealing with different kinds of problems.

Disputing irrational thoughts. Once you decide that an automatic thought is maladaptive, consider all the ways in which it is counterproductive. Ask yourself whether or not it is logical, testable, and supported by evidence. Most important, ask yourself whether or not it is constructive in its long-term effect on your welfare. If it is none of these and makes you feel bad, then it is an inappropriate thought that makes no sense to retain, no matter how valid it may seem at the moment. Your job, then, is to get rid of it.

One way to get rid of it is to dispute it every time it occurs. If you keep on reminding yourself of all the ways it is unreasonable, ultimately the arguments will filter down into your experiential mind. Instead of taking the irrational thought seriously, you will get bored with it, and it will gradually fade away. Keep reminding yourself that thoughts are simply tools for adjusting to life, and no law says you have to keep tools that are defective.

Let us consider some specific examples of disputing destructive thoughts. First, assume you experience some setback that instigates the automatic thought that you are worthless. Dispute the thought by asking yourself how you would test it to determine whether or not it is right. The answer is that there is no possible way you could test it. What is the effect of the thought on your feelings? Clearly, it makes you feel bad. What are its long-term effects on your well-being? It contributes to low self-esteem, which increases the amount of stress you experience, and it reduces your confidence, which reduces your overall effectiveness. In sum, it does lots of harm and contributes nothing worthwhile, so there is no reason to retain it. Every time it comes up, remind yourself of why it is a foolish thought: it is untestable, its immediate effect is to make you feel bad, its long-term effect is to undermine your self-esteem, and it makes you perform worse, not better.

A client complained to me that he was not able to sleep because he kept worrying about his daughter. She had just been divorced, and her husband was not sending her the money he was supposed to.

I asked him, "How does it make you feel to think that?"

"Terrible," he replied. "I keep tossing and turning and worrying about how she will make ends meet."

"What would happen if you didn't worry like that?"

After thinking a moment, he said, "It would be terrible. It would mean I didn't care."

I repeated my question, accenting the word *happen*.

"I guess nothing different would happen," he admitted, "except that I would probably be able to sleep." He looked a little surprised at the self-evident wisdom of his statement. For the first time in his life, he realized that there was no great virtue in worrying; it simply made him miserable without accomplishing anything.

The questions I asked my client come from a technique developed by Barry Kaufman. Kaufman asks three standard questions that help people dispute their maladaptive thoughts:

1. "How does it make you feel to think that?"
2. "What would happen if you didn't think that?"
3. "How do you know that would happen?"

In the previous example, the third question was unnecessary. Often, however, it is necessary. People frequently state that they feel strongly that something awful would happen if they did not have the distressing thought they are reporting. Their answer to the third question generally reveals that their concern is based on an unsupported assumption.

Reframing. Sometimes problems that seem insurmountable from one perspective can easily be solved from another. The more emotionally involved people are in an issue, the more they tend to revert to well-grooved familiar thoughts. That is why breakthroughs in science are often brought about not by working harder on an established theory, but by going outside the theory in a complete shift of perspective. Puzzles and riddles offer an easy way to grasp this principle. Try the following:

John went into a pitch-black basement to find a pair of socks. There were seven black socks and seven white socks hanging on a line. What was the smallest number of socks he could take to be sure he had a pair? (The answer is given in the next paragraph, so do not read ahead until you have answered the question.)

Why do people have trouble with this problem? Because they get hung up on the extraneous information about the number of black and white socks. They assume that if information is given, it should be used. Once they shift their perspective and ignore the extraneous information, the solution is ridiculously simple: namely, three socks ensure a matching pair.

In her book *Mindfulness*, psychologist Ellen Langer gives many examples of how people are able to solve problems in living by reframing. She cites the case of "the Birdman of Alcatraz," who was sentenced to a lifetime in prison without hope of reprieve. One day, when a crippled bird happened into his cell, he nursed it back to health. When word got around, guards, visitors, and prisoners began bringing him sick birds. He eventually became a respected authority on the diagnosis and treatment of diseases in birds. Instead of leading a dull existence in prison, he made his life interesting and rewarding simply by changing his perspective.

You have already had practice shifting construals. This procedure can be extended to shifting broader contexts of interpretation. When you are faced with difficult situations, practice using your imagination to create new contexts in which you can experience situations differently.

One of the most broadly useful shifts you can make is to shift from viewing an event as a threat to viewing it as a challenge. At the end of Chapter 15, I told the story of Patricia, who experienced considerable stress each time she spoke out in public to protest the closing of a women's shelter. She initially framed these novel situations "as representing the threat of failure by my own standards as well as disapproval and rejection by others." She worried about "sounding stupid" or forgetting what she had to say. Naturally, then, she found public speaking stressful. Patricia succeeded in reducing this stress by reframing her civic activities as "novel," "exciting," and "empowering." She thought to herself, "I've never done this before, so whatever I can accomplish is a plus for my growth as well as for the cause I'm promoting." Although she did not altogether lose her nervous jitters, her shift of focus from the threatening to the challenging aspects of public activism made it a more positive experience for her, and she actually began to look forward to facing crowds and microphones.

When I was in the army, I was punished for failing to salute an officer. The punishment was that I had to mow the lawn in front of the officers' quarters by tearing the blades of grass with my hands. Here is where a little reframing came in handy. It occurred to me that I was in comfortable surroundings with nothing to do but a mindless job that no one could take seriously. It was like being on vacation. I sat on the ground, casually tearing blades of grass, enjoying the warm sun, and singing my favorite songs, when the lieutenant who had given me the punishment strode over to me.

"You're supposed to be punished," he said irritably, "not singing."

"Yes, sir," I replied. "I won't sing anymore."

"And, damn it, you're not supposed to be happy when you're being punished."

"No, sir, I'll try not to be happy."

I watched him leave, looking sheepish. I got back to tearing the grass feeling even better than I had before. A little reframing can go a long way.

Thought stopping. Once you identify a destructive thought, how do you get rid of it? A simple, surprisingly effective technique is called "thought stopping." Simply yell "Stop!" to yourself. Some people find it helpful to wear a rubber band around their wrist and snap it when they yell "Stop!" In thought stopping, your rational mind is giving a direct command to your experiential mind, much as a parent orders a child to stop doing something destructive. Snapping the rubber band is like backing up the order with a mild punishment that adds emphasis to the command.

Distraction. If ordering your experiential mind to desist doesn't do the job, get your experiential mind out of a destructive rut by giving it something else to think about. Counting sheep in order to fall asleep is a well-known example of this technique. It works by diverting you from the distressing thoughts that prevented you from sleeping. There are many other ways you can distract yourself. All that matters is that the thoughts or activities are completely absorbing. Ellen Langer describes a useful technique that is always conveniently available: Think of a word. Then think of another word that begins with the last letter of the first word. Then think of a third word that begins with the last letter of the second word, and so on. See how many words you can put together before getting stuck.

Meditation: one-pointed concentration. There are two basic forms of meditation: one-pointed concentration, in which you focus your attention on a specific stimulus until it blocks out awareness of all other stimulation, and insight meditation, in which you remain open to all stimuli and thoughts that occur. Insight meditation, a more ambitious procedure that opens a window into your experiential mind, is discussed in the next chapter.

One-pointed concentration seems, on the surface, like just another distraction technique. However, it produces more profound changes, including deeper relaxation and a more positive state of mind than simple relaxation, and its effect lasts longer. It is not clear exactly why it has these effects. Perhaps it is because you are not simply occupying your mind but also learning to concentrate your attention, to correct your mind's wandering in a gentle and patient way, and to accept your thoughts without evaluation.

You begin by selecting a mantra on which to focus. A mantra is a word or phrase that can be "chanted." A good mantra is supposed to have a resonant quality that makes it pleasing to say. Traditionally, mantras used in meditation have symbolic meaning. Actually, as Herbert Benson demonstrated in *The Relaxation Response*, it is just as effective to simply say the word *one*.

To put yourself into a meditative state, find a quiet place where you can relax without being disturbed. Sit on a hard, straight-backed chair, where you can assume an erect position and not fall asleep. Let yourself relax. Adopt a passive attitude. Breathe in and out through your nose in a relaxed way. Say the word *one* to yourself every time you breathe out. Continue doing this for fifteen to twenty minutes.

Some people prefer to focus on their breath instead of a mantra. To practice this variation, concentrate carefully on the sensation of your breath as it enters and leaves the tip of your nostrils. With each in-breath, say *in*, and with each out-breath, say *out*.

Whichever technique you use, you can expect your mind to do a great deal of wandering at first. If your mind wanders, don't get upset; just note that it is wandering and gently bring it back to the word *one* or your breath. As your concentration improves, your mind will wander less, but it will still wander. Do not evaluate each meditation, as it will interfere with the passive, nonjudgmental attitude you need to meditate.

Positive thought and imagery substitution. Substitute thoughts or images of soothing, comforting scenes for distressing images or thoughts. Begin by putting yourself into a relaxed state. Breathe deeply and clear your mind. Let a pleasant scene or memory come to mind. Visualize it in as much detail and clarity as possible. If it is an actual memory, re-create the sights, the sounds, the smells, and, most important, the intensely pleasant feeling of the real experience. Always pick the same scene and keep working on it until you can call it up and immerse yourself in it at a moment's notice. You need not practice this long on any given occasion—five minutes will suffice—but you need to work on it regularly for about a month before you can expect to gain proficiency.

When you are able to immerse yourself in the scene to the point where you are oblivious of other stimuli, it is time to condition your reaction to some simple act, such as pressing your thumb and index finger together. If you do this every time you are about to go into your state of visualization, it will take you more quickly and reliably into that state, and eventually you will be able to call up the image and the feelings associated with it just by pressing your fingers together.

The procedure I have just described is an example of self-hypnosis. I learned about it from a colleague after I complimented her on a professional talk she gave. When I told her how impressed I was with the serenity that radiated from her, she confided that she had been nervous before the talk. She then practiced image substitution by pressing her fingers together, which instantaneously produced a state of relaxation. She has even used this procedure to undergo minor surgery without anesthesia, much to her physician's incredulity.

INFLUENCING THE EXPERIENTIAL MIND THROUGH DIRECT EXPERIENCE

The most direct way to correct your experiential mind is to provide it with corrective experiences. One way of having corrective experiences is to be lucky. For example, if your problem is that you feel unlovable, someone may happen to fall madly in love with you and provide you with just the kind of experience you need to change your maladaptive automatic thinking. But don't count on it. People who feel unlovable have a way of sabotaging whatever possibilities arise for having constructive love relationships. They are likely to keep away from situations where they might meet the right person. Moreover, even if they meet such a person, their insecurity is likely to make them so cautious or demanding that the relationship never develops.

A more reliable approach to having constructive experiences is to cultivate them. Keep in mind that it is not events themselves but how you interpret them that is important, that experimentation is useful, and that it is better to take on new experiences gradually rather than confront your problems in a sink-or-swim manner. Following is an example of how to go about influencing your experiential mind through direct experience.

Jeanne Collins, a shy young woman, decided to overcome her shyness by providing herself with corrective learning experiences. She gave herself the assignment of introducing herself to three strangers in a week. The first opportunity presented itself when she was waiting in line to see a movie. When she thought about introducing herself to the man in front of her, she had the following automatic thoughts: "What if he doesn't respond? What if he considers me intrusive?" She answered these constructively: "Jeanne, you are making too big a deal of it. If he's nasty when you're friendly, that's his problem. His behavior will be only as threatening as you make it, so observe how you react and learn something. At the very least, be proud of yourself for trying. Now, get on with it!"

Jeanne caught the man's eye, smiled, and said, "I'm really looking forward to seeing this movie. I heard it is very good." The man smiled back and said, "I don't know anything about it. I had some time to kill, so I decided to take in a movie. What did you hear about it?"

"I heard it has a surprise ending. That's all my friend would tell me because she didn't want to spoil it for me. By the way, I'm Jeanne Collins."

The man replied by introducing himself. Soon afterward, he and Jeanne parted with a friendly acknowledgment as they found separate single seats in the movie. "Now that wasn't half-bad," Jeanne said to herself.

On other occasions, when people were less friendly, Jeanne observed her old destructive thinking reasserting itself: "I guess I'm uninteresting. I shouldn't bother people. It hurts so much when people are rejecting." She now nips these thoughts in the bud and substitutes more constructive thoughts. Gradually, as she masters each level of difficulty, she gives herself more demanding assignments, such as attending a dance as a single. She takes special care to correct any self-blaming tendencies and to maintain a tolerant, sympathetic, problem-solving orientation. Eventually, she hopes to reach a level where the constructive responses become automatic, and shyness is no longer a serious problem for her.

In a book called *Rapid Relief from Emotional Distress*, Gary Emery and James Campbell outline a straightforward and compelling, action-oriented form of cognitive therapy that is based on three steps.

1. *Accept your current reality.* You begin by accepting whatever problems exist in your life, including your distressing emotions. Don't fight the way things are or bemoan your fate. Just accept the reality of it all, including your unpleasant feelings. Keep this in mind as you think about the situation you intend to change.

2. *Create a vision of how you would like things to be.* Imagine an attainable, practical goal and visualize it as vividly as you can. Hold the picture in your mind's eye and focus on it. Make it as pleasant as possible. In Emery and Campbell's words, "let light and warmth surround it and fill it until all that light spills into your current reality." Don't worry if this sounds silly to your rational mind; it is, after all, aimed at your experiential mind.

3. *Take action to achieve your goal.* Remember that your aim is to solve your problems by your own behavior. Don't expect other people to change! You have no control over what others do. If you try to change others, at best you will simply fail, and at worst you will alienate those you are trying to influence. Ironically, if you make favorable changes in yourself, it will very likely initiate the changes in others you would like to see.

Here is an example of the three steps, taken from Emery and Campbell:

I accept the fact that I was unfairly fired from my job and that I am furious about it.

I choose to create my vision of feeling good and having a job I love.

I will take action by applying for similar positions in other companies; looking into other types of jobs I might like to do; seriously examining if I have other interests I might be able to turn into a career by more schooling; and finding out about financial aid at schools that could help me broaden my skills.

BEYOND COGNITIVE THERAPY

As valuable as cognitive therapy is, like any other form of therapy, it has its limitations. Its practitioners tend to overestimate how much rational approaches by themselves can correct all kinds of maladaptive automatic thinking. Unfortunately, certain problems in living cannot be treated effectively with purely cognitive approaches. Sometimes these problems respond temporarily to cognitive treatment, but this improvement is followed by relapse. Cognitive therapists acknowledge that relapse occurs but find it most puzzling.

I believe that the roots of these problems lie deeper in the experiential mind than can be reached by simply correcting maladaptive cognitions. A person's irrational behavior may be maintained for reasons that the cognitive therapist does not suspect, and these underlying reasons, not just the surface cognitions, must sometimes be treated. The key to treating them is to communicate with the experiential mind in its own terms and to learn what it needs. Procedures for doing this are presented in the next chapter.

Our experiential minds have adaptive capacities no less impressive than those of our rational minds, but of a different nature. As you will see in the next chapter, the rational mind can learn from the experiential mind as well as teach it.

RECOMMENDED READING

Beck, A. T. *Cognitive Therapy and the Emotional Disorders*. New York: International Universities Press, 1976.

> This is a classic book on cognitive therapy by one of its founders. Although intended primarily for professionals, it is simply and clearly written and can be read profitably as a self-help book. The basic principles of cognitive therapy are explained and illustrated with many helpful examples.

———. *Love Is Never Enough* New York: Harper & Row, 1988.

> This is a self-help book for resolving problems between couples. It applies the principles of cognitive therapy to problems in marriage and to the dating and mating game. It contains many informative examples and engaging exercises.

Benson, H. *The Relaxation Response*. New York: Avon, 1975.

> This is the book that took the mysticism out of meditation and made it available as a secular, mainstream technique for reducing stress and concentrating one's mental and emotional energy.

Burns, D. D. *Feeling Good. The New Mood Therapy*. New York: New American Library (Signet paperback), 1980.

> This is a clearly written, best-selling self-help book on the treatment of depression with cognitive therapy procedures. The book describes general principles of cognitive therapy that can be applied to problems other than depression. It contains self-administered tests and many examples.

Ellis, A. *Humanistic Psychotherapy*. New York: McGraw-Hill Paperbacks, 1973.

> A classic by one of the founders of cognitive therapy. Useful both for professionals and as a self-help book. Presents the fundamentals of cognitive therapy simply and clearly and illustrates their application to a wide variety of psychological disorders.

Ellis, A., and R. A. Harper. *A New Guide to Rational Living*. N. Hollywood, Calif.: Wilshire, 1975.

> This is the most comprehensive presentation of rational-emotive therapy (one of the major cognitive therapies) for the lay reader. It features a detailed,

step-by-step procedure for disputing irrational beliefs and substituting constructive interpretations.

Emery, G., and J. Campbell. *Rapid Relief from Emotional Distress*. New York: Rawson Associates, 1986.

This self-help book presents what the authors, who were trained in cognitive therapy, call rapid cognitive therapy. Their emphasis is on an action-oriented approach for solving problems in living. The book contains many examples and exercises.

Kaufman, B. N. *To Love Is to Be Happy With*. New York: Fawcett Crest, 1977.

A self-help book that presents a form of cognitive therapy based on questions that one asks oneself. Contains many examples and questions to ask yourself.

Langer, E. J. *Mindfulness*. New York: Addison-Wesley, 1989.

Langer, a social psychologist, introduces a concept she calls "mindfulness," which overlaps with principles of cognitive therapy and cognitive-experiential self-theory. The book describes many interesting experiments that demonstrate how the principles of mindfulness can be used to increase effectiveness on the job, reduce pain, promote healing, reduce prejudice, and help the aged renew their interest in living.

Meichenbaum, D. *Stress Inoculation Training*. New York: Pergamon Press, 1985.

A manual for cognitive psychotherapists that is exceptionally lucidly written and can be profitably read as a self-help book. It provides a systematic program for identifying and treating maladaptive cognitive and behavioral responses.

Seligman, M. E. P. *Learned Optimism*. New York: Knopf, 1991.

Seligman, a world-renowned clinical and research psychologist, describes the advantages of an optimistic orientation to life. He presents compelling research findings on the relationship between optimism and performance in the workplace and in athletics, as well as between optimism and mental and physical well-being. The book contains many useful techniques and exercises for increasing optimism.

Chapter 18

The Wisdom of the Experiential Mind

Up to this point, your job has been to use your rational mind to train your experiential mind. But your experiential mind is more than just a wayward child that needs to be disciplined. Indeed, because it operates by holistic principles, metaphors, and associations and because it is sensitively attuned to the emotional outcome of events, your experiential mind is capable of a level of insight that often eludes the straightforward logic of the rational mind. At its lowest level of functioning, the experiential mind processes information in the quick-and-crude way I have described throughout much of this book. At its highest level, it is a source of intuitive wisdom, inspiration, and creativity. In these vital respects, your rational mind has much to learn from your experiential mind.

You can learn from your experiential mind in several ways. You can use your feelings (emotions, vibes, and moods) to put you in touch with your preconscious automatic thinking, you can use techniques such as insight meditation to tap into your stream of consciousness, and you can communicate with your experiential mind through fantasy and imagery, the languages it knows best.

The techniques presented in this chapter are variations of these three ways of gaining access to the wisdom of your experiential mind. I will give you the initial instructions you need to practice each technique, which you can then explore in further depth, if you wish, in the books listed at the end of the chapter.

LEARNING FROM YOUR FEELINGS

Just as you have learned to use your emotions to locate one level of automatic thinking, you can use your vibes and moods to locate other levels. Remember, emotions, such as feelings of fear, anger, joy, or sadness, are easy to identify, since they are triggered by specific situations of which people are usually aware. Vibes, such as feelings of agitation, frustration, and a vague sense of discomfort, or disquietude, and moods, which are like prolonged emotions, are more difficult to identify. This is why people commonly attribute their vibes or moods to the wrong source and put their energy into trying to solve the wrong problems. If you don't understand your vibes and your moods, they will control you. All your intelligence will do for you then is to enable you to carry out their bidding more effectively and to rationalize your behavior more convincingly. Your negative vibes and moods bear heeding as they point to basic needs that you are failing to fulfill.

Learning from Your Vibes: Two Techniques

1. *Tune into your vibes in real-life situations.* Scan your body and notice how you feel in particular situations. Since your rational mind is strongly influenced by how it thinks you should react, it confuses what should be with what is. Your experiential mind simply reflects how things are for you. You may find that your rational mind thinks you like certain situations when, in fact, you really don't and vice versa.

Let's say that in your conscious, rational thinking you admire Bernice because you consider her to be a thoughtful and intelligent person. Yet your vibes in her presence are not good. Evidently, your experiential mind is computing things differently from your rational mind. This does not necessarily mean that your vibes are valid and should be the basis for your behavior. They may be produced by inappropriate associations from past experiences with others; for example, Bernice may remind you of someone who treated you badly when you were a child. On the other hand, the vibes may reflect some subtle awareness on the part of your experiential mind that eludes your rational mind. Once you identify your vibes, you are at least in a position to decide whether you want to heed or discount them.

2. *Attend to your vibes when imagining situations that are important to you.* Larry had been going with a young woman for several years. He felt sure that he loved her very much, but whenever the topic of setting a wedding date came up, he found a reason to put it off. Since he was very intelligent, he had no problem in finding reasons to justify the delays. This was not the first time he had acted this way in a relationship, and he feared that if he continued to do so, he would never have a family and children, which he thought he wanted very much.

In order to understand his puzzling behavior, Larry carefully attended to his vibes when he imagined being married and coming home to his wife and children after work. To his surprise, the vibes were distinctly unpleasant. He then imagined the closest experience he had ever had to the one he had just imagined. His mind turned to his childhood, when he had deeply resented his mother for paying more attention to his younger siblings than to him. He was the oldest child in the family who had been dethroned by a new arrival on three occasions. This feeling, together with the interpretations that had produced it, resulted in a wish to get back at women.

After this experience, it was evident to Larry that his experiential mind and his rational mind had very different ideas about the desirability of getting married and raising a family. It was now up to him to decide which mind to heed. The path of least resistance would be to go with the vibes and decide that marriage was not for him. If he decided to go in the opposite direction, he would have to consider how best to cope with his unpleasant vibes. Knowing their source would help him to identify inappropriate feelings toward his wife and children that were based on his earlier experiences with his mother and siblings.

This vignette illustrates how you can use your imagination to learn from your vibes when you are faced with difficult decisions. Practice the following three steps so that you can use them when you need them most:

1. Vividly imagine solutions to problems as they arise, while attending carefully to the accompanying vibes.
2. Determine whether and, if so, how your vibes are related to past experience by imagining the most similar past experience that produces similar vibes.
3. In making your decision, evaluate the validity of your vibes and decide whether you should heed or override their message or effect a compromise between your two minds.

You may decide to act in accordance with, or contrary to, the promptings of your vibes, but in either case you will have made an informed decision based on the relevant information in both your experiential and rational mind. If you follow your heart (experiential mind), you run the risk that your behavior will be destructively irrational. If you follow your head (rational mind), you run the risk of making a decision that will be a continuous source of misery.

Learning from Your Moods: Focusing

Whereas emotions indicate how you automatically interpret specific events, moods indicate how you automatically interpret your overall life situation. You have a great deal to gain, therefore, by being able to uncover the automatic construals that instigate your moods. A procedure called focusing, developed by psychologist Eugene Gendlin, can enable you to do just that.

A colleague of mine who had been a paratrooper during the Second World War and had participated in some very dangerous missions, had an anxiety attack many years after the war while riding in a train. When he realized that the sight of the terrain rolling by reminded him of being about to jump from an airplane, the anxiety immediately vanished. This incident was a spontaneous demonstration of what happens in focusing: in labeling an underlying disturbing feeling correctly, the feeling often goes away or, at the least, becomes less distressing.

Focusing is based on two assumptions: first, that there are two levels of knowledge, one associated with feelings and the body and the other with intellect; second, that tension occurs whenever the two levels of knowledge are not in agreement. This tension can be relieved by putting the two levels into contact with each other so that the difference between them can be resolved.

The following example, taken from Gendlin's book, illustrates how focusing is done and what can be gained from it. Kevin was angry at his wife, Lynne. He had come home from work tired and hungry, and Lynne wasn't there. She came home shortly, eager to tell him about an exciting new development in her job. "I'm really happy for you," he said, "but can't you just once get home on time?" She snapped back, and before long they were having a full-scale argument. They had been arguing this way for a couple of weeks now, and Kevin was beginning to think that their marriage was in serious trouble. Everything Lynne did annoyed him, and sex with her no longer had any appeal.

Since Kevin had experience with focusing, he decided to see if it could help him clarify what was going on. He went to his special quiet place and put himself into a meditative state. Re-creating the feeling he had when he was distressed by Lynne's absence, he paid careful attention to how it felt deep in his body. As he concentrated on the feeling, he waited for a thought to arise spontaneously, as if directly from his body. He was careful not to force the thought. He asked himself, "What is the quality of this feeling? What do I feel to be the sense of it?" The word *anger* came to mind. "Yes, it's anger," he acknowledged, "but that's not the whole of it." He stayed with the feeling longer, and the word *sad*, which surprised him, came to mind. "No, that doesn't fit completely, either," he said, "although there is a trace of it." The word *jealous* came to mind, and he felt a definite click. It really fit, he knew, because as he thought of the word, there was a decided shift in the underlying feeling, and the tension suddenly lessened. As he thought further about his feeling, it clarified what was going on between him and Lynne. She was doing exceptionally well in her job, and he was going nowhere. He resented her success in comparison to his failure, and he was taking out his frustration on her.

Later that evening, Kevin apologized to Lynne for his behavior, admitted his jealousy, and acknowledged that the real problem was not with her behavior but with his feelings of failure. He had known all along that he should quit his job, which was at a dead end, and look for another, but he hadn't wanted to face it. Lynne was sympathetic, and after their talk they felt close to each other, as they had in the past.

As this example illustrates, focusing is an excellent technique for getting in touch with your experiential mind. The essence of focusing is to become a passive observer of your feelings and let thoughts arise spontaneously. When a thought arises, you check it against the feeling you are attempting to clarify, until one occurs that "clicks." How will you know when you have hit on the right label? When you do, you will feel a shift in the feeling. That doesn't mean you should quit after the first small shift; in fact, it's important not to. Stay with the feeling until your understanding of it is complete.

LEARNING FROM YOUR STREAM OF CONSCIOUSNESS IN INSIGHT MEDITATION

Unlike one-pointed concentration (described in Chapter 17), where you shut out all other stimulation by keeping your mind focused on a specific stimulus, such as a mantra or your breath, insight meditation requires you to passively observe the continuous flow of the contents of your mind. In practice, the difference is not so clear-cut because even in one-pointed concentration your mind invariably drifts, and you thereby become aware of your stream of consciousness. In both techniques it is important that you not become involved with, or, as they say in meditation language, "attached to," any of your thoughts. You simply note them and let them go. The difference between the two techniques of meditation is one of degree. You can concentrate more on bringing your attention back to a specific stimulus, or you can remain more open to a free flow of consciousness. Because the two procedures have much in common, mastering one is helpful in mastering the other.

To practice insight meditation, begin as if you were practicing one-pointed concentration. Let us assume you begin by focusing on your breathing, saying *in* when you breathe in and *out* when you breathe out. When your mind drifts from observing your breath, as it most surely will, passively note the content of your thoughts without evaluating them. If a voice from the outside penetrates into your consciousness, simply note it without concentrating on the meaning of the words. If you feel an itching sensation somewhere in your body, passively observe the quality of the feeling and do not evaluate it. If worries or other thoughts come to mind, such as how you will get certain chores done, passively note them and let them go.

Is it necessary for your mind to return to the breathing? There are two variations of insight meditation you can use. In one, you attend to your breathing as an anchoring point, observing the drift of your mind from it. In the other, you drop the use of the anchor and let your consciousness drift with the tide, simply noting the stream of your consciousness. Try both techniques and choose the one with which you feel more comfortable.

When you practice insight meditation, you are learning to observe the contents of your mind without judgment—that is, to accept and then let go of whatever thoughts occur to you without becoming involved with them. By adopting this attitude of passive-receptive observation, your mind will open itself up to all kinds of thoughts that would otherwise be unavailable. The "insight" in insight meditation is that you become aware at a deep, experiential level of how much *you* construct the reality you experience, including your emotions and moods. You learn that both your mental anguish and your joy in living are produced not so much by what happens objectively to you but by the way you interpret what happens.

Insight meditation is also useful for learning to let go of distressing thoughts by accepting them, instead of empowering them by trying to shut them out. As I previously noted, it has been well demonstrated in carefully conducted research that the more desperately people try to shut a thought out of consciousness, the more they become obsessed with it. So, if you want to forget something, don't try to forget it; just accept it without fussing about it.

At this point, if you have been reading this book carefully and attempting to apply its principles, you might be asking, "So what's new? Isn't the idea that we construct our own reality just what we've been learning right along?" It is, indeed. Insight meditation goes right along with the principles for facilitating constructive thinking that I have presented in this book. Still, to know something intellectually is not necessarily to know it experientially. Your eyes can take in page after page, chapter after chapter, but simply acquiring information by reading will not make it part of the way you experience life. For the knowledge to change the way you automatically think and react, it must penetrate your being, and that takes practice. If you doubt this, imagine trying to learn to play tennis or the piano by reading a book.

The practice of insight meditation has spread throughout the world since it was introduced by the Buddha 2,500 years ago, because people have found it an effective way to make these fundamental truths real for them. Some who practice the discipline day after day for many years enter a state of nirvana in which their inner experience is utterly transformed, and they develop a degree of centeredness that is extremely rare. You are not likely to travel that far along the path to wisdom, but, in company with many others, you may find insight meditation a useful tool for implementing what you are learning in these pages.

LEARNING FROM YOUR FANTASY AND IMAGINATION

The experiential mind encodes events mainly in the form of images. For this reason, fantasy is an invaluable tool for communicating with your experiential mind and therefore for both influencing it and learning from it.

A simple exercise will demonstrate how imagery comes closer to real experience than verbal abstractions. If I ask you to imagine a house, you imagine a specific house with specific features. You can tell me whether the house has one, two, or three stories; whether it has a flat or a peaked roof; and whether or not it has a chimney. If you look at the word *house*, the letters in no way resemble a house. Their meaning is an abstraction that represents all houses in general, but no house in particular. But when you experience a house, either a real one or in your mind's eye, you never see houses in general, only a specific house.

The fact that your experiential mind reacts to fantasy and reality in the same imagistic terms puts a tremendously powerful technique at your disposal. You can influence your experiential mind and thereby improve your constructive thinking not only by having real experiences but by having imaginary experiences. Experience in fantasy has several advantages over real experience: it is safer, more convenient, and more flexible, as you can do things in fantasy that you could not possibly do in reality. Most important, fantasy can reach levels of the mind that are inaccessible by any other means.

Using fantasy as a stand-in for reality involves visualization. "That lets me out," you may be thinking. "I'm not a visual person, and I don't have a good imagination." That usually turns out to be a groundless concern. Everyone can visualize, although some people are better at it than others. People think they cannot visualize because they assume that visualization consists of having mental images as clear as those in a photograph or a movie. Actually, few, if any, people have such precise mental images. More typically, people visualize vague, general impressions of things.

To prove to yourself that you have the ability to visualize, imagine that you are meeting with a painter to discuss painting your house. The painter asks how many windows the house has and what kind they are. How do you go about supplying this information? Most likely you will conjure up a mental picture of the outside of your house and count the windows, noticing whether they are casements, double-hung, picture windows, or whatever. In doing this exercise, you have demonstrated not only your ability to visualize but also your ability to fantasize, for you have counted the windows in an imaginary house for an imaginary painter.

A good way to improve your ability to visualize is to draw an object from a mental image of it. Pick out an object and observe it carefully. Form an impression of it and retain the image in your mind. Check the accuracy of your visualization by going back and forth between your visualization and the real object. Then draw the object on paper. You will see that there is at least some resemblance, showing that you do have the capacity to visualize. You can sharpen that capacity by practicing this exercise repeatedly with different objects. Each time, note the details you did not record in your mind's eye and make an effort to do so next time. The more you hone your visualization skill, the more effectively you can utilize the techniques I will now describe.

Mental Experimentation: The Use of Fantasy as Vicarious Experience

Trying out new ways of behaving in fantasy before trying them out in reality can be very helpful. For example, if you are unsure of just how to assert yourself, imagine different ways of doing so and what the short- and long-range consequences might be—that is, how you would feel about yourself and how others would react. You can proceed as follows:

1. *Vividly re-create the situation and your feelings when you act in a certain way.* What is it like when someone takes advantage of you, and you don't do anything about it? Imagine vividly how you feel about it. Then imagine the likely consequences of your behavior, both short-term and long-term.

2. *Imagine alternative ways of behaving and their consequences.* Imagine being aggressive, devastating the person either with your rapier-sharp wit or with a blatant, all-out attack, verbal or physical. How does your aggressive behavior make you feel? What are its short- and long-term consequences? Now imagine asserting yourself in a more diplomatic way in which you firmly make your views and desires known without attacking the other person. Imagine the feelings and consequences associated with this way of responding.

   Which solution seems more desirable? Consider both the immediate consequences with respect to your feelings about yourself and the long-term consequences with respect to your relationships with others. Most important, consider the consequences of the different ways of behaving in terms of ultimately becoming the kind of person you want to be.

3. *Practice your desired alternative both in fantasy and in reality.* Having decided on the course of action you prefer, first practice it in your imagination. Once you feel confident about what is the appropriate behavior, try it out in reality. Don't expect perfect success the first time. Keep working back and forth between fantasy and reality. Learn from the real experience what you have to improve; make the improvements in your fantasy; then try it out again in reality.

Using Fantasy to Enhance Motivation

I am sitting at my computer correcting this chapter. Week after week, month after month, I have been reviewing chapters, each one requiring several drafts. It seems that the book will take forever. It is a beautiful day outside, crisp and invigorating. The snow has melted, and the pond near my house is beginning to thaw. It is tempting to drop what I am doing and go for a walk on one of the many trails in the woods. What is keeping me at this task?

My mind begins to fantasize. Before long the book will be finished. People will tell me how much it has improved their lives. Professionals and laypeople will say that my theory of personality has helped them understand themselves and others better than any other theory. I will become famous and widely appreciated for having made a significant contribution. Crazy daydream? Probably, but why not? Note its power to motivate: I decide to work another hour before taking a walk.

Fantasy can be an extremely helpful motivational tool. However, it can also backfire if you use it as an escape from reality or if you take your fantasies so seriously that you become demoralized when they fail to materialize. When the job is done, and the fantasy has served its motivational purpose, you have to be ready to give it up.

Using Fantasy to Reach Deeper Levels of the Experiential Mind

Some problems in living are not readily alleviated by direct methods because they have their roots in remote past experiences that are not easily accessible. Fantasy offers a way to communicate with your experiential mind so as to uncover and help you resolve these problems. Such therapy is normally beyond the scope of self-help procedures and is best conducted with the aid of a trained professional. Nevertheless, to give you an appreciation of the power of the experiential mind and to suggest the range of application of fantasy techniques, I will briefly illustrate this approach to therapy in the case of the recovery of my wife, Alice, from cancer.

As you recall, Alice was diagnosed as having terminal cancer and was thought to have only three months to live. That was twelve years ago. Today Alice is in excellent health, with no detectable signs of cancer. To bring about this result, we resorted to a psychological approach after we had exhausted all reasonable medical treatment.

Although Alice had always been a highly successful person by conventional standards, her happy and congenial personality masked an underlying feeling of despair. The psychotherapy she undertook both with me and with another therapist, Dorothy Firman, a practitioner of a school of psychotherapy called psychosynthesis, was aimed at contacting and changing her deep-rooted automatic thinking, based on early life experiences, that caused her to experience life in this negative way. As Alice's underlying mood changed in therapy, her cancer began to shrink until it completely disappeared.

Here is just one example of the fantasies Alice used in her expedition into her experiential self. She had told me that a deep, pervasive fear of loneliness had inexplicably come over her. I asked her to put herself into a relaxed meditative state of mind and let a scene come to mind that represented the loneliness. This is a verbatim transcript of what followed as it is described in her book, *Mind, Fantasy, and Healing.*

Slowly and with much effort, the vision came. I saw some figures with shrouds—very unclear. Then as they took on a more distinct form, I saw that they were witches standing around a fire. Sy [therapist's name] told me to ask them to come over to talk to us. They were frightening to me in the light of the fire, but they were more horrible as they came closer. They laughed at me and started to poke at me with their sticks. The visualization was so real and their presence was so chilling to me that I burst into tears over the interaction with them.

Sy told me to ask them what I could do to get rid of the awful fear of isolation. Finally they revealed their price: it was that I make a sacrifice so that they could become beautiful and mingle with other people. When I heard their price, I began to tremble. In an almost inaudible voice I whispered, "They want my children so they can turn them into witches like them, but I'll never do it. I'll never give them my children!"

Sy then told me to destroy them, but I told him that I couldn't possibly do it. He urged me to try to turn my fear to wrath, to try to imagine a creature that could help me. The image that came to me was a white winged horse. He told me to mount the horse and to supply myself with a weapon that would destroy them. I refused to kill them myself, but said that the wings of the horse would fan the flames of their fire, which would turn back on them and destroy them.

There was only one problem with this scenario—the horse and I were one now and I couldn't get airborne. The wings were so heavy that I couldn't flap them hard enough to catch the breeze. The harder I tried, the more I failed and the more the witches laughed at me. Sy joined my fantasy for real when he told me that another horse who loved the first horse very much would join her and together they would destroy the witches. The other horse flew above me and made a vacuum into which I could take off. Once in the air, I flew effortlessly and fanned the fire into a huge blaze. The witches ran here and there trying to avoid the flames, but in the end they were consumed by the fire.

The use of fantasy in therapy was new to me at the time. We had decided to experiment with it because I was disappointed with the rate of progress that Alice and I had been making. As soon as Alice began using fantasy, things began to happen. The fantasies took on a life of their own and were extremely emotionally engaging. We had no doubt but that an important process had been set in motion.

Through her fantasies, Alice confronted deep-seated problems from her childhood, and, within three months, a major reorganization of her personality occurred. Lifelong feelings of helplessness and hopelessness disappeared, as did the cancer that had spread from her kidney to both lungs. Alice and I believe she could not have made the same progress without the use of fantasy, which seemed to provide a direct line of communication to the deeper levels of her experiential mind.

How can fantasy produce such significant changes in someone's personality as to improve that person's health? The answer, I believe, is that the experiential mind stores much of its information in the form of symbols and fantasy. This information is associated with feelings (emotions, vibes, and moods), which, in turn, are associated with bodily functions, including the functioning of the endocrine and immune systems. Thus, accessing the experiential mind through fantasy can produce changes not only in feelings but also in bodily functions that are critically related to health. It is not even necessary for the person to work out the problems uncovered by this process in his or her conscious mind, although this can, at times, be helpful. Instead, the person can work things out symbolically at the fantasy level.

A technique that many people find helpful is fantasizing a figure who serves as an adviser and comforter, whether the figure is called God or a "wise guide." The political columnist Max Lerner attributed his success in combating several life-threatening illnesses to his deeply intimate relationship with a personalized God. He had never before been a religious person, but now he began to take long walks in which he spoke with God in a more intimate way than he could possibly speak with any real person. Lerner was well aware that he had invented this figure as a way of communicating with his unconscious mind. His case dramatically illustrates the healing power of fantasy. It has an important lesson to convey to people who overestimate the power of rationality and look askance at fantasy.

USING THE PRINCIPLES OF CEST IN CREATIVE WAYS

Now that you understand how the experiential mind operates, you can make unlimited use of that information both to influence and to learn from it. Your only limitation is in the creative ideas you can come up with in applying the principles. The following two examples illustrate how you can tailor-make exercises for influencing your experiential mind to think more constructively.

Facilitating Self-Love

James Laird, a professor of psychology at Clark University, did some experiments on mutual eye-gazing in which he found that people's affection for each other increases when they maintain eye contact. It seems that the experiential mind, on the basis of past experience, associates eye contact with intimacy. Remember, the experiential mind does not operate by logic but is, instead, strongly influenced by the similarity between present and past experiences.

When I heard about this research, I wondered if it would be possible to increase self-love by gazing intimately into one's own eyes in a mirror. I tried it, and some interesting things happened. When I looked at myself at the usual distance in the mirror, I was neither pleased nor displeased with what I saw. Mainly, I noticed that I needed a shave. As I brought my face closer and established eye contact, a smile spontaneously appeared on my face, and I said to the figure in the mirror, "I love you, and I will always be there for you." I then gave myself a big hug. A memory of a photograph that I had recently seen of myself as a pouting five-year-old came to mind. I imagined taking the child's hand and going for a walk with him. I told him that he needn't be unhappy and that I would always be there when he needed me.

After the session with the mirror, which lasted about three minutes, I felt pretty good. I now use the technique whenever I feel a need to boost my self-esteem. I have also tried it with my students and clients and find that many benefit from it. Some, however, are so resistant to the idea that they can love themselves that they cannot bring themselves to do the exercise.

Here is how to do the exercise: Look at yourself in a mirror from the usual distance. How do you like what you see? What are your thoughts and feelings? What do you feel like saying to yourself? Your rational self may have harsh things to say, which will wound your experiential self and therefore not do much for your self-esteem. Now gradually bring your face closer to the mirror until you establish a feeling of deep, intimate eye contact. Concentrate on looking deeply into your soul. Tell your experiential self (the one in the mirror) that you love it very much and that it can always count on your support. Say whatever else comes to mind that will reassure your experiential self. You may wish to combine your eye contact with a comforting hug by wrapping your arms around yourself. Try it; it feels good. Pay no attention to your rational mind's criticism that this is foolish. Try out the eye-gazing technique by doing it routinely for at least a week, once in the morning and once in the evening, perhaps when you brush your teeth.

This is how one of my clients who suffered from low self-esteem described her reactions to the mirror exercise:

As I looked at myself from the usual distance, my rational mind began to criticize the image in the mirror: "Your face is a mess, you are so fat, and your hair is ugly." My experiential self didn't have a voice. It just silently took in everything I was saying. The image in the mirror started to look very sad. I approached the mirror more closely and established eye contact. My experiential self still did not say anything. I looked into her eyes, and I saw a lot of sadness and fear there. I said, "I'm going to help you!" The image was still silent. Finally, my experiential self said, "You know, it's about time. I really need it!" The expression on my face changed from one of sadness and helplessness to one of warmth, and a little smile appeared on it. I wasn't yet ready for the "I love you" comment and hugging myself, but next time I'll try that. As I moved back to normal distance from the mirror, the negative thoughts were no longer there. I was no longer being harsh with myself.

If you don't like yourself on a particular day, you may view yourself in the mirror disapprovingly rather than lovingly. However, those negative feelings about yourself give you all the more reason to express unconditional love for yourself. It is hard not to be sympathetic and supportive to yourself when you are looking deeply into your eyes and hugging yourself. Does it still sound silly to you? Of course it is, but try it anyway; your experiential self will like it.

Resisting Temptation

On the first spring day warm enough to enjoy tennis, I tried on my tennis shorts, only to find that either they had shrunk, or I had expanded. I decided that I must cut down on the cookies I have with my coffee breaks. Unfortunately, it is easier said than done, as I enjoy my cookies. Since my willpower was not up to the task, it was time to put my knowledge of the experiential mind into practice. I know that the experiential mind responds to immediate gratification and also to fantasy. The problem is that if I eat the cookie now, I get instant gratification, whereas the thought of fitting into my tennis shorts is a more remote reward.

The solution was to put fantasy to work in bringing the reward for abstaining and the punishment for indulging into the immediate present. I vividly imagined having finished eating the cookie and the disappointment and bad vibes that would follow my lapse in self-control. I also imagined the bad vibes that would follow when I next wore the tight tennis pants. I next imagined the good, enduring vibes that refraining from eating the cookie would produce. Once my imagination brought the future into the present, the "net weight" of the different kinds of vibes was clearly in favor of abstinence. By using my imagination to re-create vividly the good vibes I would get from abstaining and the bad ones I would get from indulging, I reduced my cookie consumption.

The same technique can be used for any other kind of training in abstinence or moderation. Indeed, versions of it have been incorporated into innovative behavior-modification programs for overeating, smoking, and other addictions. However, the question for you is not what works for me or for someone else but what works for you. If this way of putting fantasy to use does not do anything for you, invent your own, based on what you know about the experiential mind and what you know about yourself.

A PARTING WORD ABOUT YOUR CONSTRUCTIVE THINKING

You now have at your disposal an understanding of the basic principles of constructive thinking and procedures for implementing them. Apply them well, and they will transform your life. As emphasized in CEST, the reality you experience is largely of your own construction. To be sure, there are realistic constraints, but it is always possible to interpret whatever the objective reality that presents itself in more or less constructive ways. My parting wish for you is that you shall ever-increasingly succeed in constructing the kind of reality that fosters your own happiness and fulfillment as well as happiness and fulfillment of all whom you touch.

RECOMMENDED READING

Epstein, A. H. *Mind, Fantasy and Healing: One Woman's Journey from Conflict and Illness to Wholeness and Health.* New York: Delacorte, 1989.

  Epstein describes her experience in overcoming a cancer from which the chances of recovery were negligible. The book is a fantastic journey into the mind, with many examples of the therapeutic use of fantasy. It is available for $18.00 (includes postage) from Balderwood Books, 37 Bay Road, Amherst, MA 01002.

Ferrucci, P. *What We May Be.* Los Angeles: J. P. Tarcher, 1982.

  This book explains the therapeutic procedure of psychosynthesis, which includes the technique of contacting subpersonalities through fantasy. Psychosynthesis is as much a philosophy as a form of psychotherapy. It will give you some interesting new perspectives on how to lead your life, including a consideration of the place of spirituality, integration, and transcendence.

Gendlin, E. T. *Focusing.* New York: Bantam, 1979.

  Gendlin is the founder of the therapeutic technique of focusing. This is an excellent self-help book that describes a valuable technique for learning from your experiential mind so as to bring about harmony between it and your rational mind. The technique can profitably be used by itself or in conjunction with other therapeutic procedures.

Singer, J. L., and K. S. Pope. *The Power of Human Imagination.* New York: Plenum, 1978.

  This is a compilation of articles by different authors. It will give you valuable background information about theories and research on the use of imagination in psychotherapy.

Epilogue: Constructive Thinking in Broader Context

The realization that human beings operate by two different minds has extremely broad implications. It can account for perhaps the greatest puzzle of all: why a species that is capable of the most remarkable intellectual accomplishments, such as sending rockets to the moon and learning the secrets of the atom, cannot solve much simpler problems, like living peacefully with other members of its own species and preserving its environment. Why is it that, given our intellectual intelligence, war is the way we continue to solve international problems, ethnic strife is prevalent, at least half the marriages in our country end in divorce, parents who themselves have been abused and know its cost abuse their own children, and many outwardly successful people who have everything they thought would ensure happiness are often inwardly miserable? The answer is that we obviously do not operate by intellect alone. Successful adjustment requires effective functioning of the experiential as well as the rational mind. It follows that it is no less important to train the experiential mind than the rational mind. Yet, as matters stand, considerable effort is devoted to training the rational mind, whereas training the experiential mind, with rare exception, is left to chance.

Some particularly important areas of social concern where irrationality can ill be afforded but nevertheless is prevalent are advertising, politics, the environment, and education, topics to which we turn next.

APPEALS TO THE EXPERIENTIAL MIND BY ADVERTISERS AND POLITICIANS

Advertisers and politicians intuitively know all about the experiential mind; for evidence, just look at any of the well-known exposés of the use of advertising techniques, from *The Hidden Persuaders* in the 1950s to *The Selling of the President* a decade later. We, the objects of this manipulation, need to be better informed about the assaults on our experiential minds so that we can more effectively resist their influence.

Advertising appeals to the experiential mind by using images of people fulfilling their basic needs through the products being advertised. Satisfaction of people's needs for pleasure, relationships, and self-esteem are all suggested by ads showing happy, fulfilled individuals smoking, drinking, and socializing in idyllic surroundings in the company of attractive partners. As for the need for understanding, or making sense of the world, think of the political slogans that tell you that all will fall into place if you just elect the candidate who paid for the ad.

Unfortunately, advertising techniques are often used to sell harmful products, such as sugar-laden foods, cigarettes, alcohol, fuel-inefficient cars, and self-serving politicians. Advertisers know all too well how to tap the power of the experiential mind through pictures and associations. Their influence is only ineffectively countered by contrary written messages addressed to the rational mind, such as the surgeon general's warnings printed on cigarette packages about the health hazards of smoking.

In political advertising, the techniques of manipulation were perfected in the 1988 presidential election. The images of convicted rapist-murderer Willie Horton and of the pollution of Boston Harbor (which was as much a federal as a state responsibility), together with suggestions that Dukakis was unpatriotic because he did not exalt the flag and lead people in the pledge of allegiance as did Bush, may have had more impact on people's voting decisions than any reasoned examination of George Bush's and Michael Dukakis' long public records or their positions on issues. Bush on more than one occasion referred to Dukakis as "an admitted card-carrying ACLU member." Making the statement in the form of an accusation, using the word *admitted*, and suggesting an association with the phrase *card-carrying member of the Communist Party* were clearly calculated to suggest that Dukakis was perhaps even pro-communist. Very likely, many of the people hearing the message did not know that ACLU stood for the American Civil Liberties Union, an organization concerned with protecting a fundamental principle of the U.S. Constitution. These successful appeals to people's fears and prejudices made any discussion of issues futile. They were devised with the help of opinion polls and "focus groups," techniques used by commercial advertisers to identify the thoughts and feelings that influence people's purchasing decisions and then to cater to the preferences that are revealed.

Emotional appeals are nothing new in politics, of course, and they have a legitimate role in motivating people to dedicated action. But as a result of the increasing sophistication of the advertising industry, political debate both in advertisements and in news broadcasts is being reduced to shorter and shorter "sound bites" that do not leave time to counter even the most inaccurate or misleading appeals to the experiential mind with rational discussion. We are in danger, therefore, of the utter subversion of meaningful democratic decisions by an informed citizenry able to think with its rational as well as its experiential mind.

What, if anything, can be done to counter the destructive effects of advertising and emotional appeals by politicians? One approach is to counter destructive appeals to the experiential mind with constructive ones, which amounts to "fighting fire with fire," or, more precisely, to fighting emotions with emotions. As it stands, many people find the surgeon general's rational message about the ill effects of smoking that is conveyed in words less compelling than the opposite message that is conveyed by advertisers in emotionally arousing pictures. What if the health-promoting messages, too, were conveyed in pictures and associations? Why not level the playing field by countering one message to the experiential mind with another? For example, an antismoking ad might show a picture of someone connected to a life-support system who is dying of cancer. Grieving loved ones stand at the bedside, and a caption states, "Is it really worth it?" Or an attractive young woman might say of a young man shown smoking in the background, "I won't go out with him. He smokes." Some public health agencies are experimenting with such ads, including ones that poke fun at the absurdity of cigarette advertising.

CONSTRUCTIVE THINKING IN THE SCHOOLS

One way to protect people from inappropriate appeals to their experiential minds is to teach them to identify such appeals. Children can be taught how their rational and experiential minds work and how the two need to supplement each other. They could receive training and practice in distinguishing between appeals to their experiential and rational minds. Training materials could consist of advertisements and political statements as well as everyday events from their own experience. In addition to all the other benefits that this training would provide, the children would emerge from school better equipped to react critically to irresponsible attempts to manipulate them through emotional appeals.

Children can also more generally be taught to improve their constructive thinking. It is time to begin redressing the imbalance of expending all our educational resources on training the rational mind and ignoring the experiential mind. The latter training cannot legitimately be dismissed as a frill, because research on constructive thinking, our own as well as that of others, has demonstrated that constructive thinking is related to academic performance. Children who are poor constructive thinkers often fail to function at their intellectual potential. Moreover, to the extent that the thinking in their experiential mind is maladaptive, it is likely to direct their intelligence to function in counterproductive and even antisocial ways.

Dan Goleman has described some programs in both private and public elementary schools that provide training in some combination of social competence, emotional adjustment, self-control, and responsible behavior. Although, as I noted previously, it is probably a mistake to include all of these as aspects of emotional intelligence, there can be no doubt that every one of them is extremely important no matter what one calls them, and any training program that can foster their development warrants serious consideration. What these programs accomplish from the perspective of CEST is to improve constructive thinking, the intelligence of the experiential mind, which is a basic contributing factor to social competence, personal adjustment, practical intelligence, and self-control and therefore can be considered the key to the attributes that have been included under emotional intelligence. These programs use real-life experiences and special exercises that engage the experiential mind. Consider the following example provided by Goleman of how a dispute between two students in the Self Science class at the Nueva Learning Center was used as a learning experience. Following escalating angry exchanges between the students, the teacher encouraged each child to express his or her views and feelings in a nonaccusatory way, to listen carefully to the other child, and to attempt to understand the other's viewpoint. The result was that the children resolved the conflict amicably. This is clearly an example of learning by experience and therefore involves training the experiential mind.

The subject matter of Self Science reads like a manual in constructive thinking. One of the major topics it addresses is self-awareness, which includes recognizing and labeling one's feelings; observing the relations between thoughts, feelings, and behavior; establishing to what extent thoughts and feelings are the source of decisions; evaluating alternative decisions with respect to specific issues, such as sexual behavior and drug consumption; identifying personal strengths and weaknesses; and viewing oneself in a positive, yet realistic, way. A second major topic is managing emotions, which includes identifying the sources of emotions, such as recognizing the frustration or fear behind a feeling of anger, learning to delay acting on emotions, and learning ways to cope with specific emotions, such as anger, fear, and sadness. A third major topic is assuming responsibility for one's behavior, and a fourth is interpersonal relationships, which includes listening well, empathizing, taking other people's viewpoints, and asserting oneself without reacting defensively or offensively. These are all obviously invaluable lifelong skills that are important for success in a wide variety of endeavors, and therefore teaching them is anything but a frill.

It would be of interest to adapt the procedure that I have found so useful for teaching constructive thinking to college students for use with elementary and high school students. This would entail having students describe distressing incidents in their lives by noting what objectively happened, how the person interpreted (construed) what happened, what the person's secondary mental reactions were, and what the person finally did. Other members of the class could then indicate what their reactions to the same situation would be, and class discussion could center on the different ways the same situation can be construed and on alternate secondary mental reactions and behavioral reactions. They then could evaluate each and discuss which are the most constructive construals, secondary mental reactions, and behavioral responses. Better yet, the scenes could be acted out rather than just reported, which would more effectively engage the experiential system, and be particularly useful for younger children. Other techniques that could be used to reach the experiential system are the use of emotionally engaging stories to illustrate adaptive and maladaptive ways of construing events and behaving, and the use of fantasy and imagery to practice alternative ways of behaving. At a more general level, it is important to recognize that CEST provides a broad theoretical framework for understanding adaptive and maladaptive thinking and behavior that can be implemented in a wide variety of ways.

CONSTRUCTIVE THINKING AND THE ENVIRONMENT

What could be more inimical to our long-term welfare than running out of fresh air to breathe or clean water to drink? What success can we claim for our society if our children are not provided with an opportunity to live out a normal, healthy, secure life?

In his book *Earth in the Balance: Ecology and the Human Spirit*, Senator Al Gore cites the maladaptive automatic thinking—in particular, denial—that prevents us from acting to forestall what our rational minds know to be destructive consequences. He emphasizes the clash between short- and long-term consequences, together with people's tendency to experience effects on others as of little consequence compared to effects on themselves. That is how the experiential mind works when it is left to its own lower-level devices—that is, when it is neither tempered by the rational mind nor given training in accessing its own intuitive wisdom. If nothing else, enlightened self-interest (such as a concern for our own and our children's future and for the survival of the things we have created) would dictate that we care about the state of our physical and social environment. But that is the kind of enlightenment that is beyond the scope of the experiential mind in its normal, everyday functioning. Informing people via their rational minds that "there is a hole in the sky over Antarctica" does little to shake them out of their complacency about the environment. What does influence people is a concrete, tangible, nearby event: garbage washing up on a beach, parents grieving for children who have died from cancer caused by industrial pollution, or a nuclear accident at Three Mile Island. Even then, these experiential lessons lose their effect if they are not continuously reinforced and made current.

We need to present environmental issues to the public in ways that supplement appeals to the rational mind by engaging the experiential mind. People have to be made to *see* the future and to emotionally *feel* the consequences of current policies on long-term outcomes. This can be accomplished through pictures, metaphors, imagery, drama, and other emotionally and personally engaging communications. Organizing people into action-oriented groups is also an effective technique for engaging the experiential mind, as group belongingness, particularly in combination with the use of symbols, slogans, and songs, is a powerful experiential motivator.

CONCLUSION

What is the answer to the personal and social crises that confront us? Can the same intelligence that created our problems be used to solve them? I believe the answer is that it is not likely to succeed if we use it in the same way we have used it in the past, but it can if we do things differently. But what has to be done differently? Einstein said that humankind is doomed unless we can change our way of thinking. He was concerned, when he made this statement, with nuclear war. His message, however, applies equally well to other crises that confront us, such as global warming, pollution, overpopulation, drugs, crime, ethnic strife, and the failure of our social institutions. How can we learn to think differently?

The first task is to use our intelligence to understand how we do think. The next is to implement our knowledge with appropriate procedures. Both tasks will require consideration of the emotional as well as the intellectual aspects of human thought. That is, we will first have to accept and understand our two minds. We will have to learn to cultivate the higher reaches of both and to use them in a supplementary, rather than antagonistic, manner, for only by doing so will we be able to attain peace of mind. Failing that, we will be at war with ourselves, which will be externalized in the form of conflict with our fellow human beings and an inharmonious relation with our environment. Achieving that, our technology will become a boon rather than a threat to human welfare.

Two general paths can be taken to reach the integration and broad social perspective that are required. The path of enlightened self-interest emphasizes the higher reaches of the rational mind, while the path of spirituality engages the higher reaches of the experiential mind. Enlightened self-interest should lead to the recognition that we live in one world and that the welfare of each of us is tied to the welfare of all. Enlightened self-interest should lead us to recognize that we are emotional creatures and to observe the conditions that make us feel good and bad. We will then recognize that love feels better than hate and that it is to our advantage to nurture the development of love in ourselves and in others. Enlightened self-interest should also lead us to distinguish between short-term and long-term interests and to discipline ourselves so that we are able and willing to forgo the former when it exacts too great a price in terms of the latter.

The beacon for the spiritual path is faith in some power or force that transcends ordinary human understanding. Such faith can be the source of a broad perspective and a feeling of connectedness with a greater whole than exists in one's immediate environment. People with a spiritual orientation can experience a spontaneous sense of alignment and oneness with the natural and human worlds. Depending on a person's preference, such an orientation may or may not include some manner of conceptualization of God. The important consideration is that a deep spiritual identification is achieved that transcends rational calculation and enables people to take the long view and experience its ultimate consequences without effort and unimpeded by the biasing effects of destructive emotions. At this, its highest level of functioning, the experiential mind becomes not the betrayer of long-range interests and concern for others but a means for their achievement.

Notes

CHAPTER 1: EMOTIONAL INTELLIGENCE REVISITED

P. 3, "Goleman's best-selling book, *Emotional Intelligence*": D. Goleman, *Emotional Intelligence* (New York: Bantam Books, 1995).

P. 4, "The first passage is from *My Confession*": Leo Tolstoi, *My Confession* (New York: Crowell, 1887).

P. 7, "cognitive therapists such as Aaron Beck and Albert Ellis": A. T. Beck, *Cognitive Therapy and the Emotional Disorders* (New York: International Universities Press, 1976); A. Ellis, *Humanistic Psychotherapy: The Rational-Emotive Approach* (New York: McGraw-Hill, 1973).

P. 10, "believe it is the other way around": For different views on this issue, see Paul Ekman and Richard J. Davidson, *The Nature of Emotions: Fundamental Questions* (New York: Oxford University Press, 1994).

CHAPTER 2: WHAT IS EMOTIONAL INTELLIGENCE, AND HOW CAN IT BE MEASURED?

P. 13, "a French psychologist by the name of Alfred Binet": For a history of mental testing, see F. Goodenough, *Mental Testing, Its History, Principles, and Applications* (New York: Rinehart, 1949).

P. 14, "an American psychologist by the name of Stern": W. Stern, *The Psychological Methods of Testing Intelligence*, G. M. Whipple, trans. (Baltimore: Warwick & York, n.d.).

P. 15, "mental age levels in the Stanford-Binet test": L. M. Terman and M. A. Merrill, *Measuring Intelligence* (Boston: Houghton Mifflin, 1937).

P. 15, "conducted by Thurstone": L. L. Thurstone, *Primary Mental Abilities* (Chicago: University of Chicago Press, 1938).

P. 16, "Robert Sternberg, a Yale psychologist": For a review of the studies that

Sternberg and others have conducted on practical intelligence, see R. Sternberg, K. Wagner, W. M. Williams, and J. A. Horvath, "Testing Common Sense," *American Psychologist* 50 (1995): 912–27.

P. 17, "Research has demonstrated that the two kinds of ability are unrelated": Ibid. This article by Sternberg and his associates describes studies shortly to be reviewed; S. Epstein and P. Meier, "Constructive Thinking: A Broad Coping Variable with Specific Components," *Journal of Personality and Social Psychology* 57 (1989): 332–50. This article reports a near zero correlation between constructive thinking, as measured by the CTI, and intelligence.

P. 17, "long-term study of mentally gifted children conducted by Lewis Terman": L. Terman, *Mental and Physical Traits of a Thousand Gifted Children, Genetic Studies of Genius. I* (Stanford, Calif.: Stanford University Press, 1925).

P. 17, "how very bright children fare in later life": C. K. Holahan and R. R. Sears, *The Gifted Group in Later Maturity* (Stanford, Calif.: Stanford University Press, 1995).

P. 18, "in such a confusing manner": However, there are some interesting beginnings, as in the research of Robert Sternberg on practical intelligence and of Salovey and Mayer on emotional intelligence that I discussed in Chapter 2. A particularly promising study was recently reported by Professors Jack Block and Adam M. Kremen at the University of California at Berkeley. In that study, they used a self-report test constructed by Block to measure what he refers to as "ego-resilience," which he considers to be a broadly adaptive ability that includes aspects of social intelligence as well as the ability to control impulses, delay gratification, and recover from frustration. It also includes finding life interesting and having an inquiring mind that is open to new information and experiences.

Having constructed a measure of ego-resilience, Block and Kremen sought to answer the question of how people with high IQs who are not also high on ego-resilience differ from people who are high on ego-resilience but not on IQ. They referred to the former as representatives of "pure IQ" and the latter as representatives of "pure ego-resilience." The representatives of pure IQ were described by a group of judges who interviewed them and examined records of their performance in various experiments as competent, effective people in the world of work but not in the world of social relations and emotions, with which they tended to feel uncomfortable. In a sense, they were all head and no heart. The representatives of pure ego-resilience, in contrast, were described as self-accepting, warm, sociable, open-minded, able to recovery quickly from frustration, and having a zest for life. Thus, the objective ratings of behavior validated the picture provided by the self-report test. Of course, these two groups are extremes, and one need not be all one or all the other. It would be most desirable to be a combination of both, an intelligent person with heart, social intelligence, and a zest for living, what I would describe as the outcome of good constructive thinking. That is, ego-resilience refers to a way of experiencing the world, whereas constructive thinking describes what you have to do, in your automatic thinking, to get there.

The Block and Kremen study is most promising with respect to the existence of a broad ability that is somewhat similar to what Dan Goleman and others have speculated about emotional intelligence. However, it is no accident that Block refers to his scale as a measure of ego-resilience and not of emotional intelligence. The items in the test include several that refer to social adjustment and openness to new information and experiences but only one that refers to an emotion (anger). Moreover, as a single study, it remains to be seen whether it can be verified in future research with other samples of people and with more extensive and reliable measures of the proposed components of ego-resilience.

P. 19, "highly valid for predicting school performance": For a recent review of what intelligence tests predict and fail to predict, see U. Neisser, G. Boodoo, T. J. Bouchard, Jr., A. W. Boykin, N. Brody, S. J. Ceci, D. F. Halpern, J. C. Loehlin, R. Perloff, R. J. Sternberg, and S. Urbina, "Intelligence: Knowns and Unknowns," *American Psychologist* 51 (1996): 77–101.

P. 20, "Peter Salovey and John D. Mayer": Salovey and Mayer have written several articles on emotional intelligence and their attempts at measuring it. They have continuously revised their thinking as a result of research and theoretical considerations. The following article presents a definition of emotional intelligence, including identification of its primary components, a review of the relevant literature on intelligence, and a discussion of the role of emotional intelligence in mental health: P. Salovey and J. D. Mayer, "Emotional Intelligence," *Imagination, Cognition, and Personality* 9 (1990): 185–211. Their most recent definition of emotional intelligence and methods for measuring it are described in the following manuscript: J. D. Mayer, P. Salovey, and D. R. Caruso, *Emotional Intelligence Test, Research Edition* (Private publication, 1997).

P. 21, "John Gottman, a psychologist at the University of Washington": J. Gottman, *The Heart of Parenting: Raising an Emotionally Intelligent Child* (New York: Simon & Schuster, 1996).

P. 22, "Howard Gardner, a professor of education at Harvard University": H. Gardner, *Frames of Mind: The Theory of Multiple Intelligences* (New York: Basic Books, 1983).

P. 22, "In studies of high school students": A. J. Tannenbaum, *Adolescent Attitudes toward Academic Brilliance* (New York: Bureau of Publications, Teachers College, Columbia University, 1962); J. S. Coleman, "The Adolescent Subculture and Academic Achievement," *American Journal of Sociology* 65 (1960): 337–47; B. Cramond and C. E. Martin, "Inservice and Preservice Teachers' Attitudes toward the Academically Brilliant," *Gifted Child Quarterly* 31 (1987): 15–19; C. H. Solano, "Teacher and Pupil Stereotypes of Gifted Girls and Boys," *Talents and Gifts* (1977): 4–8.

P. 23, "school programs on training emotional intelligence": Several such programs are described in D. Goleman, *Emotional Intelligence* (New York: Bantam Books, 1995).

P. 23, "no research support": For a review of the relevant research, see R. S. Feldman, P. Philippot, and R. J. Custrini, "Social Competence and Nonverbal Behavior," in R. S. Feldman and B. Rime, eds., *Fundamentals of Nonverbal Behavior* (Cambridge, England: Cambridge University Press, 1991).

P. 23, "a study by Walter Mischel and his associates": The study of delay of gratification is reported in Y. Shoda, W. Mischel, and P. K. Peake, "Predicting

Adolescent Cognitive and Self-Regulatory Competencies from Preschool Delay of Gratification," *Developmental Psychology* 26, 6 (1990): 978–86.

CHAPTER 3: CONSTRUCTIVE THINKING: THE INTELLIGENCE OF THE EXPERIENTIAL MIND

P. 26, "the correlation between the two types of intelligence is zero": S. Epstein and P. Meier, "Constructive Thinking: A Broad Coping Variable with Specific Components," *Journal of Personality and Social Psychology* 57 (1989): 332–49.

P. 26, "a most revealing pattern emerged": Ibid.

CHAPTER 4: TESTING YOUR CONSTRUCTIVE THINKING

P. 35, "who had studied the influence of thinking on behavior": A. Ellis, *Humanistic Psychotherapy: The Rational-Emotive Approach* (New York: McGraw-Hill, 1973); A. T. Beck, *Cognitive Therapy and the Emotional Disorders* (New York: International Universities Press, 1976).

P. 38, "six basic patterns": S. Epstein and P. Meier, "Constructive Thinking: A Broad Coping Variable with Specific Components," *Journal of Personality and Social Psychology* 57 (1989): 332–50. Except where otherwise noted, all research findings mentioned in this chapter are taken from this source.

P. 44, "overgeneralize from bad experiences as well as good experiences as they get older": M. A. Green, "Occupational Stress: A Study of Public School Administrators in Southeast Massachusetts," doctoral dissertation, University of Massachusetts at Amherst, 1988.

CHAPTER 5: EVIDENCE FOR THE EXISTENCE OF THE EXPERIENTIAL MIND

P. 50, "hitting a target with a tetherball": J. Piaget, "The Affective Unconscious and the Cognitive Unconscious," *Journal of the American Psychoanalytic Association* 21 (1973): 249–61.

P. 50, "Timothy Gallwey": W. T. Gallwey, *The Inner Game of Tennis* (New York: Random House, 1974).

P. 53, "Amos Tversky and Daniel Kahneman and others": The following edited book contains a good sample of studies on "judgment under uncertainty" that contributed importantly to the cognitive revolution: D. Kahneman, P. Slovic, and A. Tversky, eds., *Judgment under Uncertainty: Heuristics and Biases* (New York: Cambridge University Press, 1982).

P. 54, "The research reveals": The studies that used vignettes with arbitrary outcomes are described in greater detail in the following publications: S. Epstein, "Integration of the Cognitive and the Psychodynamic Unconscious," *American Psychologist* 49 (1994): 709–24; S. Epstein, A. Lipson, A. C. Holstein, and E. Huh, "Irrational Reactions to Negative Outcomes: Evidence for Two Conceptual Systems," *Journal of Personality and Social Psychology* 62 (1992): 328–39.

P. 58, "the delayed reactions often follow those of the rational mind": This study is reported in S. Epstein, "Integration of the Cognitive and the Psychodynamic Unconscious," *American Psychologist* 49 (1994): 709–24.

P. 59, "Linda is described as a thirty-one-year-old woman": My associates and I have published the following Linda studies: S. Epstein, V. Denes-Raj, and R. Pacini, "The Linda Problem Revisited from the Perspective of Cognitive-Experiential Self-Theory," *Personality and Social Psychology Bulletin* 11 (1995): 1124–38; S. Donovan and S. Epstein, "The Difficulty of the Linda Conjunction Problem Can Be Attributed to Its Simultaneous Concrete and Unnatural Representation, and Not to Conversational Implicature," *Journal of Experimental Social Psychology* 33 (1997): 1–20; S. Epstein, S. Donovan, and V. Denes-Raj, "The Missing Link in the Paradox of the Linda Conjunction Problem: Beyond Knowing and Thinking of the Conjunction Rule, the Intrinsic Appeal of Heuristic Processing," *Personality and Social Psychology Bulletin* (in press).

P. 60, "Imagine that you are presented with two trays of jelly beans": The jelly bean studies are of particular interest because they present a conflict between the experiential and rational ways of processing information. We have done the following studies with this experimental paradigm: L. A. Kirkpatrick and S. Epstein, "Cognitive-Experiential Self-Theory and Subjective Probability: Further Evidence for Two Conceptual Systems," *Journal of Personality and Social Psychology* 63 (1992): 534–44; V. Denes-Raj and S. Epstein, "Conflict between Experiential and Rational Processing: When People Behave against Their Better Judgment," *Journal of Personality and Social Psychology* 66 (1994): 819–29; V. Denes-Raj, S. Epstein, and J. Cole, "The Generality of the Ratio-Bias Phenomenon," *Personality and Social Psychology Bulletin* 10 (1995): 1083–92; R. Pacini, F. Muir, and S. Epstein, "Depressive Realism from the Perspective of Cognitive-Experiential Self-Theory" (in press).

P. 61, "Individual Differences in People's Use of Their Two Minds": The study on individual differences in people's use of their experiential and rational minds is reported in greater detail in the following publication: S. Epstein, R. Pacini, V. Denes-Raj, and H. Heier, "Individual Differences in Intuitive-experiential and Analytical-rational Thinking Styles," *Journal of Abnormal and Social Psychology* 71 (1996): 390–405.

P. 63, "A great deal of research has been conducted with the CTI": S. Epstein and P. Meier, "Constructive Thinking: A Broad Coping Variable with Specific Components," *Journal of Personality and Social Psychology* 57 (1989): 332–49; L. Katz and S. Epstein, "Constructive Thinking and Coping with Laboratory-Induced Stress," *Journal of Personality and Social Psychology* 61 (1991): 789–800; S. Epstein, "Coping Ability, Negative Self-Evaluation, and Overgeneralization: Experiment and Theory," *Journal of Personality and Social Psychology* 62 (1992): 826–36; S. Epstein, "Constructive Thinking and Mental and Physical Well-Being," in L. Montanda, S. H. Filipp, and M. J. Lerner, eds., *Life Crises and Experiences of Loss in Adulthood* (Hillsdale, N.J.: Erlbaum, 1992); S. Epstein and L. Katz, "Coping Ability, Stress, Productive Load, and Symptoms," *Journal of Personality and Social Psychology* 62 (1992): 813–25.

CHAPTER 6: HOW YOUR EXPERIENTIAL MIND THINKS

P. 69, "powerless to resist an overwhelming impulse": S. Peele, *Diseasing of America: Addiction Treatment Out of Control* (Boston: Houghton Mifflin, 1991).

P. 70, "corresponding features of the rational mind": The list of attributes of the experiential and rational minds is adapted and expanded from S. Epstein, "Cognitive-Experiential Self Theory: Implications for Developmental Psychology," in M. R. Gunnar and L. A. Sroufe, eds., *Self Processes and Development: The Minnesota Symposia on Child Development*, vol. 23 (Hillsdale, N.J.: Erlbaum, 1991), 79–123. It was derived from an analysis of people's thinking when they discuss highly charged emotional issues as compared with impersonal issues, as well as from an analysis of the appeals made in advertising and politics; from research on constructive thinking (e.g., S. Epstein and P. Meier, "Constructive Thinking: A Broad Coping Variable with Specific Components," *Journal of Personality and Social Psychology* 57 [1989]: 332–50); from social-cognitive research (e.g., R. E. Nisbett and L. Ross, *Human Inference: Strategies and Shortcomings of Social Judgment* [Englewood Cliffs, N.J.: Prentice-Hall, 1980]; A. A Sappington and J. C. Russell, "Self-Efficacy and Meaning: Candidates for a Uniform Theory of Behavior," *Personality and Social Psychology Bulletin* 2 [1979]: 327; A. A. Sappington, J. C. Russell, V. Triplett, and J Goodwin, "Self-Efficacy Expectancies, Response-Outcome Expectancies, Emotionally-Based Expectancies and Their Relationship to Avoidance Behavior," *Journal of Clinical Psychology* 37 [1980]: 737–44); and from cognitive research on heuristics and counterfactual thinking (e.g., D. Kahneman and D. T. Miller, "Norm Theory: Comparing Reality to Its Alternatives," *Psychological Review* 93 [1986]: 136–53; D. Kahneman and A. Tversky, "The Simulation Heuristic," in D. Kahneman, P. Slovic, and A. Tversky, eds., *Judgment under Uncertainty: Heuristics and Biases* [New York: Cambridge University Press, 1982], 201–8).

P. 77, "inappropriate beliefs, feelings, and behavior": B. Fischhoff, "Hindsight ≠ Foresight: The Effect of Outcome Knowledge on Judgment under Uncertainty," *Journal of Experimental Psychology: Human Perception and Performance* 1 (1975): 288–99. See also H. J. Bursztajn, R. I. Feinbloom, R. M. Hamm, and A. Brodsky, *Medical Choices, Medical Chances: How Patients, Families, and Physicians Can Cope with Uncertainty* (New York: Routledge, 1990), 218–19.

P. 79, "as a result of accumulated life experience": S. Peele and A. Brodsky with M. Arnold, *The Truth about Addiction and Recovery: The Life Process Program for Outgrowing Destructive Habits* (New York: Simon & Schuster, 1991).

P. 79, "(consciously or otherwise) to move on": Ibid.

CHAPTER 7: WHY WE DO WHAT WE DO: A NEW UNDERSTANDING OF HUMAN BEHAVIOR

P. 80, "*cognitive-experiential self-theory* (CEST)": S. Epstein, "The Self-Concept Revisited or a Theory of a Theory," *American Psychologist* 28 (1973): 404–

16; S. Epstein, "The Self-Concept: A Review and the Proposal of an Integrated Theory of Personality," in E. Staub, ed., *Personality: Basic Issues and Current Research* (Englewood Cliffs, N.J.: Prentice-Hall, 1980), 82–132; S. Epstein, "Cognitive-Experiential Self-Theory," in L. A. Pervin, ed., *Handbook of Personality: Theory and Research* (New York: Guilford, 1990), 165–92.

P. 81, "the experiential mind operates": S. Epstein, "The Unconscious, the Preconscious, and the Self-Concept," in J. Suls and A. Greenwald, eds., *Psychological Perspectives on the Self*, vol. 2 (Hillsdale, N.J.: Erlbaum, 1983), 219–47.

P. 82, "more than 4 million years ago": R. Gore, *National Geographic* 191 (1997): 72–99.

P. 83, "Aaron Beck, Albert Ellis, Donald Meichenbaum, and Martin Seligman": A. T. Beck, *Cognitive Therapy and the Emotional Disorders* (New York: International Universities Press, 1976); A. T. Beck, *Love Is Never Enough* (New York: Harper & Row, 1988); A. Ellis, *Reason and Emotion in Psychotherapy* (New York: Lyle Stuart, 1962); A. Ellis, *Humanistic Psychotherapy: The Rational-Emotive Approach* (New York: McGraw-Hill, 1973); A. Ellis, *How to Stubbornly Refuse to Make Yourself Miserable about Anything—Yes, Anything* (Secaucus, N.J.: Lyle Stuart, 1988); A. Ellis and R. A. Harper, *A New Guide to Rational Living* (N. Hollywood, Calif.: Wilshire, 1975); D. H. Meichenbaum, *Cognitive Behavior Modification* (Morristown, N.J.: General Learning Press, 1974); D. H. Meichenbaum, *Stress Inoculation Training* (New York: Pergamon Press, 1985); M. E. P. Seligman, *Helplessness: On Depression, Development, and Death* (San Francisco: W. H. Freeman, 1975); M. E. P. Seligman, *Learned Optimism* (New York: Knopf, 1991).

P. 84, "one or two of these needs": Psychoanalytic theory and learning theory give primacy to the need for pleasure. Phenomenological psychologists (e.g., P. Lecky, *Self-Consistency: A Theory of Personality* [Long Island, N.Y.: Island Press, 1945]; C. R. Rogers, *Client-Centered Therapy* [New York: Houghton Mifflin, 1951]; D. Snygg and A. W. Combs, *Individual Behavior* [New York: Harper & Row, 1949]) emphasize the need for a belief system that organizes experience and directs behavior. Object-relations theory (e.g., S. Cashdan, *Object Relations Therapy: Using the Relationship* [New York: Norton, 1988]) centers on the need for close relationships with others. Psychologists such as Gordon Allport (*Pattern and Growth in Personality* [New York: Holt, Rinehart, & Winston, 1961]) consider self-esteem the most important of human needs. In *Client-Centered Therapy*, Carl Rogers combines the need to maintain a belief system and the need for self-esteem into a need "to enhance and maintain the self-concept." Psychoanalytic self-psychology (see Cashdan, *Object Relations Therapy*) also brings together these two needs.

P. 89, "*sudden* changes in basic beliefs": G. Catlin and S. Epstein, "Unforgettable Experiences: The Relation of Life Events to Basic Beliefs about Self and World," *Social Cognition* 10 (1992): 189–209; R. Janoff-Bulman, "The Aftermath of Victimization: Rebuilding Shattered Assumptions," in C. Figley, ed., *Trauma and Its Wake*, vol. 1 (New York: Brunner/Mazel, 1985), 15–35;

R. L. Silver and C. B. Wortman, "Coping with Undesirable Life Events," in J. Garber and M. E. P. Seligman, eds., *Human Helplessness* (New York: Academic Press, 1980), 279–340; S. E. Taylor, "Adjustment to Threatening Events: A Theory of Cognitive Adaptation," *American Psychologist* 38 (1983): 1161–73. The effects of emotionally significant events on basic beliefs are discussed and documented more fully in Chapter 12.

CHAPTER 8: CONSTRUCTIVE THINKING AND SUCCESS IN THE WORKPLACE

P. 100, "a person is likely to be in the workplace": G. V. Barrett and R. L. Depinet, "A Reconsideration of Testing for Competence Rather Than for Intelligence," *American Psychologist* 46 (1991): 1012–24; J. E. Hunter, "Cognitive Ability, Cognitive Aptitudes, Job Knowledge, and Job Performance," *Journal of Vocational Behavior* 29 (1986): 340–62; L. Mansnerus, "Coming of Age: Predicting Adult Success from a Student's Status," *New York Times Education Supplement* (Nov. 5, 1989), 31.

P. 100, "are influenced by constructive thinking": R. J. Sternberg and R. K. Wagner, *Practical Intelligence: Nature and Origins of Competence in the Everyday World* (Cambridge, England: Cambridge University Press, 1986). Additional documentation for this statement is provided by various sources cited later.

P. 100, "from their college years to middle age": G. E. Vaillant, *Adaptation to Life* (Boston: Little, Brown, 1977).

P. 100, "over a comparable period in their lives": J. K. Felsman and G. E. Vaillant, "Resilient Children as Adults: A 40-Year Study," in E. J. Anthony and B. J. Cohler, eds., *The Invulnerable Child* (New York: Guilford, 1987), 289–314.

P. 100, "class valedictorians for ten years": D. E. Lewis, "Fast Track: News in the Workplace," *Boston Globe*, Sept. 1, 1991.

P. 102, "which is exactly what happened": B. Wein, "Got a Lot of Living to Do," *New Woman*, Oct. 1989, 76–81.

P. 102, "my research on constructive thinking": D. Goleman, "New Scales of Intelligence Rank Talent for Living," The *New York Times*, Apr. 5, 1988, C1, C11.

P. 102, "the magazine *Personal Selling Power*": G. Gschwandtner, "The *Personal Selling Power* Superachiever Survey Report: How Superachievers Think to Reach Consistent Success," *Personal Selling Power*, Mar. 1990, 11–19.

P. 105, "school administrators cope with job-related stress": M. A. Green, "Occupational Stress: A Study of Public School Administrators in Southeast Massachusetts," doctoral dissertation, University of Massachusetts at Amherst, 1988.

P. 106, "Center for Leadership Studies": L. Atwater and F. J. Yammarino, "Personal Attributes as Predictors of Military Leadership: A Study of Midshipmen Leaders at USNA" (Center for Leadership Studies, Report Series: ONR-TR-7, 1989).

P. 107, "who will quit or do poorly": M. E. P. Seligman and P. Schulman, "Explanatory Style as a Predictor of Productivity and Quitting among Life Insurance Sales Agents," *Journal of Personality and Social Psychology* 50 (1986): 832–38.

P. 107, "with the Metropolitan Life Insurance Company": P. Schulman, M. E. P. Seligman, and D. Oran, "Explanatory Style Predicts Productivity among Life Insurance Sales Agents," unpublished manuscript (1989).

P. 108, "a large sample of college students": S. Epstein and P. Meier, "Constructive Thinking: A Broad Coping Variable with Specific Components," *Journal of Personality and Social Psychology* 57 (1989): 332–50.

P. 109, "associated with feelings of helplessness and depression": See Chapter 10.

P. 109, "lead to poor school performance": M. E. P. Seligman, L. P. Kamen, and S. Nolen-Hoeksema, "Explanatory Style across the Life Span: Achievement and Health," in E. M. Hetherington, R. M. Lerner, and M. Perlmutter, eds., *Child Development in Life-Span Perspective* (Hillsdale, N.J.: Erlbaum, 1988), 91–114.

P. 110, "concentrate on the task itself": R. J. Sternberg and J. Kolligian, Jr., eds., *Competence Considered* (New Haven, Conn.: Yale University Press, 1990).

P. 110, " 'I'm usually right' ": Dennis Littky, principal of Thayer High School, Winchester, New Hampshire, quoted in Mansnerus, "Coming of Age," 31.

P. 112, "emotional burnout later down the line": J. Edelwich with A. Brodsky, *Burnout: Stages of Disillusionment in the Helping Professions* (New York: Human Sciences Press, 1980).

P. 112, "gets into his or her mid-forties": C. Peterson, M.E.P. Seligman, and G. E. Vaillant, "Pessimistic Explanatory Style Is a Risk Factor for Physical Illness: A Thirty-Five-Year Longitudinal Study," *Journal of Personality and Social Psychology* 55 (1988): 23–27.

CHAPTER 9: CONSTRUCTIVE LOVE

P. 116, " 'another's spiritual growth' ": M. S. Peck, *The Road Less Traveled: A New Psychology of Love, Traditional Values and Spiritual Growth* (New York: Touchstone, 1978), 81.

P. 116, " 'unless we love ourselves' ": Ibid., 82.

P. 116, " 'they are indistinguishable' ": Ibid., 83.

P. 116, "tend to be good constructive thinkers": S. Epstein and P. Meier, "Constructive Thinking: A Broad Coping Variable with Specific Components," *Journal of Personality and Social Psychology* 57 (1989): 332–50.

P. 116, " 'love is as love does' ": Peck, *The Road Less Traveled*, 120.

P. 119, " 'in which he participated externally' ": D. H. Lawrence, *Women in Love* (Middlesex, England: Penguin, 1960 [orig. pub. 1920]), 315.

P. 119, " '*I* shouldn't be in the world, either' ": Ibid., 336.

P. 119, "use drugs, alcohol, or food": S. Peele with A. Brodsky, *Love and Addiction* (New York: New American Library, 1976).

P. 121, " 'the things I've done for her' ": This case is taken from C. G. Hindy, J. C. Schwarz, and A. Brodsky, *If This Is Love, Why Do I Feel So Insecure?* (New York: Fawcett Crest, 1990), 165.

P. 123, "than those who were not": Epstein and Meier, "Constructive Thinking."

P. 124, "are more accepting of others": S. Epstein and G. J. Feist, "Relation between Self- and Other-Acceptance and Its Moderation by Identification," *Journal of Personality and Social Psychology* 54 (1988): 309–15; W. Fey, "Correlates of Certain Subjective Attitudes toward Self and Other," *Journal of Clinical Psychology* 13 (1957): 44–49; E. L. Phillips, "Attitudes toward Self and Other: A Brief Questionnaire Report," *Journal of Consulting Psychology* 55 (1951): 79–81; E. T. Sheerer, "An Analysis of the Relationship between Acceptance of and Respect for Self and Acceptance of and Respect for Others in 10 Counseling Cases," *Journal of Consulting Psychology* 13 (1949): 176–80; D. Stock, "An Investigation into the Intercorrelations between the Self Concept and Feelings Directed toward Other Persons and Groups," *Journal of Consulting Psychology* 13 (1949): 176–80.

P. 124, "this is, in fact, the case": Epstein and Meier, "Constructive Thinking."

P. 126, "precautions to avoid being victimized": S. Peele and A. Brodsky with M. Arnold, *The Truth about Addiction and Recovery: The Life Process Program for Outgrowing Destructive Habits* (New York: Simon & Schuster, 1991), 151–53, 322.

P. 126, "attachment between mothers and infants": J. Bowlby, *Attachment and Loss: L. Attachment* (New York: Basic Books, 1969); J. Bowlby, *A Secure Base: Parent–Child Attachment and Healthy Human Development* (New York: Harper & Row, 1988).

P. 127, "love relationships throughout their lives": Hindy, Schwarz, and Brodsky, *If This Is Love.*

P. 127, *"Mind, Fantasy, and Healing"*: A. H. Epstein, *Mind, Fantasy and Healing: One Woman's Journey from Conflict and Illness to Wholeness and Health* (New York: Delacorte, 1989). This book is out of print. However, copies can be obtained by sending $18.00, which includes postage and handling to: Balderwood Books, 37 Bay Road, Amherst, MA 01002.

CHAPTER 10: BETTER CONSTRUCTIVE THINKING MEANS BETTER ADJUSTMENT AND LESS STRESS

P. 130, "particularly in emergencies": C. Darwin, *The Expression of Emotions in Man and Animals* (New York: Philosophical Library, 1955 [orig. pub. 1872]).

P. 132, "anger, fear, sadness, and joy": S. Epstein, "A Research Paradigm for the Study of Personality and Emotions," in M. M. Page, ed., *Personality—Current Theory and Research: 1982 Nebraska Symposium on Motivation* (Lincoln: University of Nebraska Press, 1983), 91–154.

P. 132, " 'I'm OK, you're not OK' ": E. Berne, *Games People Play* (New York: Ballantine, 1985).

P. 134, "mental health and effective performance": E. J. Langer, *Mindfulness* (New York: Addison-Wesley, 1989); M. E. P. Seligman, *Learned Optimism* (New York: Knopf, 1991); S. E. Taylor, *Creative Self-Deception and the Healthy Mind* (New York: Basic Books, 1989).

P. 135, "stuck with the kids": B. Wein, "Got a Lot of Living to Do," *New Woman,* Oct. 1989, 76–81.

P. 135, *"and the Healthy Mind"*: Taylor, *Creative Self-Deception and the Healthy Mind.*

P. 135, *"Learned Optimism"*: Seligman, *Learned Optimism.*

P. 135, "than others to be depressed": C. Peterson and M. E. P. Seligman, "Causal Explanations as a Risk Factor for Depression: Theory and Evidence," *Psychological Review* 91 (1984): 347–74.

P. 135, "and having a low opinion of oneself": S. Epstein, "Coping Ability, Negative Self-Evaluation, and Overgeneralization: Experiment and Theory," *Journal of Personality and Social Psychology* 62 (1992): 826–36; S. R. Maddi and S. C. Kobasa, *The Hardy Executive: Health under Stress* (Homewood, Ill.: Dow Jones-Irwin, 1984); C. Peterson and M. E. P. Seligman, "The Learned Helplessness Model of Depression: Current Status of Theory and Research," in E. E. Beckman and W. R. Leber, eds., *Handbook of Depression: Treatment, Assessment, and Research* (Homewood, Ill.: Dorsey, 1985), 914–39.

P. 136, "with various measures of adjustment": S. Epstein, "Cognitive-Experiential Self-Theory," in L. A. Pervin, ed., *Handbook of Personality: Theory and Research* (New York: Guilford, 1990), 165–92; S. Epstein, "Constructive Thinking and Mental and Physical Well-being," in L. Montada, S.-H. Filipp, and M. J. Lerner, eds., *Life Crises and Experiences of Loss in Adulthood* (Hillsdale, N.J.: Erlbaum, 1992), 385–409.

P. 137, "in a laboratory study": L. Katz and S. Epstein, "Constructive Thinking and Coping with Laboratory-Induced Stress," *Journal of Personality and Social Psychology* 61 (1991): 789–800.

P. 137, "occurred in people's lives": S. Epstein and L. O. Katz, "Coping Ability, Stress, Productive Load, and Symptoms," *Journal of Personality and Social Psychology* 62 (1992): 813–25.

P. 138, "more demanding workloads": M. A. Green, "Occupational Stress: A Study of Public School Administrators in Southeast Massachusetts," doctoral dissertation, University of Massachusetts at Amherst, 1988.

CHAPTER 11: HOW YOU THINK CAN AFFECT YOUR HEALTH

P. 140, "airplane at several thousand feet": S. Epstein, "Theory and Experiment on the Measurement of Drive and Conflict," in M. R. Jones, ed., *Nebraska Symposium on Motivation, 1961* (Lincoln: University of Nebraska Press, 1962), 127–209; S. Epstein, "Toward a Unified Theory of Anxiety," in B. Maher, ed., *Progress in Experimental Personality Research*, vol. 4 (New York: Academic Press, 1967), 1–89; S. Epstein and W. D. Fenz, "Steepness of Approach and Avoidance Gradients in Humans as a Function of Experience," *Journal of Experimental Psychology* 70 (1965): 1–12; W. D. Fenz and S. Epstein, "Gradients of Physiological Arousal of Experienced and Novice Parachutists as a Function of an Approaching Jump," *Psychosomatic Medicine* 29 (1967): 33–51.

P. 142, "a 'meta-analysis' in which 101 studies were combined": H. S. Friedman and S. Booth-Kewley, "The 'Disease-Prone Personality': A Meta-Analytic View of the Construct." *American Psychologist* 42 (1987): 539–55.

P. 142, "back pains than others do": N. Cousins, *Head First* (New York: Dutton, 1989); L. Katz and S. Epstein, "Constructive Thinking and Coping with Laboratory-Induced Stress," *Journal of Personality and Social Psychology* 61 (1991): 789–800; S. Locke and D. Colligan, *Healer Within* (New York: New American Library, 1987); K. Pelletier, *Mind as Healer, Mind as Slayer* (New York: Delta, 1980); C. Peterson and M. E. P. Seligman, "Explanatory Style and Illness," *Journal of Personality* 55 (1987): 237–65.

P. 142, "for nearly forty years": C. Peterson, M. E. P. Seligman, and G. E. Vaillant, "Pessimistic Explanatory Style Is a Risk Factor for Physical Illness: A Thirty-Five-Year Longitudinal Study," *Journal of Personality and Social Psychology* 55 (1988): 23–27.

P. 143, "can influence their health": S. Epstein, "Constructive Thinking and Mental and Physical Well-being," in L. Montada, S.-H. Filipp, and M. J. Lerner, eds., *Life Crises and Experiences of Loss in Adulthood* (Hillsdale, N.J.: Erlbaum, 1992), 385–409.

P. 143, "Gernot Gollnisch found": G. Gollnisch, "Drug Use in Methadone Maintenance Clients: A Multidimensional Model of Personality, Coping, and Motivation," doctoral dissertation, University of Massachusetts at Amherst, 1991.

P. 144, "bother to take care of themselves": For a list of "vulnerabilities" (destructive assumptions that lead people not to take care of their needs), see J. Edelwich and A. Brodsky, *Group Counseling for the Resistant Client: A Practical Guide to Group Process* (New York: Lexington, 1992), 98–99.

P. 144, "and possibly to cancer": Locke and Colligan, *The Healer Within*.

P. 146, "Dr. Redford Williams": *The Trusting Heart* (New York: Times Books/Random House, 1989).

P. 146, "Carnegie Mellon University, and his colleagues": M. F. Scheier, K. A. Matthews, J. F. Owens, G. J. Magovern, Sr., R. C. Lefebvre, R. A. Abbott, and C. S. Carver, "Dispositional Optimism and Recovery from Coronary Artery Bypass Surgery: The Beneficial Effects on Physical and Psychological Well-Being," *Journal of Personality and Social Psychology* 57 (1989): 1024–40.

P. 146, " 'cancer-prone personality' ": L. LeShan, *You Can Fight for Your Life* (New York: Evans, 1977); Pelletier, *Mind as Healer*; B. Siegel, *Love, Medicine, and Miracles* (New York: Harper & Row, 1988); C. S. Simonton, S. Matthews-Simonton, and J. Creighton, *Getting Well Again* (New York: Bantam, 1980).

P. 147, "neglect or rejection in childhood": LeShan, *You Can Fight for Your Life*.

P. 147, "commotion of the laboratory": P. J. Rosch, "Stress and Cancer," in C. L. Cooper, ed., *Psychosocial Stress and Cancer* (New York: Wiley, 1984), 3–19.

P. 147, "the mice on a turntable": Ibid.

P. 147, "combative manner had smaller tumors": Ibid.

P. 148, "showed a 'fighting spirit' ": S. Greer, T. Morris, and K. W. Pettingale, "Psychological Response to Breast Cancer: Effect on Outcome," *Lancet* 2 (1979): 785–87. A research group at Johns Hopkins University obtained similar findings, as reported in L. R. Derogatis, M.D. Abeloff, and N. Melisaratos, "Psychosocial Coping Mechanisms and Survival Time in Metastatic

Breast Cancer," *Journal of the American Medical Association* 242 (1979): 1504–8.

P. 148, "The overall findings . . . are, to say the least, confusing": B. L. Andersen, J. K. Kiecolt-Glaser, and R. Glaser, "A Biobehavioral Model of Cancer Stress and Disease Course," *American Psychologist* 49 (1994): 389–404.

P. 148, "A particularly promising recent study": D. Spiegel, "Can Psychotherapy Prolong Cancer Survival?" (Editorial), *Psychosomatics* 31 (1990): 361–66.

P. 149, "other kinds of cancer": Andersen, Kiecolt-Glaser, and Glaser, "A Biobehavioral Model of Cancer Stress and Disease Course," 389–404.

P. 149, "LeShan": LeShan, *You Can Fight for Your Life.*

P. 149, "Lori Katz": L. Katz, "Past and Current Emotions and Attitudes: How Survivors of Cancer and Heart Disease Adjusted to Their Illness," doctoral dissertation, University of Massachusetts at Amherst, 1992.

P. 149, "suggestive evidence from individual cases": B. O'Regan and C. Hirshberg, *Spontaneous Remission: An Annotated Bibliography* (Sausalito, Calif.: Institute of Noetic Sciences, 1993).

P. 149, "transformed her personality": A. H. Epstein, *Mind, Fantasy and Healing: One Woman's Journey from Conflict and Illness to Wholeness and Health* (New York: Delacorte, 1989).

P. 150, "developing and recovering from cancer": Pelletier, *Mind as Healer*; Simonton et al., *Getting Well Again.*

P. 151, " 'want your cancer to spread?' ": Spiegel, "Can Psychotherapy Prolong Cancer Survival?" 363.

P. 153, " 'chance' as well as 'choice' ": H. J. Bursztajn, R. I. Fembloom, R. M. Hamm, and A. Brodsky, *Medical Choices, Medical Chances: How Patients, Families, and Physicians Can Cope with Uncertainty* (New York: Routledge, 1990).

CHAPTER 12: ONCE A CONSTRUCTIVE THINKER, ALWAYS A CONSTRUCTIVE THINKER?

P. 158, "self-fulfilling prophecies": W. B. Swann, Jr., "Self-Verification: Bringing Social Reality into Harmony with the Self," in J. Sulc and A. G. Greenwald eds., *Social Psychological Perspectives on the Self* (Hillsdale, N.J.: Erlbaum, 1983), 33–66.

P. 159, "resulting from 'luck' ": M. E. P. Seligman, "Why Is There So Much Depression Today? The Waxing of the Individual and the Waning of the Commons" (Washington, D.C.: G. Stanley Hall Lecture Series, vol. 9, 1988).

P. 159, "their writing many years later": M. O. Burns and M. E. P. Seligman, "Explanatory Style across the Life Span: Evidence for Stability over 52 Years," *Journal of Personality and Social Psychology* 56 (1989): 471–77.

P. 160, "tends to become 'fixated' ": R. R. Sears, "Experimental Analysis of Psychoanalytic Phenomena," in J. McV. Hunt, ed., *Personality and the Behavior Disorders* (New York: Ronald, 1944), 306–32.

P. 160, " 'a young man has no experience' ": Aristotle, "The Nichomachaean Ethics," in R. McKeon, *Introduction to Aristotle* (New York: Modern Library, 1947), 433.

P. 165, *"approval-oriented"*: C. S. Dweck, "Motivational Processes Affecting Learning," *American Psychologist* 41 (1986): 1040–48.

P. 167, "never been out of school": S. Epstein, "Cognitive-Experiential Self-Theory," in L. A. Pervin, ed., *Handbook of Personality: Theory and Research* (New York: Guilford, 1990), 165–92.

P. 168, "ranged in age from 35 to 70": Ibid.

CHAPTER 13: PARENTING GOOD CONSTRUCTIVE THINKERS

P. 170, "never been out of school": S. Epstein, "Cognitive-Experiential Self-Theory," in L. A. Pervin, ed., *Handbook of Personality: Theory and Research* (New York: Guilford, 1990), 165–92.

P. 171, "somewhere in between": J. Kagan and N. Snidman, "Temperamental Factors in Human Development," *American Psychologist* 46 (1991): 856–62.

P. 171, "fathers in their thinking styles": M. E. P. Seligman, C. Peterson, N. J. Kaslow, R. L. Tanenbaum, L. B. Alloy, and L. Y. Abramson, "Attributional Style and Depressive Symptoms among Children," *Journal of Abnormal Psychology* 93 (1984): 125–238.

P. 171, "thinking in parents and young children": S. Epstein, A. Levinger, and C. Holstein, "A Study on Relations between Children's and Parents' Constructive Thinking," unpublished.

P. 172, "fathers' more than their mothers' ": Epstein, "Cognitive-Experiential Self-Theory."

P. 172, "constructive thinkers than their mothers": Ibid.

P. 172, "not nearly as strong as we had expected": Epstein, Levinger, and Holstein, "A Study on Relations between Children's and Parents' Constructive Thinking."

P. 174, "their parents' reactions": A. Freud and D. Burlingham, *War and Children* (New York: Ernest Willard, 1943).

P. 174, "problems by physical violence": M. M. Lefkowitz, L. R. Huesmann, and L. D. Eron, "Parental Punishment: A Longitudinal Analysis of Effects," *Archives of General Psychiatry* 35 (1978): 186–91; C. Widom, "Child Abuse, Neglect, and Adult Behavior: Research Design and Findings on Criminality, Violence, and Child Abuse," *American Journal of Orthopsychiatry* 59 (1989): 355–68.

P. 175, "emotional abuse on constructive thinking": S. Epstein and T. Welsh, "Parental Discipline Practices, Constructive Thinking, and Adjustment," unpublished.

P. 176, "reasonable discipline in childhood": C. G. Hindy, J. C. Schwarz, and A. Brodsky, *If This Is Love, Why Do I Feel So Insecure?* (New York: Fawcett Crest, 1990).

P. 176, "also borne out by our research": Epstein, "Cognitive-Experiential Self-Theory."

P. 177, "less protective relationships with their parents": G. Catlin and S. Epstein, "Unforgettable Experiences: The Relation of Life Events to Basic Beliefs about Self and World," *Social Cognition* 10 (1992): 189–209.

P. 178, "teach about coping with adversity": B. Bettelheim, *The Uses of Enchant-*

ment: The Meaning and Importance of Fairy Tales (New York: Knopf, 1976).

P. 178, "propensity toward depression": M. E. P. Seligman, *Helplessness: On Depression, Development, and Death* (San Francisco: W. H. Freeman, 1975).

P. 180, "as good constructive thinkers are": C. S. Dweck, "Motivational Processes Affecting Learning," *American Psychologist* 41 (1986): 1040–48.

P. 180, "Dr. Nancy Eisenberg": N. Eisenberg, R. A. Fabes, M. Schaller, G. Carlo, and P. A. Miller, "The Relations of Parental Characteristics and Pratices to Children's Vicarious Emotional Responding," *Child Development* 62 (1991): 1393-1408.

CHAPTER 14: HOW LIFE EXPERIENCE AFFECTS CONSTRUCTIVE THINKING

P. 183, "outcomes of good and bad events": S. Epstein, "Coping Ability, Negative Self-Evaluation, and Overgeneralization: Experiment and Theory," *Journal of Personality and Social Psychology* 62 (1992): 826–36.

P. 184, "parent–child relationship": S. Epstein, "The Self-Concept: A Review and the Proposal of an Integrated Theory of Personality," in E. Staub, ed., *Personality: Basic Issues and Current Research* (Englewood Cliffs, N.J.: Prentice-Hall, 1980), 82–132; S. Epstein and N. Erskine, "The Development of Personal Theories of Reality from an Interactional Perspective," in D. Magnusson and V. L. Allen, eds., *Human Development: An Interactional Perspective* (New York: Academic, 1983), 133–47.

P. 184, " 'eyes looking out of mine' ": D. H. George, "Eating Beautiful Women: Anne Sexton and Marilyn Monroe," *Associated Writing Programs Newsletter* (May 1988), 7.

P. 185, "come from 'dysfunctional families' ": H. Gravitz and J. Bowden, *Recovery: A Guide for Adult Children of Alcoholics* (New York: Simon & Schuster, 1987), preface.

P. 185, "regarded as one great trauma": For critical observations on the notion of widespread dysfunctionality, see P. Hobe, *Lovebound: Recovering from an Alcoholic Family* (New York: New American Library, 1990).

P. 185, "for independent thinking and growth": S. J. Katz and A. E. Liu, *The Codependency Conspiracy: How to Break the Recovery Habit and Take Charge of Your Life* (New York: Warner, 1991); S. Peele, *Diseasing of America: Addiction Treatment Out of Control* (Boston: Houghton Mifflin, 1991); S. Peele and A. Brodsky with M. Arnold, *The Truth about Addiction and Recovery: The Life Process Program for Outgrowing Destructive Habits* (New York: Simon & Schuster, 1991), 144–57.

P. 185, "what they call 'resilient children' ": E. J. Anthony and B. J. Cohler, eds., *The Invulnerable Child* (New York: Guilford, 1987).

P. 186, "establishing close relationships with others": J. K. Felsman and G. E. Vaillant, "Resilient Children as Adults: A 40-Year Study," in ibid., 289–314.

P. 186, *"Keep the Past in Its Place"*: S. Wolin and S. Wolin, *Resilience: How Survivors of Troubled Families Keep the Past in Its Place* (in preparation).

P. 186, " 'respond actively and creatively' ": Steven Wolin, quoted in "How to Survive (Practically) Anything" (interview), *Psychology Today*, Jan./Feb. 1992, 36–39.

P. 186, " 'life with its complexities and ambiguities' ": quote from Steven Wolin, ibid., 38.

P. 187, "wisdom in their crises of survival": Anthony and Cohler, *The Invulnerable Child*; R. Janoff-Bulman, "The Aftermath of Victimization: Rebuilding Shattered Assumptions," in C. Figley, ed., *Trauma and Its Wake*, vol. 1 (New York: Brunner/Mazel, 1985), 15–35; R. L. Silver and C. B. Wortman, "Coping with Undesirable Life Events," in J. Garber and M. E. P. Seligman, eds., *Human Helplessness* (New York: Academic Press, 1980), 279–340; S. E. Taylor, "Adjustment to Threatening Events: A Theory of Cognitive Adaptation," *American Psychologist* 38 (1983): 1161–73.

P. 188, "children with normal childhoods": A. Thomas and S. Chess, "Genesis and Evolution of Behavioral Disorders from Infancy to Early Adult Life," *American Journal of Psychiatry* 141 (1984): 1–9.

P. 188, "research has similar findings": Wolin and Wolin, *Resilience*.

P. 189, "as tough as they come": Roseanne (Barr) Arnold, quoted in J. J. O'Connor, "By Any Name, Roseanne Is Roseanne Is Roseanne," the *New York Times*, Aug. 18, 1991, H1, H27.

P. 189, "certain emotionally significant events": G. Catlin and S. Epstein, "Unforgettable Experiences: The Relation of Life-Events to Basic Beliefs about Self and World," *Social Cognition* 10 (1992): 189–209.

P. 190, "challenge of surmounting them": A. H. Maslow, *Toward a Psychology of Being*, 2d ed. (New York: Van Nostrand Reinhold, 1968); C. R. Rogers, *Client-Centered Therapy* (New York: Houghton Mifflin, 1951).

P. 190, "Marguerite Ofria": S. Epstein, "The Ecological Study of Emotions in Humans," in P. Pliner, K. R. Blankstein, and I. M. Spigel, eds., *Advances in the Study of Communication and Affect, vol. 5: Perception of Emotions in Self and Others* (New York: Plenum, 1979), 47–83.

P. 191, "that particular kind of trauma": I. L. McCann and L. A. Pearlman, *Psychological Trauma and the Adult Survivor: Theory, Therapy and Transformation* (New York: Brunner/Mazel, 1990).

P. 191, "previously made sense of the world": S. Epstein, "The Self-Concept, the Traumatic Neurosis, and the Structure of Personality," in D. Ozer, J. M. Healy, Jr., and A. J. Stewart, eds., *Perspectives on Personality*, vol. 3 (Greenwich, Conn.: JAI Press, 1990), 63–98; M. Horowitz, *Stress Response Syndromes* (New York: Jason Aronson, 1979).

P. 191, "Kenneth Fletcher": K. E. Fletcher, "Belief Systems, Exposure to Stress, and Post-Traumatic Stress Disorder in Vietnam Veterans," doctoral dissertation, University of Massachusetts at Amherst, 1988.

CHAPTER 15: GETTING TO KNOW YOUR EXPERIENTIAL SELF

P. 198, "or 'theory of reality' ": S. Epstein, "Cognitive-Experiential Self Theory: Implications for Developmental Psychology," in M. R. Gunnar and L. A. Sroufe, eds., *Self Processes and Development: The Minnesota Symposia on Child Development*, vol. 23 (Hillsdale, N.J.: Erlbaum, 1991), 79–123; S. Epstein and N. Erskine, "The Development of Personal Theories of Reality from an Interactional Perspective," in D. Magnusson and V. L. Allen, eds., *Human Development: An Interactional Perspective* (New York: Academic Press, 1983), 133–47.

P. 198, " 'walls is our own reflection' ": C. Castaneda, *Tales of Power* (New York: Simon & Schuster, 1974), 246–47.

CHAPTER 16: EVALUATING YOUR AUTOMATIC THINKING

P. 207, " 'catastrophizing' ": A. Ellis and R. A. Harper, *A New Guide to Rational Living* (N. Hollywood, Calif.: Wilshire, 1975).

P. 209, "at such an inopportune time": This vignette is adapted from J. Edelwich with A. Brodsky, *Burnout: Stages of Disillusionment in the Helping Professions* (New York: Human Sciences Press, 1980), 90.

P. 209, "reactions among her patients": K. Horney, *Neurosis and Human Growth* (New York: Norton, 1950).

P. 210, "conflict between people": A. T. Beck, *Cognitive Therapy and the Emotional Disorders* (New York: International Universities Press, 1976).

P. 211, "lead us astray": Ibid.

P. 211, "if they make you feel good": Ellis and Harper, *A New Guide to Rational Living*.

P. 213, "maladaptive in the long run"; S. Epstein, "Theory and Experiment on the Measurement of Drive and Conflict," in M. R. Jones, ed., *Nebraska Symposium on Motivation, 1961* (Lincoln: University of Nebraska Press, 1962), 127–209; R. S. Lazarus and S. Folkman, *Stress, Appraisal and Coping* (New York: Springer, 1984).

P. 213, "increase their chances of success": S. E. Taylor and J. D. Brown, "Illusion and Well-Being: A Social Psychological Perspective on Mental Health," *Psychological Bulletin* 103 (1988): 193–210.

P. 214, "your emotions without inhibition": For therapeutic alternatives to excessive and futile "ventilation" of emotions, see J. Edelwich and A. Brodsky, *Group Counseling for the Resistant Client: A Practical Guide to Group Process* (New York: Lexington, 1992), 111–15.

P. 214, "successful people later on": G. E. Vaillant, *Adaptation to Life* (Boston: Little, Brown, 1977).

CHAPTER 17: TRAINING YOUR EXPERIENTIAL MIND

P. 227, "tools that are defective": A. Ellis and R. A. Harper, *A New Guide to Rational Living* (N. Hollywood, Calif.: Wilshire, 1975).

P. 228, "developed by Barry Kaufman": B. N. Kaufman, *To Love Is to Be Happy With* (New York: Fawcett Crest, 1977).

P. 228, "complete shift of perspective": T. S. Kuhn, *The Structure of Scientific Revolutions* (Chicago: University of Chicago Press, 1962).

P. 229, "solve problems in living by reframing": E. J. Langer, *Mindfulness* (New York: Addison-Wesley, 1989).

P. 230, "before getting stuck": Langer, *Mindfulness*.

P. 230, "to simply say the word *one*": H. Benson, *The Relaxation Response* (New York: Avon, 1975).

P. 232, "sink-or-swim manner": D. Meichenbaum, *Stress Inoculation Training* (New York: Pergamon Press, 1985).

P. 233, "therapy that is based on three steps": G. Emery and J. Campbell, *Rapid Relief from Emotional Distress* (New York: Rawson Associates, 1986).

P. 233, " 'your current reality' ": ibid., 10.

CHAPTER 18: THE WISDOM OF THE EXPERIENTIAL MIND

P. 238, "can enable you to do just that": E. T. Gendlin, *Focusing* (New York: Bantam, 1979).

P. 245, "consumed by the fire": A. H. Epstein, *Mind, Fantasy and Healing: One Woman's Journey from Conflict and Illness to Wholeness and Health* (New York: Delacorte, 1989), 45–46.

P. 246, "a personalized God": M. Lerner, *Wrestling with the Angel: A Memoir of My Triumph over Illness* (New York: Norton, 1990).

P. 248, "and other addictions": E. Klinger, "Imagery and Logotherapeutic Techniques in Psychotherapy: Clinical Experiences and Promise for Application to Alcohol Problems," in W. M. Cox, ed., *Treatment and Prevention of Alcohol Problems: A Resource Manual* (Orlando, Fla.: Academic Press, 1987), 139–56; S. Peele and A. Brodsky with M. Arnold, *The Truth about Addiction and Recovery: The Life Process Program for Outgrowing Destructive Habits* (New York: Simon & Schuster, 1991), 244–46, 263.

EPILOGUE: CONSTRUCTIVE THINKING IN BROADER CONTEXT

P. 252, "advertising techniques": V. O. Packard, *The Hidden Persuaders* (New York: McKay, 1957); J. McGinniss, *The Selling of the President, 1968* (New York: Trident, 1969).

P. 253, "our own as well as that of others": In research that I recently completed that has not yet been submitted for publication, we examined the relation between children's performance on a simplified version of the CTI and their performance in school. We found that children with poorer CTI scores performed significantly more poorly in school than children with the same IQ who had better CTI scores.

P. 253, "Dan Goleman": D. Goleman, *Emotional Intelligence* (New York: Bantam Books, 1995).

P. 255, "*Earth in the Balance*": A. Gore, *Earth in the Balance: Ecology and the Human Spirit* (Boston: Houghton Mifflin, 1992).

Index

mism in, 84–85; parental fostering
of, 171–72, 173–78; poor, examples
of, 29–31, 92; positive thinking and,
107; productivity and, 106–8; as self-
maintaining, 157–58; in social relations, 123–24, 125; stress and, 105,
136–38; of superachievers, 103–5.
See also Global constructive thinking
Constructive Thinking Inventory (CTI),
26, 63, 124, 136, 165, 167; brief
version of, 36–38; development and
refinement of, 35–36; intepretation
of, 40–47; job performance and,
108; as predictor of success, 106
Control: through guilt, 121; through
imposed dependency, 121; love and,
120–22
Coping strategies, 198. See also Behavioral coping; Emotional coping
Corrective learning experiences, 232–
33
Creative Self-Deception and the
Healthy Mind (Taylor), 135
Criticism, 211

Danger, 89–90, 93; intuition and, 72;
irrational fears and, 50
Darwin, Charles, 129
Delayed gratification, 20, 23–24, 248
Denial, 213
Dependency, 121–22, 215
Depression, 6; bodily impact of, 141;
illness and, 143, 146–47; pessimism
and, 135–36; superstitious thinking
and, 136; treatment of, 7
Destructive thinking: classroom performance and, 109; common types
of, 215–16; construals in, 197–98,
203–4; vs. constructive thinking, 27–
31; disputing of, 227–28; fostering
insight into, 168–69; illness and,
127–28, 144–46; in intimate relationships, 125–26; maladaptive
construals as, 207–11; parents' contribution to, 178–82; related to illness and health, 142, 143–44, 146–
47; as source of sensitivities and

compulsions, 91, 93–94; substituting
constructive alternatives for, 221,
226; untestable hypotheses and, 211
Discipline, 58–59, 174, 175
Disengagement, 133, 215
Distraction technique, 230
Drug abuse, 143
Dukakis, Michael, 252
Dweck, Carol, 165
Dysfunctional families, 185

Earth in the Balance: Ecology and the
Human Spirit (Gore), 255
Einstein, Albert, 69, 256
Eisenberg, Nancy, 180–81
Ellis, Albert, 7–8
Emery, Gary, 233
Emotional adjustment, 22
Emotional coping: Constructive Thinking Inventory and, 38, 42–43, 136;
developmental changes in, 165, 166,
168; health and, 143; mental well-
being and, 136; of superachievers,
103–4
Emotional indignation, 69
Emotional Intelligence (Goleman), 3
Emotional intelligence: characteristics
of, 24; conceptualizations of, 3–4,
19–22; vs. intellectual intelligence, 4–
5; as predictor of success, 21, 23–24;
social adjustment and, 19–20, 23;
training of, 23; use of terminology,
8–9
Emotionally significant events: negative, impact of, 207; personal belief
system and, 189–92, 198; positive
impact of, 190
Emotions: alienation from, 180–82;
appropriateness of, 21; automatic
construals and, 198–99, 202–3; basic beliefs and, 88; changing of,
"neurological window of opportunity" and, 7; connected with experiential mind, 72; constructive
thinking affected by, 189–92; control of, 3, 7, 10, 64, 75, 129; dis-
owned, in parent–child relationship,
180–81; displays of, 75; evolu-

About the Author

SEYMOUR EPSTEIN is Professor Emeritus of Psychology at the University of Massachusetts, Amherst. A noted authority on personality, he has published extensively, including an earlier trade-oriented version of this book entitled *You're Smarter Than You Think* (1993).